Healing This Wounded Earth:
With Compassion, Spirit
and the Power of Hope

Healing This Wounded Earth: With Compassion, Spirit and the Power of Hope

Eleanor Stoneham

BOOKS

Winchester, UK
Washington, USA

First published by O-Books, 2011
O-Books is an imprint of John Hunt Publishing Ltd., Laurel House, Station Approach,
Alresford, Hants, SO24 9JH, UK
office1@o-books.net
www.o-books.com

For distributor details and how to order please visit the 'Ordering' section on our website.

ISBN: 978 1 84694 445 1

Design: Tom Davies

Printed in the UK by CPI Antony Rowe, Chippenham, Wiltshire
Printed in the USA by Offset Paperback Mfrs, Inc

We operate a distinctive and ethical publishing philosophy in all
areas of our business, from our global network of authors to
production and worldwide distribution.

CONTENTS

The message of this book is a wise one, and I have no doubt that the world would be a much better place if only we could bring ourselves to heed it. From the Foreword by **Dr Iain McGilchrist**, author of *The Master and His Emissary: The Divided Brain and the Making of the Western World*

Humanity is set for a time of fundamental change. Our relationship with the environment is spiritless and broken. But we have also lost sight of the spiritual essence in our communities, our economy, in medicine and our creativity, even in our faiths. With its wealth of wisdom this wonderful book explores how we have arrived at where we are and what all of those who call themselves ' religious' or are otherwise 'of good faith' need to do to heal this wounded world. **The Revd. Peter Owen-Jones**, author of *Letters from an Extreme Pilgrim* and presenter of the BBC TV programmes *Around the World in 80 Faiths* and *How to Live a Simple Life*.

This is a passionate call to all of us. It clearly reminds us how we all have responsibility for healing our fractured society and building a better world. It is both inspiring and reassuring in its wise message. **William Bloom**, author of *The Endorphin Effect: A Breakthrough Strategy for Holistic Health* and *Spiritual Wellbeing* and *Soulution, The Holistic Manifesto*.

In this book Eleanor Stoneham points to the central role of spirituality in healing the human condition in our troubled times. Nothing is more important if we are to have hope for a dignified future, come what may in the come-to-pass. **Alastair McIntosh**, scholar, activist, Visiting Professor of Human Ecology at the University of Strathclyde, author of *Soil and Soul* and *Hell and High Water*.

Interweaving environmental and social history with the roots of medicine, Dr Stoneham presents a provocative and refreshing kaleidoscope of possibilities. She shows how the spiritual, emotional and physical aspects of our humanity can find a new creative synthesis. Her clear visionary prose sings to the reader, inviting us on a journey of discovery through both the darkest corners of our psyche, and the most sublime hope that can emerge from bodies resonating with nature and spirit. She paints an inspiring picture of a possible future in which the soul takes its rightful place at the core of healing. **Dawson Church PhD**, author of *The Genie in Your Genes*

From many wisdom traditions, a key teaching is that our wounds make us whole. This paradoxical lesson has almost been forgotten in our age, in which the emphasis is on manipulation, power, control, and perfection. In this book Eleanor Stoneham shows that our hopes and plans for survival may depend on re-learning the lesson of the Wounded Healer, in which woundedness leads to the wisdom and humility that are required in meeting the challenges we face as individuals, as a species, and as a planet. **Larry Dossey MD**, author of *Healing Words* and *The Power of Premonitions*.

Passionate and fiercely intelligent, (this book) is a wake-up call for us all to engage actively, courageously and responsibly in the healing of our fractured world. Again and again, the author spells out her vital, central message - that it is our own behavior as individuals, not the intervention of governments, which will provide that healing (and she) charts a clear path … showing how we can all be part of a great global healing in this new era of consciousness. **Barry Cottrell**, artist, engraver, author of *The Way Beyond the Shaman: Birthing a New Earth Consciousness*

We have entered into a new era of transformation, perhaps the most significant one in the history of humanity…This lovely book puts us in touch with healing principles of spirituality and compassion throughout our lives, so that we may all become catalysts for social change…with all of our hearts and minds and souls… **Paul H. Ray, Ph.D.**, anthropologist and sociologist, co-author of *The Cultural Creatives - How 50 Million People are changing the World*

I can endorse your book wholeheartedly. The concept of the Wounded Healer resonates very much with me as an outsider/insider in European culture. Our world needs healing and that process has now begun; but the ultimate 'inconvenient truth' is that the outer environment reflects the inner. There must be change in the mindset - if we hope to bring about change we must first change within, heal ourselves; and this holds true for the individual as well as for society. The late **Cy Grant**, author of *Blackness and the Dreaming Soul*.

Preface

The idea for this book was conceived while on holiday in Turkey in 2004. I was in the middle of a long process of healing following a devastating mental breakdown and burnout that for a while had turned my life upside down. I was receiving excellent professional help for mind, body, soul and spirit, and to supplement this healing I had turned to the contemplative books by the Roman Catholic priest Henri Nouwen, including his short bestselling gem, *The Wounded Healer*.[1] These books became valuable and reliable sources of comfort and support in my pain.

So I was lying by the swimming pool at that Turkish villa reading Michael Ford's *The Wounded Prophet: A Portrait of Henri J.M.Nouwen*.[2]

As I thought more about what I was reading it seemed to me that the compassion and vulnerability of the Wounded Healer could have a significance for healing our dangerously fractured world far beyond the realms of the pastoral and medical professions, where it is primarily researched and understood as a means of healing and where most of the literature is to be found. Where else, I mused, can we find the Wounded Healer in our lives? How, I thought, could we hope to heal this world when so many of us have our own unhealed spiritual and mental wounds, and so much of our destructive behavior is because of those wounds; when for so many of us it is not regarded as appropriate in our working lives to show too much compassion, let alone vulnerability.

1

But I had not realized the enormity of the project I had started as my researches took me deeper and wider into so very many other fields. Meanwhile the wounds of the world become ever more serious and the healing needs more urgent.

Thus followed five years of painful gestation, involving much research, and numerous abandoned drafts along the way, before the version that you now hold was finally born!

In this book I address all those who over the years have bemoaned the state of the world and asked 'But what can I do?'

Any bias towards Anglican Christianity is simply a reflection of my own faith but the book is written for all those who are 'of good faith,'[3] those of any faith or none who have the honesty of intention to work alone or together to help heal the world.

Because never have spirituality and faith and the ancient wisdoms of all the great religions been more relevant than in today's fractured world and we need to appreciate these in a spirit of mutual respect and understanding. More than that, I believe there is an urgent need to integrate ancient spiritual wisdom and philosophy with modern scientific endeavors and rediscover the spiritual in all our material experiences. This is our responsibility and we have no choice if we are to halt the destruction all around us. This is a matter of faith for many and an obligation for all humankind.

I am grateful to many people who have helped me in so many ways along this journey.

Peter Challen, my spiritual director, has been a constant source of support, inspiration and information from the very beginning, pointing me in the direction of plenty of useful resources. He also reviewed the chapter on The Hope of a Healed Economy, and from his expertise and experience in that area made helpful comments and amendments.

Dr Iain McGilchrist, Consultant Psychiatrist, and the Reverend Canon Precentor Neil Thompson between them guided and supported me through some of the darkest years of my adult life. Iain also made valuable comments on the two chapters on soul medicine and I am enormously grateful to him for writing the Foreword. Neil unwittingly and unknowingly gave me plenty of inspiration from his sermons and homilies!

Barry Cottrell recommended O Books to me and gave me much encouragement along the path to publication.

My many friends were such a source of strength when I wavered and needed moral support. I also have cause to be thankful for those friends and colleagues who willingly stood in for me on my church duties, and my long suffering family who put up with me being away from them so often, so that I could find time for writing far away from the distractions of home and garden.

Finally of course I am grateful to O Books, to John Hunt and Trevor Greenfield who believed in my book sufficiently to agree to publish it, and to those others who have endorsed my work.

I thank them all.

And needless to say I take full responsibility for any faults and errors that remain, which are mine alone.

Eleanor Stoneham
January 2010

eleanorstoneham@hotmail.com
www.eleanorstoneham.com

Foreword

We live in an age whose rhetoric is that of power. Only by becoming stronger, more powerful, than the next person can we come to have any influence. Into this unseemly foraging for whatever one can get for oneself, some voices have continued to insist, not only that this may be the fastest way to destroy ourselves and the planet given into our care, but that this misses the fact that there is no great achievement without accepting vulnerability. Our apparent weaknesses may be in turn a source of strength, if only we can change the way we look at our relationships with one another. The wounded make the best healers, in medicine, in life.

The reality is that we are all vulnerable, and what differentiates us is only the degree to which we are aware of it. The price of unawareness can be high: we can wreak havoc through the need to avenge our wounds on the world we share – a world whose strengths and beauties are also inextricably bound up with its vulnerability.

A good book speaks with an individual voice: this is a very personal book. I have known Eleanor Stoneham for 10 years now, and in that time I have seen ample demonstration that through confronting one's vulnerability great strengths may emerge.

It would be easy to find reasons to disattend to what she is saying. Some of it is not very comfortable. As Viktor Frankl said, 'Being human means being conscious and being responsible.' Eleanor makes sure you are conscious, and holds you responsible. She points to the fact that it is no good subscribing to high sentiments if you do not put your money – sometimes literally your money (she is after all a highly qualified accountant) – where your mouth is. There is much to be said for what Gary Snyder calls 'the tiresome but tangible work' of local politics. We can all make a difference. Throwing one's hands up in despair is cheap, but it yet may kill us all. We have to continue to hope, even when the odds are against us.

This is the message of the book that you are about to read. Its message is a wise one, and I have no doubt that the world would be a much better place if only we could bring ourselves to heed it. But it also gives encouragement and practical suggestions that can help us along the arduous road towards healing and wholeness.

The word 'health' implies the need for being made whole – thus not a state from which we decline, but towards which we tend. Through awareness of that need for healing we may achieve for ourselves, and for the world of which we are guardians, a wholeness which through our fantasies of power we risk losing forever.

Iain McGilchrist

January 2010

Introduction

I used to believe that we must choose between science and reason on the one hand, and spirituality on the other, as foundations for living our lives. Now I consider this a false choice...we can recover the sense of sacredness...not just in science, but in every area of life.
Larry Dossey, *Reinventing Medicine* [1]

This is a book about human behavior and our spiritual hunger, and a fractured world in urgent need of healing.

It is a book that urges us all to take responsibility for this world before it is too late. More than that, it is a guidebook that shows us how we can between us build a more spiritual, peaceful and happier life for us all. And it is a book for all those who are 'of good faith'[2].

Most of all it is a book of hope: because I believe that our world is at the dawning of a new earth consciousness, a new deep spirituality that will enable us to build this better world for all time if we only allow it to happen. Generations to come may look back and marvel at how it took so long for us to see such obvious need for healing change.

We live at such a worrying and critical time in the history of our planet. One adult in seven is reluctant to have children, fearing for their future because of world issues such as terrorism and climate change. One in four adults apparently puts off making any plans at all for the future for the same reasons.[3]

Man's place in nature is unique. He is not only conscious of his own evolution, but he can shape his evolutionary future by how he behaves. And we behave badly! We commit acts of violence against each other and against ourselves, of a physical and brutal nature or in more subtle ways, such as verbal abuse and childhood bullying. There is aggression and violence in our homes, on our streets, and between communities and nations. It has been said: 'intimate violence and international violence are as tightly bound together as the fingers of a clenched fist.'[4] We commit acts of violence against the environment, manifested in pollution, soil erosion, species extinctions and perhaps in some of the effects of climate change we are now experiencing. We are all guilty of thoughtless and selfish patterns of behavior that can so often directly or indirectly contribute to the suffering of others.

The real problem is that on its own no amount of any rule and regulation, law or leadership, will change the way we behave. Rather than having regulation thrust upon us, we need to understand why we behave as we do. And that means tracing our behavior back to the healing needs of our own wounds. This does not mean our physical wounds, but the wounds we have inherited and those from our own suffering, from the way we react to personal experiences that life has thrown at us: our insecurities and fears, our feelings of hopelessness and despair, that can be reflected in greed and envy, in over-consumption, violence and addictions to work or harmful substances. Our unhealed wounds are potentially dangerous not only for our own personal wellbeing but for the future of the world.

We are in grave danger of being driven by our present behavior to spiritual bankruptcy and physical destruction. Action is urgent. To find healing and wholeness we need to reconnect with our roots, with our souls, rediscovering our spirituality and our faith, and healing those wounds. And once we have found healing for our wounds, we may even discover that we are uniquely equipped to understand the wounds of others, to walk alongside them and assist them in their own healing process. We will feel a profound and healing compassion towards all sentient beings. This is what it means to be a Wounded Healer. And this is our future.

This book has a mission: to explore these healing principles in our places of work and leisure, in our families and communities. It considers how we can infuse our lives and the lives of those around us with a rediscovered spirituality, born out of our own healing. Only then will we be able to build a better planet to leave for future generations to enjoy.

We will be more in tune with our own souls, more in harmony with the spiritual beauty of the natural world around us. We will experience a sense of greater fulfillment alongside the attainment of a real and lasting happiness and peace in our lives. And through our healing we will find our own spiritual wealth.

What qualifications do I have to write of these things? I am a scientist, a postgraduate plant physiologist and ecologist, but also a retired Chartered Accountant, Investment and Tax Adviser, not to mention amateur theologian and parish verger in the Anglican Church. In this book I use this somewhat unusually varied but certainly eclectic experience and knowledge to write from my heart in response to all who have a concern for the future of our world, who want to know what they can do. Here you will find plenty of ideas to explore and pursue. It is my urgent and passionate plea for all of us to sit up, take notice, and take action, individually and collectively. We must, for the sake of the future of our children, grandchildren and beyond. It is an appeal to us all to understand the vital part that we can play if we will only find our spirituality and our soul again, and emulate the compassion and vulnerability of the Wounded Healer. I will explore how taking individual responsibility in our lives can give us all the hope that our fractured world may be healed.

I have organized the book around an exploration of different life experiences that are of relevance to us all. I expose the wounds and look for the healing needs, opportunities and solutions that are to be found throughout our everyday and varied lives, within the context of the Wounded Healer certainly, but while also recognizing its place within a broader spiritual remit, seeking and finding the spirit in all matter, informing the material experience with a spiritual element.

There are many resources throughout the book that the reader can tap into for inspiration and action. There are detailed endnotes for each chapter and a final list of references, including websites, which have been used as sources of information.

The chapters all overflow into a final Appendix. This tells the story of how I was influenced and inspired to write this book, my own Journey of Hope. It then brings in a few more ideas and fills in a few details on others, and leaves us all fully equipped to start our own mission to heal this fractured world.

Perhaps you are skeptical that humankind is in any way responsible for global warming and climate change. Many still are in spite of increasing supportive evidence from respected sources. But we have wounded the earth in many other ways, driving species to extinction, polluting our land with harmful chemicals. Chapter 1 takes a look at the deep wounds we have inflicted on the creation that is planet earth and the increasingly urgent need for sustainability in our lives. Man's violence against the environment is traced from Rachel Carson's early and widely ignored warnings in her book *Silent Spring* to our current concerns about the effects of global warming, just 50 years of enormous and profound change. How long do we have? What can we do? This chapter looks for some answers. Whether the reader believes or not that Creation is the work of God, we can all still learn from the ancient wisdom of the world's different faiths and in particular the various beliefs they hold. The chapter therefore concludes by looking at a few of the many initiatives being taken by these faiths for the preservation of our natural world.

Chapter 2 explains the wisdom of the Wounded Healer and

the origins of the concept in the Greek myth of Chiron the physician and the earliest indigenous shamans, or medicine men. This chapter reminds us why our need to heal is so urgent. It deplores the current obsession with legislation put before healing human behavior. It relates our behavior to our wounds of nature and nurture. It explains the phenomenon of psychic numbing or desensitization, and the links between insecurity, fear and aggression. Starting from an unhealed position where we allow our wounds to crush us, the chapter considers the healing power of love and the ancient philosophy of Yoga. It goes on to explain various ways in which we can all find healing. It describes seven stages to becoming a true Wounded Healer, and the behavioral dangers of becoming stuck somewhere along that path of healing. Beware, the chapter concludes, the demons of ignorance, information overload and futility. We need rather to look for hope to see us through this world crisis and this leads us into the next chapter, on the Hope of Faith.

Pastoral and faith related ministry has a significant healing role to play in the world but our healing needs transcend all boundaries of faith and creed. In spite of Nietzsche's warnings, God is not dead. Not only that, but we can find hope all around us in a new era of spiritual awakening and consciousness. Faiths are divided not by their differing beliefs, but by the values of the religious totalitarians against the values of the religious pluralists. It is now more important than ever before that we reach our children and our youth to prevent them being cynically exploited for political and fundamentalist purposes. Chapter 3 explains how the Wounded Healer can play a part in pastoral ministry for social change and again finds much to celebrate in the initiatives of the many faith organizations that are working towards a healing of our world. The Chapter ends with signs of hope that are visible around us.

But while faith gives us hope, it cannot absolve us from personal responsibility. That is what chapter 4 is about. Here I begin by looking at the lessons that we can all learn from the abolition of the slave trade. What drove those abolitionists? We need to rediscover their spiritual hunger for justice. We need to understand again that the ill treatment of any of our fellow beings is an affront to our own dignity. John Donne wrote, 'No man is an island.' Martin Luther King called for compassion within the brotherhood of man. Such well-known writers in the last century as Carl Jung and Aldous Huxley, Carl Rogers and Scott Peck, recognized the social importance of spiritual healing. Instead we now have the egoistic selfishness of the 'Me Millennium' and much of the self-help industry. The chapter concludes by exploring our individual and collective responsibilities to be catalysts for social change and the dangers where we cannot see the direct effect of our own actions. And where better to start our own initiatives than within our communities, which are the foundation of a just and healthy society.

If you are complacent that you live in a sound community with all the benefits that this may bring, Chapter 5 may make you think again. If on the other hand you have an uneasy feeling that you do not really belong in any community, then this chapter offers some ideas. Real community is vital for our happiness, health and wellbeing and for our very future. This chapter therefore shows how we can recognize and build real community around us, locally, nationally and globally, and how we must beware of the dangers of false community. But there is much more than that. Were our childhoods as idyllic as we remember them? If so what is going wrong? We are failing our children and we need to be more responsible for them collectively in our communities. Different ideas of holistic education are described, along with the recognition of shamanic influences, the vulnerability of the Wounded Healer, within all genuine community. What are people doing and what can we do to help community. The chapter includes plenty of stories of community building happening around us.

'When the last tree is cut, the last river poisoned, and the last fish dead, we will discover that we can't eat money...'[5] reads the Greenpeace banner. Aldous Huxley's utopian island of Pala was doomed by financial greed. The subject of money is dear to all our hearts. That is our problem! Chapter 6 explains some of the fundamental flaws in our economy and why many believe these to be at the heart of serious global injustices that result in unrest, envy, violence and war. And our own flawed behavior just makes the situation worse. I hope to show you the relevance today of ancient and biblical wisdoms where money is concerned and why I support the belief that we need to build a 'Living Economy': a social and economic system that is sustainable, equitable and cooperative. Money is the most emotive of issues and this chapter seriously challenges our ways of thinking while hopefully encouraging us to make changes in our own financial lives.

A healed economy is also an essential prerequisite for a just and affordable healthcare system for all. But a healthcare system needs more than money. Many doctors agree that the practice of medicine is better if it is supported by spiritual values, and I hope to show why in the next two chapters, which look at healthcare in some detail. 'To be a good doctor you have to be a compassionate chameleon, a shape shifter, a shaman,' wrote Cecil Helman.[6] First in Chapter 7 I trace the demise of the holistic medical approach to mind and body and spirit and the seeming reluctance of the profession to bring the soul back into mainstream practice. Many have tried and still campaign for this fundamental change in the mindset of health professionals. The ability of the profession to reach the psychological and spiritual roots and the real healing needs of patients could have profound implications for the holistic wellbeing of individuals, communities, and ultimately our planet earth. Chapter 8 then offers much hope that soul medicine is making a comeback. And fundamental to soul medicine is the healing power of creativity. The book therefore ends as it began, with creation. This time it is our own creativity that comes under the microscope in Chapter 9.

We are all creative in our lives, whether we write or dance, make music or pottery, garden or cook, paint or doodle. We are always making something. The creative process can inspire and heal or it can corrupt, disturb or destroy. Healing and creativity are different sides of the same picture. This final chapter therefore considers the shamanic origins of art and the place of the Wounded Healer in our creativity. I find healing stories to tell among the great composers, painters and writers. But it is our own creativity that has far reaching social significance and we all have responsibilities to use our wounds and our talents through that creativity for good, not evil.

So whether in communities, or our economy, in our treatment of our planet earth, in pastoral and medical care or in our own creative endeavors, we can all make a difference by understanding and attending to our own wounds. We can discover the spiritual that informs all these experiences, we can even become Wounded Healers ourselves. We can open our hearts and minds and make our own individual contributions to the healing of our desperately fractured world.

John Bartlett wrote in prefacing his own famous *Bartlett's Quotations*: 'I have gathered a posie of other men's flowers, and nothing but the thread that binds them is mine own.'

That is not quite true of my book. I have certainly looked for inspiration to the writings and speeches of many influential persons both past and present. But the points of view and observations that bring their words all together into a coherent whole are mine, and they are very much more than simply the 'thread that binds.'

You may find some of what follows controversial. There is no one correct answer to how we solve the world's problems. You may be made to feel uncomfortable by what you read. But few would disagree that the world is in a mess, and at least we should all be pulling together and in the same direction to heal it!

If this book can make its own contribution in some way to the efforts of so many for a more sustainable and peaceful planet, a planet which we can be proud and not ashamed to leave to our descendants, my work will not have been in vain.

Robert Kennedy made a speech in Cape Town on 7 June 1966:

Each time a man stands up for an ideal, or acts to improve the lot of others, or strikes out against injustice, he sends forth a tiny ripple of hope, and crossing each other from a million different centers of energy and daring, those ripples build a current that can sweep down the mightiest walls of oppression and resistance.

It is my fervent hope that many will read this book, be inspired by it, tell other people about it, and use it for discussion in their book club, their faith group, such as a church lent group, or in another equally serious discussion forum. It is also my hope that you the reader will choose and pursue at least one action that appeals, that contributes to healing this fractured and increasingly dangerous world, so that each such deed, however small, will start its own 'ripple of hope' for a future that we may not see but that surely we would wish for those who will come after us.

As Mahatma Gandhi is so often quoted, 'You must be the change you wish to see in the world.'

I trust that we are not too late.

Dorset 2009

Chapter 1
Sustainable Planet – Healed Planet

A staggering 182 million people in sub-Saharan Africa alone could die of disease directly attributable to climate change by the end of the century. Many millions more throughout the world face death and devastation, due to climate-induced floods, famine, drought and conflict.
Christian Aid Report 2006, *The Climate of Poverty: Facts, Fears and Hope*[1]

'For example, how early do you start your science teaching?'
'We start it at the same time we start multiplication and division. First lessons in ecology.'
'Ecology? Isn't that a bit complicated?'
'That's precisely the reason why we begin with it. Never give children a chance of imagining that anything exists in isolation. Make it plain from the very first that all living is relationship. Show them relationships in the woods, in the fields, in the ponds and streams, in the village and the country around it. Rub it in.'
'And let me add,' said the Principal, 'that we always teach the science of relationship in conjunction with the ethics of relationship. Balance, give and take, no excesses - it's the rule of nature and, translated out of fact into morality, it ought to be the rule among people.'
Aldous Huxley, *Island* [2]

God's natural world can be so healing in its beauty, its peace, even in its ruggedness and wildness.

When I am tucked away in my remote hideaway where I do much of my writing, the one constant that gives me inspiration, serenity, and a profound sense of wellbeing is the landscape, and the wilder this is, the more healing it seems to become. Gales that whine around my little attic room, or whip the waves into a frenzy as they crash onto the rocks below during a storm, torrential rain that blots out the landscape: these can have a particularly soothing quality about them, a spirituality that is hard to describe. It is something that must be experienced. I have known such extreme conditions lift me out of a serious bout of depression when nothing else could! In his book, *The Solace of Fierce Landscapes: Exploring Desert and Mountain Spirituality*, Belden Lane, Presbyterian minister and theologian, describes this as the 'unaccountable solace that fierce landscapes offer to the soul. They heal, as well as mirror, the brokenness we find within.' [3]

But the landscape doesn't need to be fierce to have healing power. My father suffered chronic ill health throughout his working life as a research scientist, almost certainly induced as much by stress as by physical disorder. In mid life he was fortunate to inherit some capital from his parents. This enabled him to take up dairy farming. He was a city man until then, knowing little if anything about animal husbandry. He was also a proclaimed agnostic. But with much practical advice and help from others, plenty of hard physical labor and long relentless hours with never a day off, he succeeded in creating a compassionate farming business around a dairy herd that he adored! There was little financial reward for his efforts, but alongside a return to excellent physical fitness, without doubt he found some kind of spiritual healing and fulfillment that had been missing in his previous city life.

With increasing urbanization most of us have sadly lost contact with the land and the soil. As a result I believe that a part of our soul has died. But we do not have to own a farm to renew that connection! Many find less expensive and more readily available succor working the land within their own gardens, with healthy homegrown fruit and vegetables a valuable byproduct of their endeavors. And for those without a garden, there are community gardens, such as the thriving Clinton Community Garden[4] in New York City. This is an inspiring story of successful urban regeneration. Taking in hand an ugly lot in the heart of that city, that had been abandoned for many years and strewn with all kinds of debris including dumped cars, keen volunteer citizens have created a green garden sanctuary, a place of tranquility for all to enjoy. With more than 100 plots now actively cultivated, it has a waiting list for those who would like a share of the action.

There seems to be a real resurgence of interest in getting back onto the land, getting back to our roots, seeking a reconnection of soil and soul.

What about those who for any reason are unable to find some land with which to make such a connection? All of us can be informed and enriched by the wonderful TV images of the natural world brought into our living rooms through the efforts of the latest incredible photographic techniques and the enthusiasm of the most dedicated and knowledgeable presenters such as the broadcaster and naturalist Sir David Attenborough.

If we do not allow the natural world to speak to us, if we do not let the fierceness give us solace, or the silence reach and heal us, then we can turn our wounds, our own brokenness, against the natural world. And that is what we are doing. By our thoughtless actions we damage the very soul of nature that could help us most in our own healing.

If only we would slow down and watch and listen. If only we would allow ourselves to become more deeply aware of that spirit that infuses all matter.

This powerful source of healing is itself now hurt. Nature has become the docile dog that will savage the child who innocently pokes it in the eye. We are hurting our planet. If we do not act quickly, it may turn on us and destroy us.

But we are not innocent bystanders. Now I know that many are still skeptical about humankind's role in climate change. A Times poll in 2009 found that only two in five Britons believed that this current and visible problem was largely man made. But those that still harbor any doubts that we are in any way responsible for climate change should heed the report to world leaders by the United Nations Intergovernmental Panel on Climate Change (IPCC) following its meeting in Paris at the start of 2007. This report concludes that it is very likely (and that means a 90% chance!) that the activities of man are responsible for the increased greenhouse gases and the resultant problems of climate change now being seen and predicted for the foreseeable future.[5] As a consequence average temperatures are likely to rise by 4°C by the end of the century. This is the consensus of opinion from the combined efforts of more than 800 contributing authors and more than 450 lead authors, with more than 2500 scientific expert reviewers involved in the two-stage scientific and technical review process.

For the continuing cynics why not use an adaptation of Pascal's Wager? Pascal reasoned that whether or not one believed in the existence of God, it was a safer bet and one had nothing to lose by supposing that He existed. So it is with the global warming debate. If we allow ourselves to become more spiritually aware, more sensitive to our finely balanced place in the world, more compassionate towards the plight of our brethren across the globe, more simple in our needs, more at peace with ourselves, more in tune with our own souls and the soil beneath our feet, then surely we are all enriched? We will certainly be happier, and we will be leaving a better world for those who come after us. What do we have to lose?

There are bound to be some controversies and debates

surrounding the details of the IPCC report and the scale of its significance. Much of our best scientific research effort is being directed towards gaining a fuller understanding of all the issues involved, and what actions we can take.

We saw the distress that extreme weather can inflict in the 2005 devastation of New Orleans by Hurricane Katrina. Even those who cannot quite believe or accept the evidence for the part humankind may be playing in climate change cannot deny the extent of human suffering now seen on a global scale. This then becomes more than a debate on climate change. It becomes a matter of human compassion and justice. These injustices brew a potentially dangerous potion of civil unrest and worse. There is a social and moral imperative for us all to share everything, to watch out for each other, to work for global healing. I believe we can no longer ignore our global responsibilities.

It is also a great injustice that those countries with materially comfortable lifestyles are often least affected by the climate change that we now know is 'very likely' to have been brought about by our own profligate squandering of natural resources. The developed world has the resources to adapt most easily to any of the resultant climate change. It is the dispossessed and vulnerable in the poorer parts of the world who suffer dispro-portionately with hunger and disease and homelessness in the face of droughts, floods, tsunamis, and other natural disasters. The habitats of the poor are fragile, and they cannot afford to build defenses or replace their homes and livelihoods without our help. Does it matter whose fault, if any, it is?

Yes it does. There is actually enough productive capacity in the world to provide every living man woman and child with a decent basic way of life. It is important that we help communities become self sufficient for a better future. It is also imperative that we curb our own excesses, that we stop violating the natural world around us, that we acknowledge the integrity of our finely balanced ecosystems. Every time we drive one more animal or plant to extinction, not only are we poorer for that, but also the effect on the fragile balance of planetary life may be profound. That is why it is so important, and ever more urgent, that we do not compromise our future by today's actions, or indeed through our inactions.

What part do our governments play? As with so many of society's problems, it seems that we may be content to sit back, do nothing and rely for solutions on a stream of laws and regulations from both national and local governments. Of course we all need the leaders we have voted for to take action on the big issues. But these initiatives are only a part of any solution. Our own behavior must also change and that change begins within our own hearts and minds, it must reach out from our own souls.

We have that power within us to heal our own behavior, to define our own future. We can listen again deeply to the natural world around us and let it speak to us through the silence or the tempest. We can nurture a reverence, a love and respect for the natural world around us, and be open to its healing powers.

Then we will no longer want to destroy it. We will no longer want to defile it with our gas guzzling cars, our litter and filth, our plastics, our bottles and our cans. We will regain our spirituality and seek a simpler life. We will discover humility and vulnerability and a compassion for all living beings. We may even walk barefoot upon the earth, because we 'tread on the earth so much more gently barefoot.' [6] Then we will experience a harmony of body, soil and soul and we may even become Wounded Healers for a fractured world.[7]

Ecology and our place in evolution

In my youth at school in the early 1960s I had a passionate interest in ecology. I studied it diligently as part of my botanical school exams and later at University. But it was only as I walked through the great National Parks of Yosemite or California's Giant Redwoods, hiked the UK's Yorkshire and Derbyshire Dales or tramped the Burren in Eire, and saw all the plants and creatures in their natural habitats, that I came to discover and feel a spiritual attachment to such a wonderful and varied world, and a great respect for its complexities.

Our understanding of the need for sustainable management of the earth's finite resources, and the stewardship of our natural environment, probably owes much to the work of the American scientist Eugene Odum, often referred to as the father of ecology. His *Fundamentals of Ecology* written in 1953 with his brother was a groundbreaking American textbook of the time, even though its message was not picked up in my own English schoolbooks.

Odum introduced the concept of the study of living organic communities within their physical settings and of ecosystems interacting one with another on a global basis.

Now James Lovelock has developed and refined his Gaia Theory, born out of the Gaia Hypothesis that he proposed with Lynn Margulis in the early 1970s. The Gaia theory views the Earth '...as a self regulating system made up from the totality of organisms, the surface rocks, the ocean and the atmosphere – tightly coupled as an evolving system.'[8] The goal of the system according to Lovelock's theory is 'the regulation of surface conditions so as to always be as favorable as possible for contemporary life.' Alongside Lovelock's work the scientists were also changing their views on how the earth evolves. Conventional science used to say that life adapted to conditions on earth as both evolved separately. But these views have also changed. In 2001 more than 1000 delegates representing four important global change organizations[9] attended the first Global Change Open Science Conference in Amsterdam, where they made the following declaration: 'The Earth System behaves as a single, self-regulating system comprised of physical, chemical, biological and human components.'[10] Thus was the new discipline of Earth System Science formally declared, and it represented a significant step on the road towards formal adoption of the Gaian Theory. But the scientists fell short of giving a purpose for this single dynamic entity, which in Lovelock's Gaian terms is to sustain habitability. Scientists still do not universally accept the Theory. For those scientists Lovelock has a plea: please do not allow scientific reductionism to close your eyes to the wisdom of the ancient sacred texts or the Gaia Theory, but rather try to understand the ineffable in our creation, the God immanent but unknowable.[11] As the naturalist Francis Rose once observed, 'nature is very complex. When you start to interfere by thoughtless introduction of alien species, you do so at your own peril.'[12]

Can we afford to ignore any longer the fact that we are one living organism in an extremely intricate and complex web or ecosystem worldwide, of living interactions? I think not.

Man's violence against the environment

An early awareness of our violence against the natural environment probably came with James Lovelock's invention[13] in 1957 of the Electron Capture Detector, a device used for measuring chemical compounds in atmosphere and matter. This enabled the discovery of residual pesticides in the food we eat, the evidence for which Rachel Carson exposed to a general public in her book *Silent Spring* in 1963. In this she brought together the available research at that time on toxicology, ecology and epidemiology. She sought to put the world on alert as to the dangers ahead for humanity that she foresaw if we continued to use chemicals indiscriminately in our homes. She warned of the dangers of using such chemicals for agricultural and horticultural purposes, if we did not understand the possible long-term harm they may cause. She saw that the resultant build up of these substances in our food chain could be catastrophic to wild life environments and our own health. Most importantly, the book shattered our assumptions until then that the environment had an infinite capacity to absorb pollutants and maintain its own stability.

While much of what Carson wrote is of course now out of date, it was a pivotal book in opening the debate on modern ecology. At the time of its first publication it provoked antagonism from the chemical manufacturers and press alike. This probably only served to increase its readership and the impact of its message! It was also said to have influenced the foundation of Friends of the Earth in 1969 in San Francisco by David Brower. This non-profit advocacy organization operates independently of any political party or large corporation, to 'campaign on the most urgent environmental and social issues...challenge the current model of economic and corporate globalization, and promote solutions that will help to create environmentally sustainable and socially just societies.'[14]

From these beginnings and with Friends of the Earth to support the cause, there was little to hold back the advance of the environmental movement. The American biologist Paul Ehrlich's book *The Population Bomb* had recently been published on the connection between human population, resource exploitation and the environment.[15] This fuelled the debate.

Then in 1971 Greenpeace started up in Canada and as part of a program of organized civil protests and non-violent interference they launched an aggressive agenda to stop environmental damage. A year later Barbara Ward wrote, with Rene Jules Dubos, *Only One Earth: the Care and Maintenance of a Small Planet.* This was an exploration of man's relationship with his environment, as an ecological study on a global level. It was written for The United Nations Conference on the Human Environment, held from 5-16 June 1972, in Stockholm, Sweden, the first major international gathering of nations to address the world's environmental problems.

The American government of that time, led by President Richard Nixon, also gave high priority to environmental preservation and took a leading role in developing the concept of international cooperation to address the issues involved. He created

23

Project Independence, which set a national goal, to develop the potential to meet the country's own energy needs without relying on foreign energy. At that time, the United States imported less than a third of its oil from foreign countries, and that was regarded as an unacceptably high figure. Sadly the impetus of Richard Nixon's endeavors back in the 1970s was lost through subsequent administrations. Following the election of President Obama to the White House, Al Gore wrote, '...today, after all six of the presidents succeeding Nixon repeated some version of his goal, our dependence (on imported oil) has doubled from one-third to nearly two-thirds - and many feel that global oil production is at or near its peak.'

Amazingly, when I first conceived the idea for this book and started my research in 2004 there was very little public knowledge or awareness of the urgency of the environmental problems we now face globally. This was in spite of the plethora of research and information that clearly has been available through several decades and the best endeavors of many authors to educate us of the need for change. The controversy over *Silent Spring* is a distant memory.

Al Gore described President Obama's election success as an 'inspiring and transformative choice by the American people,' which calls for 'an emergency rescue of human civilization from the imminent and rapidly growing threat posed by the climate crisis...in a world that desperately needs to protect its primary endowment: the integrity and livability of the planet.' He continued:

...to those who are still tempted to dismiss the increasingly urgent alarms from scientists around the world, ignore the melting of the north polar ice cap and all of the other apocalyptic warnings from the planet itself, and who roll their eyes at the very mention of this existential threat to the future of the human species, please wake up. Our children and grandchildren need you to hear and recognize the truth of our situation, before it is too late.[16]

Al Gore has probably done more than anyone to bring an awareness of our global warming crisis to Americans, through his film and supporting book, *An Inconvenient Truth.* Nevertheless his views continue to be met with cynicism and hostility by many.

What are we all doing individually? Many of us already will be supporting the various aid agencies that work tirelessly and unselfishly to alleviate immediate global suffering. There are plenty of such organizations craving our support. We are also becoming much better at recycling our trash and becoming more energy efficient. We learn, I hope, to be less reliant on our cars. We use low energy light bulbs. But there are still many who disregard such initiatives. And I am sure that too often these changes are being forced by government intervention rather than coming from our own hearts and souls.

This innate ability we seem to have to ignore warnings until it is too late reminds me of the fire alarm that went off in the middle of the night in our holiday hotel. Bleary eyed and scantily dressed we stumbled out into the garden to be counted. It was only when we all thankfully returned to our beds some time later that we met a family peering round the corner of their bedroom door. 'Was it a false alarm then?' the father asked. Fortunately it was!

I feel sure that the current situation we find ourselves in is not a false alarm. And of course there is one fundamental difference between the fire alarm story and the daily choices that we all have to make on sustainable living. The fire escape decision did not involve money! Always, they say, follow the money. Financial considerations sadly color our judgment when they should not do so. And this is why laws and rules and regulations have to play a part in finding solutions to our problems. I love

Upton Sinclair's observation: 'It is difficult to get a man to understand something when his salary depends on his not understanding it.'[17]

Also, and sadly, the many blogs and websites that perpetuate silliness seem to attract a far greater following than those that attempt serious dialogue and generate calls to action. Of course we all need escapism in our lives. We need refuge from our very real underlying fears and doubts. It may be a good TV whodunit, an outrageously politically incorrect comedy, a sport event, a good novel or a musical instrument. I myself love a good hospital 'soap'. But the serious things in life must also receive our attention.

Can we afford to take our time, to sit back and hope that this is all a false alarm? The writer of the Old Testament book of Ecclesiastes commented in some exasperation on the apparent inability of man to make any lasting change in the world. 'What has been is what will be, and what has been done is what will be done; and there is nothing new under the sun.'[18]

So why does change seem so slow? Why do we continue on this course of possible self-destruction?

It seems that even if we are happy to read, to comment, to worry, debate and blog about our futures, most of us will then leave any behavioral change to the next man! There also seems to be a widespread human indifference to large-scale disasters both natural and man-made. These news stories seem to induce in us a kind of psychic numbing. Why is this?

Apparently part of the answer could be in our genetic history. We are 'wired' to care for ourselves and for those immediately around us to ensure our own security and survival. In our ancestral past we had no awareness of what was happening beyond our immediate environment. We would have been unaware of any tragedies further afield, of whatever magnitude.[19] It has been suggested that perhaps we have not adapted yet to our wider global world even though events on the other side of that world are emblazoned daily on our massive plasma television screens! We need to unscramble our wiring and start taking positive remedial action.

How long do we have?

Warnings of the potentially catastrophic effects of our violence against the environment have been made repeatedly over several decades. There is still insufficient action being taken. How much longer do we have?

James Lovelock wrote in 2006 that he believed we could be past the point of no return unless we are willing to embrace nuclear power for our energy needs. Even then, he said, it will be very difficult indeed to survive this latest crisis. North America takes the lead in this, producing 19% of its electricity needs through nuclear power.[20] Many countries are dubious of the risks, the UK included, and the debate rumbles on. Because of man's inherent resistance to change, seen also within scientific circles, Lovelock reminds us that we have wasted perhaps 20 years that we can ill afford to lose in resolving the problems of climate change. [21] In 2009 Lovelock published *The Vanishing Face of Gaia: a Final Warning*.[22] In this he not only casts doubt on some of the IPCC models: he also shows that trends based on observed data are actually far worse than the IPCC predictions and that we have gone beyond that tipping point where the earth can no longer adjust to maintain the equilibrium that sustains life as we know it. But according to Lovelock the planet can look after itself. It is humankind that urgently needs saving!

Some show more optimism. The UK Government's chief economist Nicholas Stern wrote in 2006 'There is still time to avoid the worst impacts of climate change, if we act now and act internationally.'[23]

We may have little time to lose. Meanwhile, as Lovelock points out, resources diminish daily while we make up our minds what to do!

The French Jesuit, biologist, philosopher and paleontologist, Teilhard de Chardin, died in 1955 a full ten years before Lovelock's Gaian Theory was born. But he believed the earth to be in some way the prime living force at the center of our future existence. He saw man and nature as being one inextricably linked organic and living whole. 'The world,' Teilhard wrote, 'must be compared not to a bundle of elements in artificial juxta-position, but to an organized system informed by a broad unity of growth proper to itself.'[24] He recognized that we are unique in the role we play in the evolutionary process. We are the first organisms that can collaborate with (or thwart) the evolutionary process. We can profoundly affect the course of our evolution by our actions or inactions.

The American Greek evolution biologist and futurist Elisabet Sahtouris also explores the pressing implications of the Gaia theory to mankind. She echoes de Chardin when she writes that we need to mature from competition to cooperation. She says humanity is in an adolescent crisis, brought upon ourselves by our egotistic behavior. She argues, in *Earth Dance: Living Systems in Evolution*, that our maturity as a species 'depends on our accepting the responsibility for our natural heritage of behavior freedom by working consciously and cooperatively toward our own health along with that of our planet.'[25]

Faiths and Creation [26]

All the world's faiths share a concern for Creation. Whether or not we believe that our world is God's Creation, it is instructive to look at the beliefs of some of the main faiths regarding our relationship with the environment. We should be aware of the substantial work they are all doing, often in collaboration or cooperation with others, towards ensuring the earth's future protection.

The Tanzanian island of Misali on the East African coast is an important nesting site for turtles and has wonderful corals reefs to support the fish population.[27] The local fishermen were unwittingly beginning to destroy this ecosystem by the indiscriminate use of dynamite to literally blow their fishing catch out of the water. This made their fishing so much easier, and the catch so much more certain. But of course this was not only killing young fish that were too small to catch, and would have escaped through more traditional nets. It was also destroying the coral habitat on which the fish population depends. In the long term this would seriously threaten the livelihood of the fishing community. Attempts to educate the fishermen through leaflets had no effect, and neither did the imposition of a law banning this method of fishing. The law was simply flouted, a sadly common human reaction. Scientists even suggested that there should be armed patrols to apprehend the culprits to put an end to this devastation of their environment. But by appealing to the Muslim faith of the majority involved, through the community sheik leaders, the fishermen were persuaded that what they were doing was wrong, that dynamite fishing is illegal according to the laws of Islam. In particular the Qur'an teaches 'O children of Adam!...eat and drink: but waste not by excess for Allah loveth not the wasters.'[28]

Christianity [29]

Christianity is still the faith to which 33% of the world's population and 78% of North Americans turn for their healing and spiritual nourishment. Indeed the ministry of Jesus Christ reflects the very essence of the Wounded Healer, with his compassion borne out of his own redemptive suffering for mankind.

Throughout the history of Christianity, its followers have tended to think of their relationship with God's Divine creation in terms of stewardship, which has been too often interpreted as mastery. Faced by the threat of environmental crises, the main Christian Churches have been redefining their theology, as seen in the document from a meeting of the World Council of

Churches in Granvollen, Norway, in 1988:

> The drive to have 'mastery' over creation has resulted in the senseless exploitation of natural resources, the alienation of the land from people and the destruction of indigenous cultures...Creation came into being by the will and love of the Triune God, and as such it possess an inner cohesion and goodness. Though human eyes may not always discern it, every creature and the whole creation in chorus bear witness to the glorious unity and harmony with which creation is endowed. And when our human eyes are opened and our tongues unloosed, we too learn to praise and participate in the life, love, power and freedom that is God's continuing gift and grace.

The World Council of Churches again came together in 1990 'to consider the issues of justice, peace, and the integrity of creation,' when they wrote in an affirmation of faith [30]:

> The integrity of creation has a social aspect which we recognise as peace with justice, and an ecological aspect which we recognise in the self-renewing, sustainable character of natural eco-systems. We will resist the claim that anything in creation is merely a resource for human exploitation. We will resist species extinction for human benefit; consumerism and harmful mass production; pollution of land, air and waters; all human activities which are now leading to probable rapid climate change; and the policies and plans which contribute to the disintegration of creation.

The report concludes with a challenge to all Christians,

> to discover anew the truth that God's love and liberation is for all creation, not just humanity; to realise that we should have

been stewards, priests, co-creators with God for the rest of creation but have actually often been the ones responsible for its destruction; and to seek new ways of living and being Christians that will restore that balance and give the hope of life to so much of the endangered planet.

How many of us who claim to be Christians are prepared to rise to that challenge?

Judaism [31]

Jews believe that the entire universe is the work of the Creator, and therefore to love God must mean to love everything He has created, including the inanimate, plants, animals and man. This core belief is behind the Jewish attitude to environmental issues. They also believe that nature in all its beauty has been created for man, and it is, therefore, wrong for man to spoil it. Moreover, man's connection to nature can restore him to his original character, to a natural state of happiness and joy.

In the current environmental crisis, Jewish values and laws are seen to be paramount. 'If the proper course is followed, man will not forfeit his opportunity to live a life of comfort in his environment, nor will the environment be uncomfortable with man.'

Judaism teaches that it is wrong to over exploit the earth's resources, or behave in such a way as to destroy any species, since all have been created for some purpose. Jews understand the vital importance of preserving the natural balance of creation.

Islam [32]

Islam, the third great Abrahamic Faith alongside Christianity and Judaism, teaches that:

31

humanity is the only creation of Allah to be entrusted with the overall responsibility of maintaining planet Earth in the overall balanced ecology that man found...If biologists believe that humans are the greatest agents of ecological change on the surface of the earth, is it not humans who, drawn from the brink, will, for their own good, abandon Mammon and listen to the prescriptions of God on the conservation of their environment and the environment of all the creatures on earth? The Islamic answer to this question is decisively in the affirmative.

Sikhism [33]

Guru Nanak, who laid the foundation of Sikhism in the late fifteenth century, declared that matter is only a form of spirit and spirit is the only reality. 'The current instability of the natural system of the earth, the external environment of human beings, is only a reflection of the instability and pain within humans. The increasing barrenness of the earth's terrain is a reflection of the emptiness within humans.' On creation the Sikh believes:

a concern for the environment is part of an integrated approach to life and nature. As all creation has the same origin and end, humans must have consciousness of their place in creation and their relationship with the rest of creation. Humans should conduct themselves through life with love, compassion, and justice. Becoming one and being in harmony with God implies that humans endeavor to live in harmony with all of God's creation.

Hinduism [34]

In the UK, near Birmingham, the Hindu community has reclaimed an area of polluted industrial scrubland. Here they have built a beautiful Hindu Temple within surroundings that now incorporate a historic canal, woodland and hills. From early beginnings where there was much resistance from local communities, there is now a place of beauty that is available not only for Hindu worship, but also cultural and educational events. The Hindus have healed the earth and restored a green and healthy environment to wildlife and the local community.

Here is another religion that teaches its followers to live simply and to see God in everything in the Universe. 'Conserve ecology or perish,' says the *Bhagavad Gita*, (or Song of God), the Hindu sacred scripture.

'God's creation is sacred. Humanity does not have the right to destroy what it cannot create. Humans have to realize the interconnectedness of living entities and emphasize the idea of moral responsibility to oneself, one's society, and the world as a whole.' Hindus teach that we can learn spiritual happiness and find fulfillment by living simply and without chasing after material wants and pleasures:

> They have to milk a cow and enjoy, not cut at the udder of the cow with greed to enjoy what is not available in the natural course. Do not use anything belonging to nature, such as oil, coal, or forest, at a greater rate than you can replenish it...do not destroy birds, fish, earthworms, and even bacteria which play vital ecological roles; once they are annihilated you cannot recreate them. Thus only can you avoid becoming bankrupt, and the life cycle can continue for a long, long time.

Buddhism [35]
Of all the great faiths and philosophies, the Buddhist seems to understand most clearly not only our need to live more simply and altruistically within the natural world but also the healing power of nature.

The Vietnamese monk Venerable Thich Nhat Hanh writes:

Buddhists believe that the reality of the interconnectedness of human beings, society and Nature will reveal itself more...as we gradually cease to be possessed by anxiety, fear, and the dispersion of the mind. Among the three - human beings, society, and Nature - it is us who begin to effect change. But in order to effect change we must recover ourselves, one must be whole. Since this requires the kind of environment favorable to one's healing, one must seek the kind of lifestyle that is free from the destruction of one's humanness. Efforts to change the environment and to change oneself are both necessary. But we know how difficult it is to change the environment if individuals themselves are not in a state of equilibrium.

Daoism

Daoism is one of the smallest religions of all. Actually Daoism, like Buddhism, is more a philosophy of life than a religion, as Daoists worship no god as such. The Daoist believes that nature has its own limits, that if recklessly exploited by greed or desire, we will see extinction and destruction. Daoists see in the deepening world environmental crisis that ways of human thinking have unbalanced the harmonious relationship between human beings and nature, and overstressed the power and influence of the human will over nature. The number of thriving species on our planet measures the affluence of the true Daoist. If one considers the continuing destruction of life forms on this earth, the many species threatened with a man induced extinction, then by Daoist standards we are now becoming very poor indeed.

It seems to me from these brief vignettes that the Ancient Wisdom of the great Eastern faith traditions recognizes a deeper spiritual commune of mankind with nature. Many of us hunger for that spirituality. We could learn so much about the links between the unrest in our wounded souls and the wounds of the

34

natural world if we would only allow our hearts to be receptive to what all these great faiths and philosophies have to offer. Between them they provide a wonderful tapestry of beliefs. But equally they are all united in the same mission. We all have a duty of care to the world, whether based upon our sensitivity and compassion or the beliefs of our faith, or indeed both. We surely have to look beyond our own horizons more and appreciate our place in a much wider world.

As the Sikh teaches us,

All life is interconnected. A human body consists of many parts; every one of them has a distinct name, location, and function, and all of them are dependent upon each other. In the same way, all the constituents of this universe and this earth are dependent upon each other. Decisions in one country or continent cannot be ignored by others. Choices in one place have measurable consequences for the rest of the world. It is part of the same system.[36]

The protection of the coral reefs and the turtle sites in Misali, and the success of the Hindu Temple available for all to enjoy, are just two of the many achievements of the Alliance of Religions and Conservation (ARC), a secular organization founded in 1995 by The Prince Philip Duke of Edinburgh. Nine years before that, as President of the World Wide Fund for Nature (WWF) International, Prince Philip had initiated discussion between five major world religions (Buddhism, Christianity, Hinduism, Islam and Judaism) and leading environmental organizations. Representatives were asked to bring to that first meeting at Assisi, in Italy, details of the various environmental projects that they were running at that time. Surprisingly, it transpired that these projects were few. But each faith was also asked to prepare a statement explaining their place in the context of creation and ecology, and that proved to be a real catalyst for change.

This initial meeting developed into a worldwide network of faith groups working on ecological and development issues and by the time the ARC was launched at Windsor Castle in 1995 there were nine religions involved and thousands of environmental projects in hand, initiating much extremely valuable and far reaching conservation work. Both the World Bank and the BBC World Service were invited to the talks and launch since the faith leaders saw two of the greatest obstacles to world conservation as being the power of world economic forces and the satellite technology that was spreading Western values worldwide.

The ARC has a vision 'of people, through their beliefs, treading more gently upon the earth,' and a twofold strategy 'to help faiths realize their potential to be proactive on environmental issues and to help secular groups recognize this and become active partners.'[37]

While the great faiths share much common ground in their concern for creation and environmental sustainability, they also have their differences, which must be respected if we are to appeal to the hearts and minds of any faith group for real change. This most certainly does not mean a watering down of all beliefs and faiths to a lowest common denominator. The slogan adopted in the early days of the ARC was 'Come, proud of what you bring of your own, but humble enough to listen.' As Rowan Williams, Archbishop of Canterbury, explained on his visit to the new Hindu Temple of Shri Venkateswara (Balaji) in Birmingham on 15 November 2008, 'interfaith dialogue is not a way of obliterating our differences, it's a way of living creatively with them. A way of living gratefully with them, so that our compassion, our love and our fellow feeling do not stop simply with those who are like us.'[38]

The work and vision of the ARC continues. In November 2006 they organized a conference in Oslo[39] alongside the Norwegian Government, in recognition that international work for sustainable development and respect for creation and ecology should from now on directly involve the faiths. It was important to reflect on and coordinate the many individual initiatives already launched by those faiths. By provision of education and information, and by involving, listening and resourcing, it was hoped that the impact of these faith initiatives would be enhanced. My book is a part of that process: this is my vision.

The Oslo conference was a vital step forward and its longer-term influence remains to be seen. Government initiatives alone by their very nature can become part of a nation's own political agenda. And they do not necessarily survive changes in leadership. On the other hand the almost unique international structure of the world's great religions enables them to coordinate and promote changes on a global scale. Faith involvement introduces continuity, and accordingly the potential for greater impact and the promise of real ongoing change. We can all play our part in ensuring a continuity of focus, through our own faith, through our votes and through our actions.

Conclusion

Too often in the past we have been arrogant enough to believe that humanity is in some way in charge of the world's ecosystems. We have either seen ourselves as the dominant stewards of God's creation or believed that our superior intelligence and consciousness entitles us to manipulate the world's resources solely for our own needs. I believe that both views are wrong. I believe we need to become more sensitive to our place within this web of life that God has created. I believe that our future depends on that understanding. I am not alone.

Lovelock has described our desire to use this Earth for our benefit alone, particularly in our wholesale burning of fossil fuels, as 'breathtaking insolence'. [40] Cottrell calls it the 'arrogance of the superiority of intellect'.[41] When we truly regain our sense of belonging to earth, he says, 'this elemental awareness automatically brings with it a gentleness and humility towards all other expressions of life.'

We have indeed sinned in all our excessive use and abuse of nature, showing our greed and selfishness. In the past this often may have been due to ignorance, but we can no longer claim that as any sort of excuse for our behavior.

We need to come with humility and awe to apologize to our own higher spiritual power, whether that is God, Dao, Yahweh, Allah, or perhaps simply our own inner conscience. We need to beg forgiveness and resolve in our healed hearts and souls here and now to do all we can to amend what we have caused and prevent further ravaging of the natural and wonderful creation of which we are but a relatively small but so destructive part. 'We have followed too much the devices and desires of our own hearts,' we lament in the beautiful prose and poetry of The Order for Evening Prayer in the 1662 Book of Common Prayer for the Church of England. Do we go out and live our faith?

It seems that too many of us follow the mechanics of our religion to the near exclusion of prayerful living and discipleship. I believe there is a need for much more spirituality in our Western religions, for more ministry directed to the healing of our own souls for the sake of the spiritual health of the world around us, and for underpinning our mission to the world, not just for our own personal redemption.

While controversy and debate continues over the facts surrounding climate change and our role in handling this, the ecologists have little doubt that we are part of a complex web of life and we are damaging this fragile global ecosystem. We have become aware that any of our actions must weave into that whole living system. Traditional indigenous cultures understand that and we need to work with them. They have wisdom that we have lost in our urbanization. As Lovelock reminds us, we need 'to renew that love and empathy for nature that we lost when we began our love affair with city life.'[42]

There is increasing pressure to produce more and cheaper food with little regard for our health or the health of the stock and the land. This puts farming at risk, caught up as it is in a new business culture, driven primarily by profit motivation, where all too often science has become a tool to help fight against the natural rhythms of the land.[43] We need to rediscover the craft of genuine agrarian farming where farmers are sensitive to the role of nature in the process.[44]

We are getting better at buying local produce but the continuing vast success of hypermarkets is testimony to the work still needed in that direction. Food supermarkets continually jostle with each other in price wars to stock the cheapest produce, thereby prejudicing animal and plant welfare and the quality of the end product.

So I urge you the reader to please stop believing that our carbon emissions and climate change are something that can be solved by attacking the symptoms. Let's treat the disease rather than the symptoms. Stop expecting instant action from governments and corporations to combat the ills of society as if they alone must solve these problems while we continue to carry on our lives in the same selfish and unsustainable ways. We all need wake up calls from time to time to bring us back to reality. Angina attacks tell us we need to be looking after our heart; stress related illnesses might warn us that we need to review our work/life balance. It is true that climate change is now far too big an issue to sort out as individuals alone without government and scientific intervention. But it is a strident wake up call for many of the world's other problems: all are symptoms of serious disease, disease that needs healing not just curing. And healing must start within us. We can then inform and inspire those around us, in our workplaces, our communities, and our churches. This is an imperative for every day of the week, not only our Holy Days.

We have a responsibility to leave a cleaner healthier

environment for our children and grandchildren. We need to end the suffering of all our fellow human beings. No one should be hungry or thirsty or subjected to unnecessary disease and suffering. There must be justice and peace on a global scale. Then we will all find a profound spiritual wealth.

So, you may ask, where is the Wounded Healer in our world? The next chapter will combine spirituality with compassion and healing and take a journey back to the origins of the archetypal Wounded Healer in the Greek myth of Chiron and in indigenous shamanism. Later chapters will then show the reader how the compassion of the Wounded Healer, within a broader spiritual paradigm, has fundamental importance in all our lives. Because, as Carl Jung recognized, it is our own hurts and wounds, and how we have healed them, that determine our own abilities to heal others. And this has a profound significance for the future health of our world. As John Sentamu, Archbishop of York, reminded us in his inaugural address,

"The trouble with virtually all forms of revolution and modernising strategies is that they change everything − except the human heart. And until that is changed corporately, nothing is significantly different in the long run."[45]

Chapter 2
From Chiron to Shaman
(Wounded Healers for a Fractured World)

Myths are the mirrors in which we can study human life.
Petrusca Clarkson, *The Transpersonal Relationship in Psychotherapy* [1]

Pain and loneliness are forms of energy that can be transformed if we turn them outward, using them to recognize and redeem someone else's pain or loneliness.
Jonathan Sacks, *To Heal a Fractured World* [2]

In Greek mythology there was a Centaur called Chiron.[3] Centaurs are normally portrayed as clumsy and brutal beasts. Chiron was different. He was kind, gentle and well educated and tutored many of the Greek gods. Famous pupils included Jason, the leader of the fifty Argonauts, who sailed aboard the Argo to bring back the golden fleece to Pelias. Another was Achilles of the vulnerable heel legend, killed by an arrow from Apollo's bow.

Much of Greek mythology is highly intricate and complex and the myth of Chiron varies in precise details depending on its source. The story goes that he was the love child of an affair between the Greek God Cronus and the Earth Nymph Philyra. Before making love to Philyra, Cronus changed her into a horse to allay the suspicions of his wife Rhea. And so the centaur

Chiron was conceived. Abandoned by his parents at birth, Chiron was adopted and brought up by Apollo, The Divine Physician, who trained him to be a great and wise teacher, physician and healer.

Centaurs were known for their over indulgences and Chiron was probably no exception. One day there was a bloody fight between Centaurs over a carafe of wine and Chiron was accidentally shot in his knee by a stray poisoned arrow from the bow of Heracles (or Hercules). The wound would not heal and it gave him much pain. Centaurs also had the gift of immortality. Such was Chiron's suffering, from both the mental wounds of his abandonment at birth and from this painful physical wounding, that he prayed to the gods to let him surrender his own immortality and die. He then spent the rest of his life trying to find a cure for his physical wound and became an expert in the healing power of plants, particularly the herbal remedies he developed for war wounds. But the healing abilities for which he was renowned came especially from the empathy he developed for the suffering of others, acquired from his struggle to overcome his own physical and mental wounds. Chiron allowed his own wounds to be a source of healing for others. He became a Wounded Healer.

What became of Chiron? His prayer was eventually answered and after his death he was placed in the sky by the king of the Greek gods, Zeus (the Roman Jupiter and the only surviving son of Cronus and Rhea), where he can be seen in the night sky as the constellation Sagittarius (the archer), otherwise known as Centaur (the man/horse).

Greek mythology is of course a collection of fables, of the Greek gods, goddesses and heroes. But many of them encompass a deeper wisdom about human behavior even if few have any basis in fact.

One of the legacies left by the analytical psychologist Carl Jung was the idea that in our psyche we all share deep inherited and unconscious ideas and images together known as our 'collective unconscious.' This collective unconscious, Jung said, is made up of different recognizable human models or archetypes. He saw in the Greek myth of Chiron a reflection of the archetypal Wounded Healer of the indigenous medicine man or shaman, first recorded in the earliest known hunting and fishing communities of Siberia and Sub Arctic North America. In fact it was probably from the language of a small group of hunters and reindeer herders from the Arctic Tungus that the name shaman comes, meaning 'he who knows'.

The true shaman was both priest and healer and prophet. The essential prerequisite of the shaman was that he would have suffered a serious mental or physical illness or both, which would often be long and drawn out. As healing progressed, the shaman acquired the capacities for inspiration and healing and with recovery he came to understand the spirits and how to master them. He would also train and initiate assistants into the role of healer. Shamans can therefore be seen as people who have come through their own serious illness as a result of which they are stronger in themselves and more able to safeguard the souls of others, either into the next world or to heal them in this world. Michael Lerner has aptly called them 'spiritual midwives'.[4]

Shamanism is still widespread today among indigenous tribes in Central and South East Asia, some of the Pacific Islands, South America and among some of the North American Indians. It has been the subject of many detailed studies[5] and there is reason to believe that the traditions in these tribes have been passed down largely unaltered from the earliest records of shamanic activity.

This then is the concept of the Wounded Healer. The idea is well researched, documented and understood within the traditional fields of medical and pastoral care. Those will be considered in later chapters. But I believe that the Wounded Healer holds a much wider significance for us all.

This book is based upon a simple notion. The world's problems are largely caused by our own bad behavior. Why do we behave as we do? Because we are all wounded. Some would say it is part of the 'human condition'.

By developing a better self-awareness and understanding of our own wounds, and by healing them, we can transform and transcend our own traumas that caused our wounds. This enables us to become more fully receptive to the wounds of others and be able to reach out to be alongside them in their own healing process. To achieve that we have to rediscover our own spirituality, recognize with new eyes the spiritual in all our material experiences, and feel that spiritual awakening in our own individual consciousness.

Why should we do this? Certainly we will all be much happier if we recognize our shamanic origins, allow our vulnerabilities to surface and discover a more sensitive and compassionate interaction with those around us.

But by reconnecting with the spiritual and the wounds within each of us, we not only become a potential source of healing for others, but a powerful healing catalyst for social change within the world around us, in all our work and leisure activities. Surely we have an individual and collective responsibility to do this, for the sake of our wounded world.

This is a healing imperative for us all.

And this is not unrealistic. The author and physician Rachel Naomi Remen, one of the earliest pioneers in the mind/body holistic health movement, is well known and widely respected for her work on the Wounded Healer. She believes that it is possible for many of us to find that inner healing ability.

Remen explains the Wounded Healer response thus: 'my wound evokes your healer. Your wound evokes my healer. My wound enables me to find you with your wound where you have the illusion of having become lost.'[6]

So how can we take this idea forward to heal our world? Why

is our need to heal so urgent? Let me remind us all where our wounded behavior is currently leading us.

Bad behavior

I was brought up in the mid 1950s, a generation when there was much less paranoia about safety and 'stranger danger'. Children had freedom to play outdoors together with minimal adult supervision, [7] and we cycled or walked or were bused to school. The concept of the supermarket had not arrived, and there were no out of town shopping centers. These of course could only become viable once car ownership became the norm rather than a privilege for the wealthy few.

We lived simply in those early post war years, and the material changes we have seen since then have been immense. But material wealth does not apparently bring us happiness, peace and contentment. We now live in a culture where success seems to be based on celebrity status and wealth. The material possessions of others often create envy and greed, and this fuels its own social problems. Do we buy what we want rather than what we need? Is our purchase fuelled by need or greed?

The continual urge to maintain an expensive lifestyle can cause stress and depression, both of which are now epidemics in the western world and the cause of many other health problems. The links that can exist between mental ill health and physical disorders, such as certain cancers and heart disease, are well documented.

The stark fact is that most of us now have a love affair with our car, our house, our computer technology and our other material possessions. And we all love a bargain. So much so that many of us are unwilling to pay the premium for fairly traded and fairly priced organic or local goods. We love our sanitized, standardized, pre-packaged meat and perfectly blemish free fruit and vegetables. But when we chase the cheapest mass-produced goods we are at the same time casting aside any ethical considerations regarding the production of those goods. We really do not want to think about the possible sweat-shop conditions of the laborers, the unrealistically low wages that may have been paid, the cruelty inflicted on helpless animals, that our purchasing behavior may be promoting. But we need to!

We know that our oil consumption is unsustainable, that our landfill sites are nearly overflowing with the waste of consumerism, that it makes sense to walk or cycle to work, or send our children to school by bus or train or cycle or foot. But how many of us are making a sustained effort to curb these excesses? And because everyone else crowds out the rush hour roads with the 'school run' we do not regard it as safe for our children to even think of 'green' travel options.

While we enjoy material riches, real poverty is rife and 923 million people across the world are hungry.[8] In addition, almost 16,000 children die every day from hunger-related causes. That's one child every five seconds.[9]

These statistics are an affront to our humanity. The injustices of the rich/poor divide bring discontent and envy, particularly with the globalization of information. Poverty brings disease and lack of education, which itself perpetuates that poverty. Lack of resources also increases vulnerability to natural disasters that in the developed nations we are broadly speaking better able to handle. Inadequate and poor quality housing exacerbates the impact of floods, hurricanes, tsunamis and earthquakes. Although we often call such disasters 'Acts of God' there is evidence that some of these 'natural' disasters are linked to man's own interference with the planet. There is widespread homelessness, and a devastating AIDS/HIV crisis. I have seen various estimates of the number of children who will be orphaned by AIDS in Africa by 2010, ranging from 20 million to 50 million. Even the lower figure is appalling. We have global warming, a depletion of the ozone layer, and the inexorable destruction of rain forests that is profoundly affecting climate and the fragile survival of wildlife.

We have trade barriers, civil unrest, ethnic and racial problems, terror, violence, public disorder, crime waves, the 'yob culture' on our streets, binge drinking, terrorist attacks and metal detectors in schools to combat knife crime. Many of these problems were unheard of, even unimaginable, in my own childhood and youth.

Our generation remembers the Cold War, with the Suez crisis of 1956/57 and the Cuban Missile crisis of 1962. We recall the sense of euphoria when the Berlin Wall, a symbol of the Cold War since 1961, was dismantled in 1989, marking the end of European communism. We hailed a New Era and a new and peaceful world.

In his acceptance speech following receipt of the 1989 Nobel Peace Prize the 14th Dalai Lama remarked, 'As we enter the final decade of this century I am optimistic that the ancient values that have sustained mankind are today reaffirming themselves to prepare us for a kinder, happier twenty-first century.'[10] Sadly his prediction looks tenuous as we enter the second decade of the new millennium. We now live in a more perilous world than we could possibly have foreseen as children of the fifties. There are more wars worldwide than ever before. It is true that in the Western world many of us have experienced unbroken peace since the end of the Second World War. But we can no longer ignore the wider global picture. In those terms the future is bleaker, with so much war and civil unrest obvious from our daily news.

But not everything is gloom and doom.

When I was a child I remember the family physician boiling a terrifyingly enormous hypodermic syringe in a saucepan on the stove to sterilize it before giving my mother an extremely painful injection. Many of the recent advances in medical science are wonderful and extend far beyond making a more humane hypodermic needle! We can now cure cancers that only 25 years ago claimed the lives of some of my own dear friends. We have effective drug treatments and amazing surgical techniques that our parents could only have dreamed of. Meanwhile in the developing world children still suffer the misery of harelips and blindness that cost so relatively little to treat, if only they had the money. How with a clear conscience can we let any of this happen to our fellow human beings?

Why not solve our problems through legislation?

Because that will not work on its own! There is a disconcerting trend throughout the developed Western world towards more and more legislation. It seems that governing and regulatory bodies try to combat every ill of society as it arises by what can only be interpreted as knee-jerk or panic-button reaction. We see ever more complex and burgeoning laws and regulations. The individual is not blameless, as we look to a government to 'do something' in response to society's problems. Governments are not entirely innocent either if we believe, perhaps cynically, that new laws can grab headlines and be good for Public Relations and Opinion Polls!

But examples of the undesirable effects of excessive regulation can be seen all around us. Small businesses find it difficult to keep up to date with the continual red tape handed out to them. Private investors have to be protected with overly complex investment and money laundering regulations for the simplest of transactions. Schools and hospitals struggle to cope with more tests and targets and league tables. In fact life is becoming far too complex and stressful for us all. Where will this all end?

It was observed, with reference to Britain under the Labour Government in November 2006, that, 'If legislation was a guarantee of greater public safety, this country would be the safest nation on earth.'[11] I am sure Britain is not unique.

But herein lies another problem. Overzealous legislation can be dangerous in itself. It can take away from us our individual sense of ethical, spiritual and social responsibility. We have personal responsibilities towards ourselves, towards each other, towards our communities, our nations and ultimately to our living planet earth Gaia. And of course legislation fails to address our underlying behavioral problems, our selfishness and aggression, our greed and our envy, the seemingly prevalent albeit petty dishonesty among so many of us. Such behavior can cause even the normally law-abiding citizens among us to sometimes ignore the rules and regulations. Simple examples are the widely disregarded restrictions on speeding and the use of a hand held mobile phone or cellular while driving. Such behavior is obviously selfish. It exposes our fellow road users, pedestrians, cyclists, horses, pets, wild life and other vehicles to mortal danger. Why do we do it? Would we change our driving behavior if we knew that every other user on the roads around us was a cherished friend or relation? Of course we would! If we always drove with consideration and care and indeed love for every other person sharing the road with us, traffic regulations would not be needed at all. This I know is unrealistic given human nature!

Simone Weil, the French philosopher, Christian mystic and activist, was known for her support of the cause of the working classes in early twentieth century France. She recognized that for any real and positive change to come about, a spiritual awakening must occur in the individual. To achieve this she thought it was necessary to experience for herself the lives and hardships of those she sought to help. She recognized that she had to enter completely into their pain and suffering. She described this as allowing the experience to permeate her entire spirit and being. One must become a slave, she wrote, to understand what a slave endures.

So we see that we cannot rely only on Government interventions to achieve lasting and real solutions to these seemingly intractable problems of the twenty first century world. The world's many fractures will not be healed in that way. Positive change must come from within our own hearts, through a healing of our own wounds and our own behavior.

In his 'Call to Renewal' Keynote Address to a Sojourners conference in 2006, Barack Obama reminded the audience 'the problems of poverty and racism, the uninsured and the unemployed, are not simply technical problems in search of the perfect ten point plan. They are rooted in both societal indifference and individual callousness - in the imperfections of man. Solving these problems will require changes in government policy; it will also require changes in hearts and minds.'[12]

'There are a thousand hacking at the branches of evil to one who is striking at the root,' wrote Henry David Thoreau.[13] We all have to start striking at those roots.

Our wounds

The Dutch Roman Catholic priest and popular spiritual writer Henri Nouwen certainly knew suffering in his own life. Firstly he had a domineering and pushy father. This meant that Nouwen grew up always fearful of criticism and needing constant praise and affirmation. He also struggled with the painful conflict he felt between his priestly vows of celibacy and his own strongly felt need for intimacy. This was a source of his loneliness and probably accounted at least in part for his bouts of depression. His life was a continual struggle to come to terms with these wounds. This is reflected in his prolific and inspirational spiritual writing. It also explains his undoubted ability through his writings to help the suffering of others.

It was the Jungian psychoanalysts who probably first started referring to the Wounded Healer archetype as a recognized tool in the healing process. But it was Nouwen who really popularized the term within a wider spiritual and pastoral healing context when he wrote his own bestselling book *The Wounded Healer* in 1979. In it he identifies the loneliness that he himself so keenly felt as the most painful of our human wounds, leaving us craving for love and attention. Loneliness, he tells us, is recognized in words such as alienation, separation and isolation. [14] But Malcolm Langford identifies four other basic types of wound: those resulting from the evil of our own life experiences and of others with whom we are involved, those from our own broken personalities and motivations, from our personal prejudices and fears and those which reflect our emotional and spiritual poverty in such a materially wealthy world.[15] We can all relate to some if not all of these examples of woundedness.

As Ian McEwan reflected on the Twin Towers collapse on 9/11:

If the hijackers had been able to imagine themselves into the thoughts and feelings of the passengers, they would have been unable to proceed. *It is hard to be cruel once you permit yourself to enter the mind of your victim. Imagining what it is like to be someone other than yourself is at the core of our humanity [my italics].* It is the essence of compassion, and it is the beginning of morality…The hijackers used fanatical certainty, misplaced religious faith, and dehumanizing hatred to purge themselves of the human instinct for empathy. Among their crimes was a failure of the imagination.[16]

And as the Chief Rabbi Jonathan Sacks explains, when bad things do happen to us, we can use these experiences to sensitize us to the pain of others. Rather than allowing such wounds to make us victims of circumstance, let them turn us into potentially life changing agents of hope.[17]

Our wounded behavior

However we define and categorize man's wounds, we now know that who we are and how we behave as adults is not only a combination of our inherited gene and possibly also our meme [18] makeup. We are also affected by subsequent influences in our upbringing and our experiences as we develop through childhood and beyond. This is what is meant when we talk about 'nature versus nurture'. So as well as our inherited physical characteristics, we pick up mental wounds from the collective experiences of our ancestors. The unhealed wounds of mankind inflicted through millennia of evolution by strife and violence and disaster mean that hundreds of millions of people are psychologically, emotionally and physically scarred and wounded and in need of healing. It has even been suggested by some psychologists that 'human culture as a whole has been saturated by unhealed wounding, which, if unchecked, will continue on a downward spiral toward inevitable disintegration.'[19] This is not a good thought.

Books abound, both popular and academic, on the psychological study of why we behave as we do. This book is not one of those. Here it is sufficient for us to understand that wounds manifest themselves in many different and undesirable personality traits. We see greed and envy, craving for love and attention, consumerism, lust for power, superiority, violence, overspending, addictions to work and substances, depression, cynicism, despair. What we need to cultivate instead is a compassionate trend, always sensitive to the pain of others. We need an instinctive urge to support the weak and the vulnerable. And we must combat violence, both against each other and against the planet. Violence is probably threatening our very future more than anything else. And the most obvious violence that we inflict upon this fragile planet is consumerism.

Consumerism

Why do we eat too much, consume too much? Mass consumerism is a disease of our overly comfortable Western lives. It is as if we are always feverishly looking for something to satisfy us, to fill some kind of hole in our lives. And the media are far from blameless. Driven by profit motives, they shamelessly exploit us in advertisements and articles to pamper ourselves, to treat ourselves, to have whatever we want at all times. This fuels greed rather than need. Competitions reward us with a supermarket trolley dash: the winner fills a trolley with as much as possible from the shelves in a frenzied grab over a given time. Color supplements publish glossy images of items we must have. Surely the fostering of pure self-indulgence is an affront to our humanity while so many starve and suffer elsewhere in the world.

That is not to say that we should deny ourselves an adequate standard of living. We cannot all live the extreme sacrificial lifestyle of Simone Weil, and anyway we have plenty of our own wounds and related behaviors to pay attention to! But neither should we live extravagantly. We should strive to live responsibly and sustainably. We should minimize our own footprint and always have regard for the needs of our fellow human beings as if they were living with us under our same family roof.

'We need an expression,' mused Alastair McIntosh to The Honorable Sir Maxwell MacLeod of Fuinary and the Isles as they shared a car journey in Scotland back in 1992. 'We need something that describes the way people mask their misery by going out shopping.' 'How about,' Maxwell pondered, 'how about 'retail therapy'?'[20] And that, according to McIntosh, is the origin of the phrase now so widely used today across the globe.

Violence against each other

If we are to hold any hope at all for the future of our race we must believe that mankind is inherently good, not evil. Even though young children can be incredibly cruel, this is something that in the normal course of healthy development they do seem to generally grow out of. Simone Weil observed that 'at the bottom of the heart of every human being, from earliest infancy until the tomb, there is something that goes on indomitably expecting, in the teeth of all experience of crimes committed, suffered, and witnessed, that good and not evil will be done.'

Anne Frank, in spite of the terrible experiences she suffered at the hands of the Nazis in the Second World War similarly wrote, 'Despite everything,...people are really good at heart.' [21]

If man is essentially good, why is there so much violence in the world?

Anthony de Mello, an Indian Jesuit Priest and psychotherapist who lived during the middle years of the twentieth century, wrote many best selling albeit sometimes controversial books on Christianity and spirituality. He writes succinctly on the cause of the violence of war:

Do you know where wars come from? They come from projecting outside of us the conflict that is inside. Show me an individual in whom there is no inner self-conflict and I'll show you an individual in whom there is no violence. There will be effective, even hard, action in him, but no hatred. When he acts, he acts as a surgeon acts; when he acts, he acts as a loving teacher acts with mentally retarded children. You don't blame them, you understand; but you swing into action. On the other hand, when you swing into action with your own hatred and your own violence un-addressed, you've compounded the error. You've tried to put fire out with more fire. You've tried to deal with a flood by adding water to it.[22]

Another Jesuit priest, Thomas Merton, tells us that our hatred of ourselves is more dangerous than our hatred of others, because we project our own evil onto others and we do not see it in ourselves.[23]

Fear can be the result of a lack of understanding, or a suspicion, of the other point of view. Thus Herod ordered the slaying of the Holy Innocents because of his fear that his power was being usurped by the birth of the boy Jesus 'born to be King'.

And fear translated into insecurity can also lead to greed and overconsumption, representing a violence against our own bodies, or against the environment, or indeed both.

If we fail to recognize these wounds in ourselves there is a danger that we allow them to crush us. We turn them in upon ourselves, and then we harbor thoughts of anger, resentment, envy, lust, greed, and all the worst character traits of mankind. They cause us to be unhappy or discontent. This impacts on our relationships with other people, in everything we do, in our work, in our creativity. Without intentionally setting out to do harm, we allow those wounds to hurt those around us, as Simone Weil explained: 'A hurtful act is the transference to others of the degradation which we bear in ourselves.' Or as Barack Obama has described this in our twenty first century world: 'When a gang-banger shoots indiscriminately into a crowd because he feels somebody disrespected him, we have a problem of morality; there's a hole in that young man's heart; a hole that government programs alone cannot fix.'[24]

A further unwelcome effect of being crushed by our own wounds is that we may suffer a physical or mental breakdown, as we turn our woundedness in upon ourselves. Thus a person who has been deprived of love and support in his past may drive himself harder and harder in his work to gain that love and acceptance. This can trigger a complete mental breakdown, even total 'burnout', as the human mind and body can only take so much punishment.

Spiritual gifts of healing

Analytical psychologists are required to undergo personal analysis in order that they may understand their own wounds and the compensations they make for them in their own behavior. This ensures that those wounds do not interfere in the therapeutic process with their clients. But this principle is not the unique property of the analytical psychologists. We can all recognize the wounds in ourselves. How we then deal with them is rather up to us! But do we not have a human responsibility to make these moves towards healing, of ourselves and of the world around us?

Responsibility is a big topic, and a chapter is devoted to this later on. First I want to consider where we may be able to start our own healing mission.

I do believe that at the very core of any healing are the spiritual gifts of faith, love and forgiveness. Anthony de Mello counseled the offering of prayer and meditation with Christ as Healer, to mend our inner conflicts and our past wounds.[25] Alastair Campbell explains 'the wounded love of Jesus Christ has a healing power because it is enfleshed love, entering into human weakness, feeling our pain, standing beside us in our dereliction.'[26] This is at the heart of the true Wounded Healer. Nouwen recognized that the traditional healing of the Christian minister is embodied in such words as 'care and compassion, understanding and forgiveness, fellowship and community.'[27]

Over 2 billion citizens worldwide find healing and spiritual nourishment in the Christian faith in its various denominations.[28] But our principles of love and compassion for all are relevant not only for Christians. They are fundamental to the teachings of all the great faiths, and can be embraced by all those of any religion or none, indeed by all those 'of good faith'.[29] More than ever before there is an urgent need for all religions to unite in a common mission of healing all the wrongs and hurts of our world. Worldwide our faiths could be a powerful strength in this healing mission.

The next chapter is devoted to the hope that faith can offer in this healing. Here I want to look a little more at the healing power of love.

The healing power of love

If violence is caused by fear, insecurity or prejudice, then the antidote is found in love. Martin Luther King spoke thus in his 1964 acceptance speech for his Nobel Peace Prize:

> ...nonviolence is the answer to the crucial political and moral question of our time - the need for man to overcome oppression and violence without resorting to violence and oppression. Civilization and violence are antithetical concepts. Negroes of the United States, following the people of India, have demonstrated that nonviolence is not sterile passivity, but a powerful moral force which makes for social transformation. Sooner or later all the people of the world will have to discover a way to live together in peace, and thereby transform this pending cosmic elegy into a creative psalm of brotherhood. If this is to be achieved, man must evolve for all human conflict a method which rejects revenge, aggression and retaliation. The foundation of such a method is love.[30]

Love is used to overcome any negative feelings we may otherwise have against others. We do not have to like others to love them. That would be unrealistic. Of course we are all very different, with widely differing attitudes, opinions, interests. But we can love others within the context of God's love for all mankind. It is important to note that we are not talking here about the romantic or sexual love, or eros, with which the word is so often automatically associated in modern parlance. Neither is it the sentimental and weak emotion that Martin Luther King calls 'emotional bosh'.[31] It is the Christian love of agape: to show unselfish concern for our fellow humanity regardless of gender, color, race and creed, regardless of their abilities or disabilities. In that delightful passage so often chosen as a reading at church weddings, from St Paul's first letter to the Church in Corinth in the first century AD, he explains that:

Love is patient and kind. Love is not jealous or boastful; it is not arrogant or rude. Love does not insist on its own way; it is not irritable or resentful; it does not rejoice at wrong, but rejoices in the right. Love bears all things, believes all things, hopes all things, endures all things. Love never ends.[32]

That is a tangible demonstration of real love. Love of course can be stern, as in the sometimes necessarily harsh discipline of our children in the spirit of love, or 'tough love' referred to by De Mello. But with such love we can overcome hatred and fear. And if hatred and fear is overcome, so too is violence. Non-violence becomes a matter of the heart. And with love will come a respect for each other and for our environment. Persons who respect each other are very much less likely to commit acts of violence against each other. And persons who respect the environment are similarly less likely to commit violence against mother earth.

Mahatma Gandhi was asked what he thought of Western Civilization. It would be a good idea, he said! [33] He is popularly remembered for teaching ahimsa or non-violence, which is better translated as 'non-hurting'. But Gandhi actually taught the spiritual yogic practice of truthfulness or satyam. Truth in Yoga is the concept that the soul is Self, the One, and the Self or the One in you is the same as the Self or One in me.

Yoga is an ancient philosophy with its origins in the Indian subcontinent some 4000 years ago, with links to both Buddhism and Hinduism. Those who practice Yoga fully today follow the Yoga Sutras, rules for living that were drawn up by the sage Patanjali[34] 2000 years ago. These rules are still very relevant to the needs of today's world. They are based on principles of non-violence to self and others, purity and truthfulness, contentment and non-possessiveness. We have seen how so many in the Western World measure success only in terms of wealth and celebrity status. But the Yoga Sutras teach us not to covet the possessions and achievements of others. We are instead taught to

accept our situation in life. This was the basis of Mahatma
Gandhi's philosophy of non-violence, based on love and truth:
truth in our thoughts, in our words and in our actions [35] that
with perseverance naturally flow into the practice of non-
hurting. Many of the crimes that beset our otherwise 'civilized'
societies, crimes of theft and fraud, result from greed and envy
of others, when we fail to accept our own lives as they are.

Unfortunately Yoga today has too often become nothing more
than the learning and practicing of physical postures to aid and
maintain physical health and fitness, flexibility and balance in
our bodies, a sort of yogi aerobics! But combined with
meditation, the use of mantras and breathing exercises, the
postures become much more than a physical fitness regime. Yoga
becomes a holistic healing system with the aim of attaining the
healthy integration of body, mind and spirit. Yoga after all comes
from the Sanskrit 'yuj', meaning to join or yoke. If practiced
completely, true to the principles of Patanjali, it is a spiritual
journey, a search for deeper self - knowledge, a source of inner
peace, and mental and physical harmony. The postures or asanas
so often isolated today into nothing more than a keep-fit class
were actually developed as an aid in concentrating the mind to
meditate more deeply.

While many find healing and spiritual growth, and an inner
peace and calm, in Yoga and meditation, others practice Tai Chi
and Chi Kung with similar benefit.

The path to the Wounded Healer
We have seen the dangers that can arise if we allow our wounds
to crush us. Thankfully most of us are able to move beyond that
stage. But other phases of healing have been identified that hold
their own perils. [36] The 'survivor' response to our wounds is
seen in the desensitization we can experience if we are continually bombarded with the wounding images of horror, either
real or in the relentless gratuitous violence of screen or computer

game. I will mention this again in Chapter 9 in the context of our responsible and healing use of creativity.

There are other stages of healing that we may recognize in us or in others. For example there are the 'martyrs' and the 'thrivers'. We all know the 'martyr'; he could also be called the moaner or whinger and hardly needs further explanation.

The thriving response to our wounds is complex and the subject of much research. In simple terms for our purpose the 'thriver' can be defined as the 'person who experiences the traumatic or stressful event and benefits or gains in some way from the experience and can apply that gain to new experiences, leading to more effective subsequent functioning.' An example would be Beethoven who overcame his deafness to find joy in his music making. But this response type may not always be what it seems. I believe it may sometimes be similar to what I think of as the 'self-help response', something I discuss more fully in chapter 4.

The next step on our journey to Wounded Healer is the 'inspirational' phase. Here we use an understanding of our own wounds to work for the benefit of others with the same afflictions. We all know these inspirational people. Superman Christopher Reeve fought paralysis after a stunt accident while filming and fought for more research to help others suffering from the same disablement. Such people campaign, they set up charities, they march for a cause, they fund-raise. This is praiseworthy but it does not make a Wounded Healer.

Mental health nursing expert Marion Conti-O'Hare describes one more stage along the road to Wounded Healer. These are the people, she explains, who have experienced trauma and are using it to help others but without understanding how they themselves are affected. O'Hare describes Diana Princess of Wales as an example of what she calls the 'walking wounded'.[37] Diana died tragically before she could transcend much of her suffering. She did however devote much of her later years to causes such as the victims of HIV infection and AIDS, almost certainly reflecting her own advanced stage along the road to Wounded Healer.

This leads us to our ultimate healing goal, to the person who has taken his wounds into his soul, fully comprehended them, transformed and transcended them, and become the Wounded Healer. From those transcended wounds we have the insight to fully understand and care about the sufferings and wounds of others. We can be with them in true empathy and compassion. Compassion literally means 'to suffer with' and means much the same in this context as empathy. We identify with you in your suffering. We can bare our own souls and walk in your shoes to share your suffering; that is true empathy. But empathy must not be confused with sympathy. If you are at this moment suffering an acutely painful illness that I suffered last week, I can certainly sympathize with you: I can make all the right sympathetic noises. Research does indeed show that nurses who have experienced intense pain are more sympathetic to another's pain. But this is surely not surprising. And it does not make them Wounded Healers.

David Smith, an Episcopal Minister, suffered a serious mental breakdown, for which he was hospitalized. During that experience he came to recognize those who put themselves forward as healers but who in fact had failed to overcome their own wounds, and were accordingly less than effective in their healing roles.[38]

And so we understand the need to heal ourselves, we have an idea as to how this may be achieved. We know there are personal benefits. But we do nothing. Why? We have to overcome those voices within us that make excuses for our inaction.

The demons of ignorance, information overload and futility

Are we ignorant? I don't think so. We have little excuse for such ignorance. We live in an information age. We cannot open a newspaper or magazine or watch television or listen to the radio or log onto the internet without being informed of the problems besetting the earth. We are bombarded with countless ways that we can reduce our individual carbon footprints. We have blogs and teleseminars, iPods and YouTube. Never before have we had such ready access to so much information. The possibilities for education and research from such media are seemingly endless. This education is important because it enables action. But sadly and indeed alarmingly the same media can bring us unnecessary images of brutality and ugliness, and much that is of no value at all. The world wide web is a wonderful tool for research, for the spread of knowledge, for constructive debate and for the rapid dissemination of information. It can help to gauge and build up public support at an international level for worthy campaigns. It can effectively build bridges across cultural and political divides. But the internet can be as destructive as it is positive and we have to learn to be discerning, to filter the valuable and truthful information from the incorrect, the misleading, the dangerous or the simply biased. And those who create the images and information should ensure they read chapter 9 on the healing and hurting powers of creativity. We all need to understand how our own inappropriate creativity can be a force for evil not good through a reflection of our own wounds.

A further problem we may find is that there is simply too much information available to us. It is increasingly difficult to keep abreast of everything that we need to know, or feel the need to know, whether at work or at home. Emails demand instant attention, real or illusory, that the humble letter never could. Now we can be in continual contact with each other through cyber space with our Tweets! What a mad world it has become! The pressures can be enormous and an inevitable result for many is stress and the various stress related illnesses.

The complexities of all the issues involved, for example balancing air miles with the support of fair-trade products in developing countries, may go some way to explain why we often seem to 'give up'. Is it any wonder that with this bombardment of problems from all corners, we develop a sense of hopelessness, of escapism, of self interest nursed with mass consumerism, drowning our confusion and sorrows in drink and other drugs? Work can even become a drug. We push ourselves too far in searching for an anesthetic to dull our guilt, or fear, or unrest or anxiety.

It is easy to become immune to bad news, to feel that nothing we do can possibly alter the situation. We shrug our shoulders at the latest media story. We may contribute to a disaster fund to temper our guilt, to somehow make us feel better, but then shut ourselves away from the horrors and bury ourselves in the escapism of self- indulgence. We might feel overwhelmed and depressed by the unraveling of horrors on our screens. Michael Mayne wrote about what he called 'redressing the balance'.[39] By remembering all the wonderful things in life we can find a sense of balance that will help us to cope with such horrors without ignoring them. He urges us to recover our sense of awe and wonder, to concentrate on the many gifts bestowed on us rather than on our afflictions and adversities. This can help us foster a more positive and fulfilling attitude towards life. As Sacks has remarked, giving thanks is better than shopping, and cheaper too!

We have to overcome such feelings of futility. As the African proverb reminds us: 'If you think you are too small to make a difference try spending one night in a room with a mosquito!' We can all make differences, however small our individual contri-bution may seem. Sacks devotes the final chapter of his book, *To Heal a Fractured World,* to how we can overcome our sense of futility, to make a difference.[40] And if we feel that we are fighting against all odds, that the dice seem to be stacked against spiritual healing in a world that we are continually and misguidedly told is secular, we can draw hope and perspective from examples in nature. The caterpillars on my cabbage patch can practically destroy the leaves as they ravenously eat their way through them before finally turning into a chrysalis. While the old immune system of the caterpillar resists the change, the tiny new cells forming in the emergent butterfly find strength in their mutual cooperation and between them overcome that resistance. The butterfly emerges triumphant.[41]

However, we must not confuse hope with optimism. Optimism is passive. We believe that something better will happen. Hope is far more than that. It is a firmly held conviction that it is worth taking action to improve something; and it is grounded in spirituality and faith.

Archbishop Desmond Tutu tells us: 'I've never been an optimist. I've always been a man of hope - I am a prisoner of hope...hope holds on even when things are seemingly doomed and dark.' 'We must,' said Martin Luther King, 'accept finite disappointment, but we must never lose infinite hope.'

In Christianity hope is one of the three great spiritual virtues or God given graces, of faith, hope and love. These form the foundation stones of the spiritual wisdoms that have served us well for 2000 years. The need to return to them is urgent!

Barack Obama has a prayer he says for America today. It is for *'hope that we can live with one another in a way that reconciles the beliefs of each with the good of all.'*[42]

In the next chapter we shall look at this hope that faith can offer.

Chapter 3
The Hope of Faith

There is only one religion, though there are a hundred versions of it.
George Bernard Shaw [1]

I was able to see faith as more than just a comfort to the weary or a hedge against death; it is an active, palpable agent in the world. It is a source of hope.
Barack Obama[2]

We may claim a particular faith as our spiritual guide and source of hope, or we may simply be 'of good faith' [3] but still have hope. However we see ourselves, the deep healing need that is within each and every one of us transcends all boundaries of faith or creed. Continuing my thesis that we need to reach that need and heal our hearts before we can hope to heal our world, how, I wonder, can we do this? How can our faith help?

Religion and ethics were once closely intertwined, but since the influence of religion has declined in so many lives, there is, warns the Dalai Lama, 'mounting confusion with respect to the problem of how best we are to conduct ourselves in life...morality becomes a matter of individual preference.'[4] Nietzsche called this an impending 'total eclipse of all values.'[5] Atheist as he himself was, his observation, he claimed, was entirely objective: we need a God and the moral codes inherent in that belief to curb our otherwise unpleasant behavioral traits.

'As at the beginning of the Christian era, so again today,' wrote Carl Jung[6] in 1957, 'we are faced with the problem of the general moral backwardness which has failed to keep pace with our scientific, technical and social progress.' Martin Luther King called this our moral and spiritual 'lag'. He observed that 'the richer we have become materially the poorer we have become morally and spiritually.' We live, he said, in two realms:

> The internal is that realm of spiritual ends expressed in art, literature, morals, and religion. The external is that complex of devices, techniques, mechanisms, and instrumentalities by means of which we live. Our problem today is that we have allowed the internal to become lost in the external. We have allowed the means by which we live to outdistance the ends for which we live.

He warned that we would put ourselves in peril if the former, the internal, does not grow apace of the external material realm. 'When the 'without' of man's nature subjugates the 'within', dark storm clouds begin to form in the world.' The result, he cautioned, is racial injustice, poverty and war, that will only be alleviated if we balance our moral progress with our scientific progress and learn the practical art of living in harmony in a 'worldwide fellowship that lifts neighborly concern beyond one's tribe, race, class, and nation.'[7]

The healing power of forgiveness

I was negotiating some hairpin bends high up in the Mallorcan mountains in our rental car when my passenger said out of the blue: 'I have no time for your Christian faith; you have such a pre-occupation with guilt and sin.' I was floored for a moment. Perhaps we do to the outside world. But doesn't that miss some of the point? Guilt gives us a chance to reflect on our actions and inactions and resolve to do better next time. None of us can possibly be perfect. I am certainly no saint. But we can all strive for improvement in the secure knowledge that with true penitence we do not need to carry a guilt burden with us along life's journey. Jesus Christ died for our sins, that we might be forgiven. He represents love and forgiveness, not guilt. Forgiveness from God through Jesus Christ, the world's greatest Wounded Healer, heals us and allows us to move on.

'To err is human, to forgive divine,' [8]wrote Alexander Pope, the renowned early eighteenth-century poet. We also have to forgive those who do wrong to us: otherwise we harbor bitterness and resentment within our own souls. Forgiveness is vital for our own spiritual wellbeing. Jonathan Sacks calls forgiveness the emotional equivalent of losing weight. It is even better for you than for the person you have forgiven! Even if our offer of forgiveness is not accepted, 'yet once we reach out our hand, we cleanse ourselves of resentment. We may remain deeply wounded, but we will not use our hurt to inflict further pain on others.' These are the words of pastor Johann Christoph Arnold, who in his book *The Lost Art of Forgiving – Stories of Healing from the Cancer of Bitterness*, [9] relates the very human stories of ordinary people scarred by crime, betrayal, abuse and war. He tells how many have learned to forgive in sometimes the most difficult of circumstances. He reminds us of Gordon Wilson, whose daughter Marie died in Enniskillen, Northern Ireland, the innocent victim of a terrorist bomb; of Chris Carrier, a ten year old abducted in Miami and subjected to the most brutal attack, who many years later exchanged mutual forgiveness with his abductor, by then an old man. Harbored bitterness, Arnold explains, is destructive and self-destructive. It 'has a disastrous effect on the soul. It opens the door to evil and leaves us vulnerable to thoughts of spite, hatred and even murder. It destroys our souls, and it can destroy our bodies as well.'

The Most Rev. Desmond M. Tutu, formerly Anglican

Archbishop of Cape Town, South Africa, oversaw the post-apartheid reconciliation in his native South Africa, as leader of South Africa's Truth and Reconciliation Commission. He has deep practical experience of the power of forgiveness. Without it, he tells us, 'there can be no future for a relationship between individuals or within and between nations.' He brought soldiers and paramilitaries face to face with their victims from the Northern Ireland Troubles to grant and receive forgiveness. This was a process, he felt, which would help individuals in Northern Ireland who had been living for decades with unresolved emotions.

Tutu has also observed that if only America could truly heal the wounds from slavery and the displacement of its Native Americans, the country could reach unprecedented heights.[10] He often speaks of such unresolved emotions as festering wounds that need opening up again and cleansing before real healing can occur.

Some of us believe that the Anglo-Catholic Church has seriously lost its way in the last 100 years or so by concentrating too much on individual redemption rather than nurturing a deeper spiritual commune with the sentient world around us, understanding our place in the wider humanity, visibly living our faith more proactively. Until the Church truly admits to its past failings, it will not be able to move on in a truly healing mission within the world.

This ability to forgive and be forgiven is an essential part of any global healing, a fact recognized by organizations such as the Fetzer Institute, based in Kalamazoo, Michigan USA. They are devoted to the furtherance of love and forgiveness in the pursuit of global healing. The Fetzer Institute has a mission that rests on 'its conviction that efforts to address the world's critical issues must go beyond political, social and economic strategies to their psychological and spiritual roots.'[11] And forgiveness, within or without a sound supporting faith, is one key to the healing of those psychological and spiritual roots.

The reality is that we all need our faith and our spirituality more than ever in these coming decades of the new millennium.

Is God dead?

'God is Dead,' Friedrich Nietzsche famously wrote in 1882.[12] We had, he said, lost our religion, our faith and our soul, to rationalism, scientific thought and Darwinism. This loss, he predicted, would be the cause of the awful wars that we did indeed subsequently experience in the twentieth century, 'wars such as have never happened on earth.' And this he attributed to our fundamental human need for a God to absolve us of our guilt. Without the comfort of this absolution and still guilt-ridden, we would go on to develop barbaric nationalistic brotherhoods, resulting in the robbery and exploitation of other human beings not of our own fraternity. Does this sound familiar?

If this all sounds like too much gloom and doom, we should not be dispirited, because God most certainly is not dead.

This is in fact an exciting time in the development of our planet. I firmly believe that there is a definite paradigm shift that is not always being recognized, although it is right under our noses. People are coming back, if not always to an organized religion, then at least as seekers of spirituality and truth, in a quest to find another level of meaning in their lives.

This spiritual awakening is gaining momentum. If we will open our hearts and minds to this awakening, nurture it and allow it to touch our souls, we will find its healing power. If we let this power infuse our lives and our faith, then this is where I believe we regain a hope for the future. Most importantly, we will experience an inner contentment, a peace of heart, 'that peace that the world cannot give.'[13] This, I submit, will be the source of the world's healing.

We saw in Chapter 1 the deeper spiritual connection with

nature that is found in the mystical traditions of the Eastern faith. It seems to me that this connection is not always as readily accessible in our Western religious worship. Indeed we often seem to smother it as we struggle to adapt our worship to reach a younger generation. But we underestimate the spirituality of the young. I observe our own young school children in the church and sense the spirituality that they feel in the setting of worship. We all have a deep human need to find the transcendent in our lives, the young and old among us alike. We therefore turn to yoga, meditation, Tai Chi and other practices in search of that higher spiritual plane that we think our religion denies us. And we find such experiences profoundly healing.

Satish Kumar reminds us that spirituality should not be confused with religion or with being religious. The two are quite distinct. Spirit is free, he tells us. Religion binds.[14] One does not have to follow any religion to be in touch with your own soul, to be spiritual. Conversely many devout followers of a faith do not find its spirituality. I believe we need both!

Perhaps John Sentamu had this partly in mind when he said of Christianity 'We've lost the joy and power that makes real disciples, and we've become consumers of religion and not disciples of Jesus Christ.'[15]

Some believe that a new type of religion must emerge to satisfy the changing spiritual needs of the twenty first century, that spirit, freedom, life and love are needed more than existing religious rites and doctrines that can stifle that spirit. 'God will be worshipped 'neither in this mountain nor in Jerusalem, but in spirit and in truth,' namely, in the mind and heart.'[16] It is true that many of today's youngsters are seeking the spiritual but rejecting the formalized religion. Some church groups are experimenting with different styles of worship, perhaps going out into the community to find the people rather than expecting to receive them into the church for Sunday worship. Maybe we should evangelize more in those great but soulless shopping malls, the twenty-first century cathedrals built to the god of commerce and material greed.

Of course this sense of need for spiritual connection is not really new at all. It represents a re-discovery in some way of that wisdom entrenched in the oldest indigenous communities. This new found consciousness builds again on those principles embodied in the core of the sacred texts of all the great world's religions, from both East and West, from ancient time. Aldous Huxley neatly encapsulates this wisdom in the definition of the Perennial Philosophy as popularized in his 1945 book of that title:

The metaphysic that recognizes a divine Reality substantial to the world of things and lives and minds; the psychology that finds in the soul something similar to, or even identical with, divine Reality; the ethic that places man's final end in the knowledge of the immanent and transcendent Ground of all being — the thing is immemorial and universal. Rudiments of the Perennial Philosophy may be found among the traditional lore of primitive peoples in every region of the world, and in its fully developed forms it has a place in every one of the higher religions.[17]

How we need a return to this philosophy now! We need to embrace these spiritual insights and wisdom into a healing imperative for our fractured world. We have ignored and grown away from them for too long and to our own detriment.

Richard Dawkins in public debate with Steven Pinker in 1999 said that it was his 'suspicion...hunch...and hope' that within the twenty first century the nature of the 'mysterious substance called consciousness', that 'spiritual part of man regarded as surviving after death, the theory that there is something non-material about life, some non-physical vital principle...vital force...mysterious energy or...spirit,'[18] will be completely mastered by scientific explanation and the soul will be definitely dispatched once and for all.

With the same reasoning Dawkins argues passionately that there can be no God.[19] This type of scientific reductionism however does our world no favors. What is more, Dawkins' hunch is thankfully losing some of its credibility. Those who only see the human being in terms of physical body and brain are challenged by the opinions of an increasing number of respected and eminent scientists and philosophers, who know there really is something more to life than mere matter, that there is something that is beyond the ability of scientists to prove or disprove empirically and that God most certainly is not dead.[20]

We have to resist scientific reductionism, a perpetuation of the view that eventually everything in nature will be described and explained scientifically: because this strikes at the heart of the fundamental beliefs in our faiths and religions, it crushes our spirit and inhibits our healing needs.

The Dalai Lama warns us that we should not 'overlook the limitations of science. In replacing religion as the final source of knowledge in popular estimation, science begins to look a bit like another religion itself. With this comes a similar danger on the part of some of its adherents to blind faith in its principles, and, correspondingly, to intolerance of alternate views.'[21]

We live in a world where those of us who talk openly of our souls and our spirits, of the influence of a living God or Supreme Being in our lives, tend to be branded as weird. This is less so in America than in the United Kingdom. Tony Blair demonstrated this during his term as UK Prime Minister when on Blair's behalf his press secretary Alistair Campbell famously said; 'We do not do God.'[22] I am delighted to see that Barack Obama clearly does 'do God'. Interestingly, now that Blair is no longer Prime Minister, he is totally open about his faith.

We should all be able to share our spiritual beliefs and religious faiths in an atmosphere of complete respect and understanding. As Albert Einstein once observed, 'If at first the idea is not absurd, then there is no hope for it.'

The Faith Line

More than one hundred years ago, the great African-American scholar W.E.B. Du Bois warned in his book *The Souls of Black Folk*[23] that the problem of the twentieth century would be the racial segregation that existed after the abolition of slavery, in 'the relation of the darker to the lighter races of men in Asia and Africa, in America and the islands of the sea.' He called this 'the problem of the color line.' With the election of President Barack Obama to the White House and only a short while before that the inauguration in the Anglican Communion of John Sentamu to be their own first black Archbishop of York, the hope must be that this color line is well on the way out.

Eboo Patel[24] is an American Muslim of Indian heritage. Brought up in Chicago, he struggled in his youth with his cultural background and came to understand how different faiths could be the source not only of mutual enrichment but as readily could become mutually exclusive. At school he witnessed religious discrimination at first hand as to his shame he turned away when his Jewish friend was subjected to anti Semitic taunts. Patel was no stranger to bullying himself on account of his faith origins. Most importantly, his own upbringing made him consider the forces that determine whether a youngster follows a route of hatred against the world or takes the alternative and happier route of love and compassion for all. He realized that much depends upon whom you meet when you are at your most impressionable. He saw firsthand that the twenty first century is being dominated not by the color line but by a different line, which he calls the faith line. This, he points out, is no less divisive and no less violent than the color line. The faith line does not divide different faiths, or separate the religious from the secular. This line is divisive between the values of religious totalitarians and the values of the religious pluralists. The former believe that their way is the only way and are prepared to convert, condemn or indeed kill, those who are different, in the name of God. It is this side of the faith line that gives religions a bad press in the eyes of the secular public. The pluralists on the other hand hold that 'people believing in different creeds and belonging to different communities need to learn to live together in equal dignity and mutual loyalty.' Pluralism is the belief, Patel explains, 'that the common good is best served when each community has a chance to make its own unique contribution.'[25] What Patel soon realized was that the dangerous religious fundamentalism we see around us is nurtured in the young, in the disaffected youth of our day who are taken advantage of and exploited for fundamental political aims. It is those youth of today who fuel the religious conflicts we witness, who martyr themselves while they kill or maim thousands. He also knew that the main faith leaders over the decades who have campaigned for justice and peace, leaders such as Gandhi, Martin Luther King, the Dalai Lama and Nelson Mandela all started young; they became active while still in their youth.

Inspired by this knowledge Patel saw that there could be no better place to make a start in trying to achieve a harmony and a common good among all America's variants of religion than with this youth of today, those who will shape and see tomorrow's world. It was against this background that in 2003 he founded the Chicago based Interfaith Youth Core (IFYC).[26]

The idea of the IFYC was simple. Its mission is to build 'a global movement of interfaith youth cooperation by generating mass public support for interfaith youth work, equipping youth-focused institutions to positively engage their religious diversity, and nurturing the emerging leaders of this movement.'

This has become an extremely successful organization with a multimillion-dollar budget. It actively involves tens of thousands of religiously diverse young people in projects that are taking the message of religious pluralism to millions across six continents.[27]

The IFYC is not alone. There are other successful organizations working for peaceful and global cooperation between the faiths. One such organization is The Peace Council, [28] a network 'of religious and spiritual individuals who are internationally known and respected and who have decided to come together 'to understand one another and work together...for the common cause of humanity.' Its Councilors include such respected leaders as H.H. Tenzin Gyatso, The 14th Dalai Lama and The Most Rev. Desmond M. Tutu. They all determine the policy and programs of the Peace Council and participate personally in its activities.

'In a world where religion too often is used to justify division, hatred, and violence,' the Peace Council says in its mission statement, 'the Peace Councilors offer an alternative: the example of religious leaders working effectively together to relieve suffering and make the world whole.'

The Peace Council has a very long list of accomplishments to its credit, in the fields of diplomacy and international advocacy, conflict resolution, disarmament and peacemaking, human rights and humanitarian aid. Examples include the participation in the successful International Campaign to Ban Landmines; the support of peace walks by Buddhist monks and nuns through combat zones in Cambodia in the late 1990's, that resulted in cease-fires between Khmer Rouge and government forces; helping to secure the release of prisoners of conscience and persons unjustly charged with civil crimes in Mexico; providing initial funding and ongoing support for the Home of Peace and Love, a shelter for victims of prostitution and rape near Bangkok, Thailand; and the provision of micro-loans to support indigenous communities in Chiapas to start bread-baking, weaving, and irrigation cooperatives in dozens of villages and refugee camps. [29]

These interfaith initiatives along with those of many other similar organizations that are working towards a just and peaceful world have been brought together within The International Interfaith Organisations Network.[30] This network enables its members to share information and find mutual support and ideas while avoiding duplications of effort and costs.

The Council for a Parliament of the World's Religions (CPWR), another member of that Network, reflects the common thinking behind all these bodies. 'Too often, religion is misused as an instrument for division and injustice, betraying the very ideals and teachings that lie at the heart of each of the world's great traditions. At the same time, religious and spiritual traditions shape the lives of billions in wise and wonderful ways. They gather people in communities of shared beliefs and practices. When these diverse communities work in harmony for the common good, there is hope that the world can be trans-formed.'[31]

We are desperately in need of a universal religious tolerance. We can all play our part, to work hard at that faith line and support in any way we can all those organizations and individuals who are striving to achieve harmony between the diverse religions of the world. Many of us are apparently blind to the fact that all the great faiths share a love, compassion and respect for all beings, sentient or not. May we all in the years to come learn to celebrate our differences and our unique perspectives in an atmosphere of tolerance, understanding and humility. This is a vital message for our future, the need to heal the rifts between religions and faiths so that we can all be a part of that great global healing, all be catalysts for healing change at society and global level.

'...I would urge people who are judgmental and moralising," said John Sentamu in his inauguration sermon in York Minster, as followers of the Prince of Peace, the friend of the poor, the marginalized, and the vulnerable, I bid you all by the mercies of God to go and find friends among them, among the young, among older people, and all those in society who are demonized and dehumanized; and stand shoulder to shoulder with them.

Christians, go and find friends among Buddhists, Hindus, Jews, Muslims, Sikhs, agnostics, atheists – not for the purpose of converting them to your beliefs, but for friendship, understanding, listening, hearing…

Buddhists, Hindus, Jews, Muslims, Sikhs, agnostics, atheists, go and find friends amongst Christians, not for the purpose of converting them to your beliefs, but for friendship, understanding, listening, hearing.

God is working in the world today quite beyond the limits of our budgets, structures and expectation. His gospel, lived out in corporate-discipleship, has the power to transform our individual and corporate lives, our families, our communities and our nations. It has the power to break beyond our timidity and insufficiency.[32]

The color line took a great deal of time to transcend and the work is not entirely finished. Can we dare hope that the faith line will follow the same path towards tolerance and respect for all, blessed as we now are with greater global information, communication and education? May this lead to a better understanding if we will only allow it in our hearts and minds. There are many organizations that work tirelessly to keep the principles of religious pluralism alive. They need our support. With leaders such as Eboo Patel our future looks considerably more promising and hopeful. Are we ready for that challenge?

The Wounded Healer
To meet our challenges we need to stay alert and fully alive to the

healing opportunities that fall in our path. We must not walk by on the other side of the road.

There is a Jewish legend from the *Sanhedrin* tractate of the Talmud. Rabbi Yoshua ben Levi came upon Elijah the prophet while he was standing at the entrance of Rabbi Simeron ben Yohai's cave. . .He asked Elijah,

'When will the Messiah come?'
Elijah replied, 'Go and ask him yourself.'
'Where is he?'
'Sitting at the gates of the city.'
'How shall I know him?'
'He is sitting among the poor covered with wounds. The others unbind all their wounds at the same time and then bind them up again. But the Messiah unbinds one at a time and binds it up again, saying to himself, 'Perhaps I shall be needed: if so I must always be ready so as not to delay for a moment.'[33]

Henri Nouwen tells this story to illustrate how the Wounded Healer must always be prepared, always ready to offer healing to others through the wounds he himself has suffered. And one of the most common and painful of those wounds, says Nouwen, is loneliness, something he himself often keenly felt in his life. According to a Duke University study, 25 percent of U.S. citizens say they have no one to confide with about personal troubles. This is more than double the number who were similarly isolated in 1985, two decades earlier.[34]

This may partly explain why so many of us seek comfort and healing in psychotherapies, in group therapies, indeed in any forum where common experiences can be shared in a safe place. But Nouwen compares our wounds to the Grand Canyon, 'a deep incision in the surface of our existence which has become an inexhaustible source of beauty and self-understanding.'[35] Those wounds that we seek to heal in ourselves should be protected and cherished as a precious healing gift. We could all be Wounded Healers, he wrote, we can all be alongside those who suffer with our respective wounds while a mutual healing is found within this openness and honesty.

And nowhere can we better share our own wounded loneliness and allow our wounds to become a source of healing for others, than in the provision of hospitality.[36]

Hospitality

Forty United Methodist churches joined together for the inauguration of President Obama in Washington in January 2009. These churches opened their doors to those very many people who had traveled from across the country to be there, from as far away as New Jersey, Ohio, Texas, North Carolina, Iowa and Georgia. They were all offered a friendly place for rest and refreshment and about 90 people slept on the floors of a Methodist Sunday school classroom. On inauguration day, again the church was able to provide hot beverage and fellowship while watching the event on a projection screen.[37] The numbers helped in this way were not great, but that does not matter. Every kind gesture is a seed sown for the future.

While hospitality is deeply rooted in Judeo-Christian tradition, it is also an essential part of most if not all faiths.

Throughout the Holy Bible the sharing of food together is often mentioned as a token of friendship and commitment. This entire code of hospitality in the Middle East was so strong that it is expressed in a biblical warning, 'Do not neglect to show hospitality to strangers, for thereby some have entertained angels unawares.'[38] And of course Jesus shared his Last Supper with his Disciples before his Crucifixion and Resurrection. We celebrate this meal each week in our Holy Eucharist.

On holiday with my family in Turkey a few years ago we experienced two memorable examples of generous Muslim hospitality. We were walking around a small isolated village, in need of refreshment: we were hot and thirsty. It wasn't long before we found ourselves engaged in a somewhat stilted conversation with a local man. He spoke very little English. Nonetheless, from the rather tenuous link that he also had a friend in London - 'did we know him?' he asked - we were invited back to his modest stone built cottage to meet the rest of the family. After much nodding and handshakes we sat on cushions on the floor among them and shared cool beer. The conversation was difficult but the genuine warmth and hospitality was undoubted.

A few afternoons later we were drawn towards the sounds of music and dancing in another village. Following the sound we found a massive party in full swing in the front garden of a huge, if rather less than grand, house. Many of the guests were wearing national costume. Displaying the worst of bad manners, I recall that we were trying inconspicuously to take a photo. Immediately we were spotted and most graciously beckoned into their midst, where we were introduced to everyone and plied with huge quantities of good food, much of which seemed to be arriving continuously from various kitchens along the street. This turned out to be a circumcision party for a twelve- year old lad, dressed in traditional white for the ceremony. We pinned the customary Turkish dinar to his clothes, to add to the many notes already there. We ate and drank heartily while some of the men and boys tried to teach their dance to my own sons, somewhat unsuccessfully I recall! It was altogether a wonderful and happy occasion.

Such hospitality is fundamentally important to Muslims. It defines who they are and they judge themselves and each other on the generosity of their welcome to strangers as well as friends.[39]

But the Muslims are not alone in this generosity of welcome. Hospitality is also seen as very important to the Sikh faith. Here it is grounded in the 500 year old tradition of langar, which is the free distribution of vegetarian food to both rich and poor, regardless of caste, color, religion or status. The United Sikh Association of New York University has organized langar events there every year since 2006. This free food from their community kitchen is offered to all students as they sit on the floor, as is traditional, in a symbolism of brotherhood, equality, hospitality, community service, and selfless-service.[40]

Hindu culture also believes that appropriate hospitality should be offered to any visitor to the home, even to an enemy. After all, they say, 'A tree does not deny its shade even to the one who comes to cut it down.'[41] The uninvited guest should be treated as good as God, says the popular Hindu proverb.

Sadly too many of us in our daily lives now seem too busy to relax and welcome the unexpected visitor into our home. Gone it seems are the days when we could all have an open house for our friends and neighbors. How often do we deny ourselves the healing of companionship? It may not always be obvious how hospitality is being used as a source of healing, although the opportunity is always present if we are sensitive enough to find it.

The idea of hospitality as a source of healing has perhaps been seen nowhere more clearly than in the international and free barbeque ministry, On The Move.[42] Founded in 1998 by Martin Graham, the idea is simple but effective. Lay Christians are recruited as leaders from the local churches across all Christian denominations to take the message of Jesus Christ into town centers, usually in the open air. There a free barbeque is served to all who stop by, in a spirit of love and generosity. There is worship and there is healing. The leaders are encouraged to move out of their comfort zones, to minister to those who are broken, needy, lonely, in fact in need of any healing. The movement takes the love of God in the power of the Spirit to the many people who are ready to receive it, as the leaders pray with the guests for the healing of these needs. The success of the movement is seen in the coverage of its missions in 26 countries and across the five continents. Its history has been described in the book *Sizzling Faith: The Dream that got the Church on the Move!*[43]

Such has been the success of On the Move that it has gathered its own momentum and the ministry is now being copied across the world through other Christian groups. On the Move has fulfilled its mission and has wound down its own program. But the success of On the Move shows that we do not have to be an ordained minister to be a source of healing to others. Certainly within the Christian churches there is an increasing interest in the use of the laity to work alongside ordained priests in their ministry. Henri Nouwen saw his ideas of a healing ministry based on the symbolism of the Wounded Healer as being practiced by all Christians, not just pastors.

Hospitality is just one aspect of an important healing ministry that is to be found across all the religions. While some religions have more established healing ministries than others, all are there for anyone in need of pastoral care and support in times of trouble and where many find nourishment for spirit and soul.

Social healing

Traditionally and historically the role of the Christian priest has been as a curer of souls, to be a Wounded Healer, as he follows the example of Jesus Christ in his own ministry. But healing has a wider social significance; Pastoral care is a healing ministry taken out into the world.

In 1983 Peter Selby[44] wrote a book on church pastoral care challenging the pastor to 'become actively involved in taking sides to try to change the dark aspects of life which brings people to counselling in the first place.' Selby stressed that such pastoral work has to be about much more than empathy and assisting an individual to personal growth and inner wholeness. 'Where two or three are pastorally gathered together,' he wrote, 'it is possible to model a new world and in the process to empower the two or three to pursue the overarching aims of justice and peace with greater strength and conviction. Caring,' he said, 'is a liberating, socialist activity.'[45] It is an essential aspect of the work for any parish priest.

Most of the faiths are represented by the work of chaplaincies within companies and businesses, in the armed forces, in prisons and hospices, as well as in our hospitals. J. J. Means, a pastoral counselor at the Des Moines Pastoral Counseling Center, Iowa USA, is certain of the social significance of his work, of the need for the Wounded Healer to become a Mighty Prophet for social change.[46]

The clients of the pastoral counselor are scouts, he observes, bringing into the consulting room not only their own problems, but also a wider message of the hurts and wounds of the culture in which they live. This is a culture, he says, that is preoccupied with speed, technology and objectivity, full of idols and false truths that lead to so much long term dissatisfaction and that hurt and destroy the very selves and souls of the person. It is all too easy to be so engrossed with the client's own problem brought to that consultation, that there is no time to listen to and properly to consider the underlying social message, that deserves far more attention. While acknowledging the general busy-ness of the practitioner, he calls all pastoral caregivers, whatever their setting, in their capacity as Wounded Healers, to the vocation of Mighty Prophet. He believes that they have a responsibility, both personal and institutional, in their capacity as Wounded Healers, to look beyond the client and what is hurting that client, to the wider world, with its needs for education and reform.

'The time is ripe and the need is great for...[pastoral caregivers]... to be wisely guided by our woundedness, and for us to courageously, faithfully and fully... become mighty prophets in a world desperately looking for direction.'

We can all heed Means' words and understand that the role of Mighty Prophet can be extrapolated not only from the world of pastoral counseling but out of the broader remit of all health professionals as Wounded Healers: all will need courage to speak out on the social issues that have wounded the patient and begin to heal those issues and the patient's world.

'This is not a small matter,' Means writes. 'In fact, our ultimate survival as a society rests upon our willingness to do three things: 1) believe the messenger that comes to us; 2) listen to their unpleasant messages about the culture in which we live, and 3) speak prophetically and courageously in response to the messages we hear.'

That same religious network that enables a faith to reach the grass roots of society in pastoral care and hospitality also facilitates dialogue on the bigger healing issues of our time. All the main faiths have their initiatives for addressing climate change and sustainability, as well as tackling violence and in the pursuit of peace. There are also many well-organized and often courageous faith-based aid efforts for the relief of human suffering, from the ravages of war, natural disaster, man's inhumanities to man, all a major source of humanity's wounds.

Religions also become involved in issues that are an affront to their faith and their beliefs as they strive towards a justice for all. For example Let Justice Roll,[47] a coalition of more than ninety faith, community, labor and business organizations, is committed to raising the minimum wage in America to a decent living wage for all, campaigning actively at federal and state level.

We should also remember that both Christianity and Islam have been significant influences in the history of the provision of health services. As we shall see in the later chapter on the Hope of Soul Medicine, the boundaries between spiritual care and health care are likely to become increasingly blurred with the passage of time. Indeed we should encourage healthcare and church to work together as far as possible, to complement one another in their respective healing skills.

And of course the religions are defenders of moral and ethical values.

Our children as catalysts of healing

If you want to explore our general moral decline, all you have to do is start a blog. Ask for people to comment on how they would behave if they went to an ATM to draw 20 dollars and received 60 dollars instead; what they would do if they are undercharged or over-changed in a shop!

Most of us seem to be generally concerned about the lack of values and morality that we see all around us.

Eboo Patel is right to target the youth of today. We also need to target our children. They are our future. We fail them if we do not ensure they are brought up with sound moral and ethical values; we fail them if we do not teach them a sense of right from wrong, fail to show them the importance of tolerance and love and compassion for all.

Parents often want their children to go to faith schools, not always for any specific religious education but rather because of the values that are taught. Indeed our local Anglican church school has been turning children away for lack of space and is now busy finding that extra space to accommodate two further classes.

Hindus put great emphasis on the importance of a holistic education for their children, for their values to be rooted in spirituality. Recognizing the destruction caused by ignorance, emphasis is placed on Hindu education from an early age, not only in the school but in the family unit and in the community. Traditional Hindu education 'covers all facets of life – economic, political, cultural, and above all religious.' Following the example of Krishna, Chaitanya, or of Gandhi, they draw 'no clear division between the economic or political and the religious or cultural facets of life. The body and mind are in the service of the heart. In the same way politics and economics are rooted in and guided by religion and culture, and ultimately by spiritual experience.' [48]

Faith schools exist for many of our established religions. They are certainly not without controversy and obviously they can be harmful when they indoctrinate and exclude. But these schools all have principals and governors, teachers and parents who can be courageous and stand up for principles of inclusivity and mutual understanding. Perhaps you are one of those?

Jobbing theologians

Even if we cannot see ourselves as Wounded Healers, we can be jobbing theologians. We must not be shy to take our faith or belief and the spiritual and moral values inherent in it, along with our own sense of vulnerability and woundedness, into our work and leisure. Those of no affiliation to organized religion, but simply of good faith, take your spiritual values out into your life. Be firm and stand up for those values! Those many who have a nominal Christian faith, don't abandon this. Nurture it, allow yourself to grow spiritually and you can become a Wounded Healer in the name of Jesus Christ. You could find it life-changing!

Some faiths are more reticent than others to display their beliefs. Christians particularly often seem to be afraid to live out their religious principles in the open. Some of our reticence is perhaps because of that ridicule that firmly held beliefs seem to often engender in others. Consequently it is easy for us to sidestep our responsibilities when we find ourselves involved in activities that are contrary to the moral and ethical beliefs and practices of our faith or to our own principles.

It was dangerous to be a Christian in the time of the apostles and there is no reason to suppose that it will be any less dangerous now if we truly live our faiths and take a stand individually and collectively against that which we know to be wrong.

All the world's great religions share common visions of peace and of love and compassion for all. And they all share the Golden Rule, albeit expressed in different ways: 'nature is only good when it shall not do unto another whatever is not good for its own self.' [49]

Signs of hope

We began this chapter with hope, the hope of faith. There are signs of hope all around us. Jim Wallis, founder of Sojourners, a US network of progressive Christians working for justice and peace, notes that the landscape is changing in America, with the young more ready to embrace Christ and take Him into the world.[50] We need to foster and cultivate such interest.

We see our church leaders taking much more of a public stand and involving themselves in vital issues of the day. The internet enables these same leaders to publish their sermons and talks to inspire us all. We have also seen the immense success of the Inter Youth Faith Core and other organizations working towards genuine peaceful religious pluralism, dedicated to working for world justice and peace. As a Christian I see the hope of a wider laity involvement, witnessed by organizations such as On the Move, because to help us along the way we need more healers, both priests and laity.

I find hope in this new age of consciousness that is dawning, in the soul medicine of doctors, in the plethora of good books that are appearing that capably answer the strident objections of the fundamental atheists. I find hope in all those who work to shed ever more light on how we can use our own wounds and spirituality to heal.

When times are hard people pull together. This was seen in Britain in the Second World War. Perhaps the deep global problems of this new Millennium will engender a similar spirit of community survival.

Even the warring factions can forget their differences in some circumstances. There were the famous Christmas truces in the trenches in the First World War when the German and British soldiers exchanged small gifts, sang carols and played football together.

This is certainly not the first record of a temporary truce from fighting. 'In the Crimean War British, French and Russians at quiet times also gathered around the same fire, smoking and drinking. In the American Civil War Yankees and Rebels traded tobacco, coffee and newspapers, fished peacefully on opposite sides of the same stream and even collected wild blackberries together.'[51]

On 29 July 2007 millions of Iraqis, Shia, Sunni, Kurds and Christians, became united for a brief interlude to rejoice over their football victory against Saudi Arabia in the Asian Cup Final. Shots were fired in the air in jubilant celebration rather than for political squabbling and killing. Iraq had been momentarily unified by eleven footballers! But the euphoria was short lived. In no time the city had reverted to its politically fuelled bombings and shootings.

The truce in war has a long tradition and is surely a sign of hope for the world?

If we can all unite for sport and athletics, at langars and in No Man's Land, why can we not work together peaceably for our own futures?

Finally I hope for more politicians who will not be shy or afraid of letting the world know their own faith-driven values. We need such politicians who can reflect those values in policies in a way that still appeals to the electorates and does not antagonize them.

This however would not be the final panacea. In the final reckoning how we live our lives and mold our futures goes back to our own behavior as responsible and healed citizens. As

Thomas Merton said, 'If you love peace, then hate injustice, hate tyranny, hate greed – but hate these things *in yourself*, [Merton's italics] not in another.'[52]

'*What is required of us now is a new era of responsibility*,' said President Obama in his inauguration speech, '*a recognition, on the part of every American, that we have duties to ourselves, our nation, and the world, duties that we do not grudgingly accept but rather seize gladly, firm in the knowledge that there is nothing so satisfying to the spirit, so defining of our character, than giving our all to a difficult task.*'

In the next chapter we discover the hope of that responsibility.

Chapter 4
Hope For Our Destiny
A New Era of Responsibility

Responsibility: A detachable burden easily shifted to the shoulders of
God, Fate, Fortune, Luck or one's neighbour. In the days of astrology
it was customary to unload it upon a star.
Ambrose Bierce

On 30 July 2008, the United States House of Representatives
passed a resolution apologizing for American slavery and for the
subsequent 'Jim Crow' discriminatory laws. In the previous year
the Virginia General Assembly had acknowledged 'with
profound regret the involuntary servitude of Africans and the
exploitation of Native Americans,'[1] and called for reconciliation
among all Virginians. Virginia became the first of the 50 United
States to recognize through their governing body the state's
negative involvement in slavery.

In that same year the UK celebrated the 200-year anniversary
of the abolition of the Slave Trade. The Church of England have
since offered a full apology for profiting from the slave trade, and
Prime Minister Tony Blair offered deep sorrow 'that it could ever
have happened' and said that we could 'rejoice at the better times
we live in today.'[2]

Among the media attention in both countries, much was made
of whether we should now be apologizing at all for what our
ancestors did all that time ago, and whether any compensation

was due. Rather less publicity or thought was given to the feelings of those in the original abolition movement. What motivated them?

The prominent American abolitionist William Lloyd Garrison said in a talk delivered in the Broadway Tabernacle, New York, 14 February 1854:

I am a believer in that portion of the Declaration of American Independence in which it is set forth, as among self-evident truths, 'that all men are created equal; that they are endowed by their Creator with certain inalienable social rights; that among these are life, liberty, and the pursuit of happiness.' Hence, I am an Abolitionist. Hence, I cannot but regard oppression in every form, and most of all, that which turns a man into a thing, with indignation and abhorrence. Not to cherish these feelings would be recreancy to principle. They who desire me to be dumb on the subject of Slavery, unless I will open my mouth in its defense, ask me to give the lie to my professions, to degrade my manhood, and to stain my soul.[3]

In the UK, a group known as the Clapham Sect drove the abolition movement. Taking their name from the Surrey village where they mostly lived and held their meetings, this group of evangelical Christians saw the treatment of slaves as an affront to their own dignity. It was the overwhelming spiritual hunger for justice that drove these and other abolitionists, often among controversy and even violence, to strive towards making a real and permanent difference to the lives of so many.

Sadly there is still slavery in today's world, alongside so many other inequalities and human suffering, even in so-called 'civilized' Western societies such as ours. So how can we make a difference today to alleviate the many injustices in the world? As it was then, so it needs to be now if there is to be any real change in the lives of so many who still suffer. We need to feel again that degradation of humanity, the affront to our dignity, that staining of our souls. We need to find again that hunger for justice that the abolitionists felt.

In the Beatitudes that Jesus preached to his followers in the Sermon on the Mount, He spoke of the happiness and joy, or blessedness, that would be felt if we 'hunger and thirst for right-eousness.'[4]

The Archbishop of Canterbury Dr Rowan Williams in his New Year message for 2007[5] spoke of the need for us to feed our own spiritual hunger. For real change to be made, to put right the injustices of the world, we have to follow, he says, the example of the Clapham Sect. We must realize that such issues are indeed an affront to our own dignity. In some way they make each of us less of a person. We will be fed and nourished spiritually only when we really and honestly wake up to the needs of our fellow human beings, learning together to reach out to them, to heal, feed, and befriend those less fortunate than ourselves. Then we will discover what it really means to be truly human.

Barack Obama, writing on the difficulties he sometimes experienced in his relationship with his grandfather, observed 'that sometimes he really did have a point, and that in insisting on getting my own way all the time, without regard to his feelings or needs, I was in some way diminishing myself.' He goes on to say: 'I believe a stronger sense of empathy would tilt the balance of our current politics in favor of those people who are struggling in this society. After all, if they are like us, then their struggles are our own. If we fail to help, we diminish ourselves.'[6] He reaffirmed this message later on the campaign trail, when he spoke of those he had met 'whose dreams and struggles become my own; they will stay with me in the White House.'

This is the message of a Wounded Healer.

The Brotherhood of Man

In his Nobel Lecture, Peace Prize Laureate Martin Luther King reminded us:

> Ultimately a great nation is a compassionate nation. No individual or nation can be great if it does not have a concern for 'the least of these.' Deeply etched in the fiber of our religious tradition is the conviction that men are made in the image of God and that they are souls of infinite metaphysical value, the heirs of a legacy of dignity and worth. If we feel this as a profound moral fact, we cannot be content to see men hungry, to see men victimized with starvation and ill health when we have the means to help them. The wealthy nations must go all out to bridge the gulf between the rich minority and the poor majority...
>
> In the final analysis, the rich must not ignore the poor because both rich and poor are tied in a single garment of destiny. All life is interrelated, and all men are interdependent. The agony of the poor diminishes the rich, and the salvation of the poor enlarges the rich. We are inevitably our brothers' keeper because of the interrelated structure of reality. [7]

Three centuries earlier the Renaissance author and Anglican priest John Donne famously wrote in 1624:

> No man is an island, entire of itself; every man is a piece of the continent, a part of the main. If a clod be washed away by the sea, Europe is the less, as well as if a promontory were, as well as if a manor of thy friend's or of thine own were. Any man's death diminishes me, because I am involved in mankind; and therefore never send to know for whom the bell tolls; it tolls for thee.[8]

The Apostle Paul, writing in his first epistle to the Corinthians, on human worth, likened the worldwide body of Christians with the human body. All parts of the body are essential for the complete welfare of the whole. In the same way we all need each other and the loss of any part weakens us all: there should be no discord between us. He taught his followers that the members of the church should 'have the same care for one another. If one member suffers, all suffer together; if one member is honoured, all rejoice together.'[9] The 'body' in this biblical context is translated from the Greek Soma, related to Sozo meaning 'to heal, preserve, be made whole.' We are not whole: we are wounded or spiritually impoverished if we are not a part of the greater body of faith in our community. We all need to feel that connectedness, that relationship. We need to find unity within the wide diversity of all our individual gifts. We all need each other and we all are special in the eyes of God.

Followers of the Baha'i faith see Earth as one country of which we are all citizens.[10] One of their guiding principles is that 'the oneness of humanity is the fundamental spiritual and social truth shaping our age.'

Whatever our faith we can be guided by these truths.

This is our responsibility.

A new organ of consciousness

Long before the era of mass cheap travel and the universal availability of personal computers, the French Jesuit and visionary Pierre Teilhard de Chardin predicted a new kind of oneness of humanity. He foresaw the massive advances in technology and communications that would create a planetary information network. He called this new organ of consciousness the 'noosphere'. This, he said, would enable a convergence of mankind at all levels, between families, communities, organizations and nations, across all boundaries, social, cultural, economic and political. With the development of the worldwide web, and the enormous advances in global communication that this made possible, these predictions have been fulfilled. What is more, Teilhard also foresaw the possible dangers of such convergence; and that this had fundamental implications for the future of humanity if we did not consciously evolve to cope with the effects of these changes.

Teilhard lived before the age of the internet and the global communications phenomenon that he foresaw so accurately. He made a life time study out of trying to integrate theories of evolution with religious experience, particularly Christian theology. Most of all he wanted to understand the place of man within evolution and the implications that would have for our future.[11] He was excited by the possibilities of his predicted new global consciousness for the future evolution of mankind. Man, he said, was at an evolutionary crossroads, and if he could overcome the dangers inherent in these changes, then he was capable of heading for a new state of peace and planetary unity. There would be a convergence of systems across the world, a coalescence of consciousness. He called this the 'Omega' point. He was equally clear that to achieve this new planetary harmony 'It is not our heads or our bodies, which we must bring together, but our hearts…Humanity…is building its composite brain beneath our eyes. May it not be that tomorrow, through the biological deepening of the movement drawing it together, it will find its heart, without which the ultimate wholeness of its power of unification can never be achieved?'[12]

However, as Martin Luther King saw, (and we do not seem to have made much progress since then!), 'We have learned to fly the air like birds and swim the sea like fish, but we have not learned the simple art of living together as brothers.' [13]

Conscience and social responsibility

Viktor Frankl observed: 'Being human means being conscious and being responsible.'[14] He was writing about the very core of our being, our human conscience, and our personal integrity.

The state of being responsible is to be 'liable to be called to account,' or to render satisfaction, or to be answerable to someone for something. In his book *To Heal a Fractured World* The Chief Rabbi Jonathan Sacks writes at length on the ethics of our responsibilities. His theme is that 'Life is God's call to responsibility.'[15] While written from a Jewish perspective, his message is equally relevant to those of all other faiths or none. The Jewish ethics of responsibility can be summed up very simply. If someone is in any kind of need, help him. And this, Sacks says, is the best answer he knows to the meaning of life, expressed in the Hebrew word *simhah* meaning *the happiness we make by sharing*. It is akin to the joy or 'blessedness' of the Christian who hungers and thirsts for justice and righteousness.

But of course in practice it is useful to be reminded from time to time of our responsibilities. Thus for example the Methodists have a special renewal service each year when they covenant to continue their lives in the service of Christ.[16]

Towards the end of his life in June 1961 Carl Jung was beginning to show increasing concern for the future of the earth and man's role in its downfall. 'Everything now depends on man,' he wrote. 'Immense power of destruction is given into his hands, and the question is whether he can resist the will to use it, and can temper his will with the spirit of love and wisdom. He will hardly be able to do so on his own resources. He needs the help of an 'advocate' in heaven.' [17] Jung wrote of the hope 'that God's good spirit will guide [man] in his decisions, because it will depend on man's decision whether God's creation will continue.'[18]

Carl Jung is well known, but there may be fewer who are aware of the work of another influential and pioneering psychologist and therapist of that time, Carl Rogers. In addition to his professional practice Rogers was an American peace activist with a strong social concern and sense of social responsibility. He recognized the potential value to mankind of his healing work with his patients and became increasingly interested in ways of resolving tensions in human relationships. He expressed his deep unease that man was developing the capacity to destroy himself and the world, and would do so unless individual, inter-personal and inter-group tensions could be understood and resolved. This was the 1960s, the world of the Suez Crisis, the 'Cold War' and the Berlin Wall. 'Out of defensiveness and inner fear,' Rogers explained,

individuals can and do behave in ways which are incredibly cruel, horribly destructive, immature, regressive, anti-social, hurtful. Yet one of the most refreshing and invigorating...(parts of my experience)... is to work with such individuals and to discover the strongly positive directional tendencies that exist in them, as in all of us, at the deepest levels. We already possess learnings which...would help to decrease the inter-racial, industrial, and international tensions which exist...and used preventively, could aid in the development of mature, non-defensive, understanding persons who would deal constructively with future tensions as they arise.[19]

Rogers developed his own theories of human behavior into what became known as his Client Centered Therapy. He became an expert on the dynamics of human behavior and relationships and spent the last ten years of his life taking his practical experience of this approach into conflict situations. He 'developed an entire way of being – a lived expression of positivity and reverence for others –(he) envisioned a new world, a place of peace and harmony'[20] of which he caught glimpses in his peace work in, for example, Northern Ireland and South Africa and the Soviet Union.

'This new world,' he said, 'will be more human and humane.

It will explore and develop the richness and capacity of the human mind and spirit. It will produce individuals who are more integrated and whole. It will be a world that prizes the individual person – the greatest of our resources.'[21]

Sadly Rogers did not live to see the complete fruition of his dreams. Because of his peace initiatives he was nominated for the Nobel Peace Prize, but this was just days before he died suddenly at the age of 85 in February 1987.

Carl Jung and Carl Rogers were not alone among twentieth century mental health professionals in wanting to use their knowledge and skills for practical and socially responsible causes. M. Scott Peck became well known in the 1970s and 1980s for his bestselling books on personal spiritual growth. He is probably best remembered for *The Road Less Traveled* and *Further Along the Road Less Traveled.* He also made a study of community building and its role in achieving world peace, and he wrote this up for the popular market in his book *The Different Drum.* His books continue to sell well and are just as relevant in today's world. I shall look at more of Peck's ideas in the next chapter on community.

The twentieth century philosopher and social commentator Aldous Huxley also recognized the essential role and responsibility of the individual in determining the events of the world. In a shift away from his early preoccupation with the mistakes of institution and state, he came to believe in later life that 'the most overlooked cure for social problems is actually the improvement of the individual citizen, and that cultures are only expressions of the collective consciousness of their people.'[22] This insight came to him with the spiritual growth he found from the practice of yoga and meditation, recommended by his friend George Heard for the relief of his chronic health problems. Huxley also became committed to the pacifist movement in Europe, taking his views on successful lecture tours with Heard in the years leading up to the Second World War.

Jung, Rogers, Scott Peck and Huxley all came from different philosophies and backgrounds. Nevertheless they shared a common vision and understanding: they all appreciated the significance, and the potential social impact, of the spiritual growth and health of the individual for the future health of the world.

If only more of us would heed all these things, ponder them in our hearts and understand the significance of our actions and our healing. The world would become a better place for us all. Surely we all have this responsibility.

Beware the self-help industry!

Peter Selby observed that 'the obsessive search for personal growth and inner wholeness without concern for the health of society is distorting.'[23]

Nowhere is this distortion more obvious, and more potentially harmful than among the self-help and self-development genre of book that is so popular today, and that fuels what has been dubbed the new egocentric 'Me-Millennium'. I suspect that quite a few of us have reached in our time to those sections of a library or bookshop tempted by books that promise to 'change our lives', or help us 'succeed'. Many of these are excellent. I have quite a few on my own bookshelves! But there are some among them that may not be quite as healing as their contents imply, particularly in the context of the world's healing needs. Sadly the emphasis of such books may too often be on the petty ego of self, the selfish desire for individual improvement, the seemingly endless drive for power and wealth. This style of self-development is often measured by the values of material gain, promotion, or celebrity status. But doesn't this approach fuel greed and envy, eschew vulnerability and threaten genuine altruism? I think so, and I fear that this then undermines attempts to establish a global world community, to convert hearts and minds to a higher plane, for a better world, as envisaged by Teilhard de Chardin. Unfortunately a huge and profitable industry has built up around this 'success' culture. What is more, many such books actively discourage contact with those who are wounded in our society, the vulnerable, the loners, the unhappy, the unsuccessful, the disadvantaged, those who are damaged emotionally. Such weaknesses are too often seen as inhibiting to our own 'development'.

By not helping such people we dig ourselves deeper into a less attractive future! We divorce ourselves from experiencing and displaying that empathy and compassion needed for real individual healing. We fail to acknowledge the powerful effect that such healing can have on the wounds of the world around us. We perpetuate an unhealthy 'divergence' at a time when we should be actively seeking Teilhard's 'convergence' and all that this entails.

We should instead appreciate that the wounded are often in a unique position to help others in the same plight, and we should not shun them. To do so contradicts the teachings of all faiths.

Perhaps you feel that I am being too hard on the self-help industry? After all, any healing can be a power for good if it is achieved in the right spirit of social responsibility.

But surely we have to beware the potentially damaging influence of a self- help industry if it becomes too self-centered on the individual at the expense of others?

Beware the danger of remoteness

Perhaps one of the greatest enemies of responsible behavior is to be found in the remoteness that often exists between cause and effect. It is so much easier not to have a conscience about our behavior where the consequences of our actions are not directly experienced.

10% of the world's population is consuming 50% of its resources. 20% of the world's population has no safe water supply. Observing our speed limits can save a liter of fuel or more per 100 miles. Are we going to slow down, stop using that pressure hose, cut our consumption?

People use the expression 'out of sight, out of mind,'[24] to mean that something is easily forgotten or dismissed as soon as it is beyond our range of vision. It can be used in everyday conversation for quite trivial incidents. The problem is that whether we realize it or not, we often live our lives by the same principle, and some incidents may be far from trivial. 'Facts do not cease to exist because they are ignored,' said Aldous Huxley.

1 in every 30 Americans, that is 10 million people, back the Humane Society of the United States, [25] an organization that seeks a humane and sustainable world for all animals and is America's 'mainstream force against cruelty, exploitation and neglect.' This means that 29 out of every 30 or 290 million Americans may not care very much about animal cruelty. That is a huge number of people. Many farm animals are subjected to the most appallingly cruel conditions in factory farms. Would those who love their own family pets be happy for them to be treated to the same kind of cruelty? By our inactions we appear to condone miserable birthing cages or farrowing crates for female pigs, where they are held for months and can hardly move let alone turn around or socialize with other pigs; we eat and apparently enjoy the French delicacy pate de foie gras which requires that ducks and geese are force-fed unnaturally large quantities of food through a metal tube that is shoved down their throats and into their stomachs two or three times each day. This barbaric treatment produces a liver that is fatty, diseased and ten times the normal size. It sounds disgusting and it is; goodness knows how those birds must suffer. We prefer not to know about the calves separated from their mothers within the first few days of birth and crammed into individual crates or stalls, tethered by their necks, so they can hardly move, for the duration of their dreadful short lives; and we ignore the plight of the 280 million laying hens in the United States which spend their lives cooped

up in tiny cages with no more than the space of an A4 piece of paper that they can (hardly) call their own.

This is not only about cruelty to animals, although that is reason enough to do something to stop these dreadful practices. Organic humanely reared food is better for our health, and usually tastes a whole lot better as well. These factory farms are pushing family farms, farms that have practiced small-scale humane husbandry sometimes through generations, to the brink of bankruptcy. 'Every new factory farm forces 10 family farmers out of business. With every small family farmer that has to leave the farm, communities lose access to fresh, healthy food and local economies are weakened.'[26]And a sustainable environment is threatened with abnormal pollution patterns and disease.

It is true that very many organizations have signed up to a commitment to use only humane farm produce and through the efforts of organizations like the Humane Society the numbers increase daily. But America's record on animal welfare does not compare well with that in Europe, where the entire European Union has already banned both veal crates and gestation crates, effective 2007 and 2013, respectively. As I write, in the United States the use of these abusive crates remains customary practice.

In the UK shock tactics have been used to change public opinion. Celebrity chefs Hugh Fearnley-Whittingstall[27] and Jamie Oliver[28] have both used powerful documentaries on prime time TV to drive home the message about unacceptable and cruel farming practices.

The Humane Society has on its website videos of animal cruelty in factory farming that I found too shocking to watch. It is shameful if we have built a society with so little compassion that these videos do not persuade people to change their eating habits and campaign for better conditions for all farm animals.

This same remoteness is seen at a global and human level, when we do not always associate the extreme manifestations of climate change happening in other parts of the world with our own excessive and consumer lifestyles.

The IPCC said in 2007 'that by 2050 up to 2 billion people worldwide could be facing major water shortages. The U.S. used more than 148 trillion gallons of water in 2000, according to the U.S. Geological Survey. That includes residential, commercial, agriculture, manufacturing and every other use — almost 500,000 gallons per person.'[29] Serious water shortages in the US are predicted sooner than 2050, caused by 'rising temperatures and evaporation rates, lack of rain, urban sprawl, waste and overuse.'[30]

We usually take our potable water supply totally for granted, because we have not experienced for ourselves and cannot begin to imagine having to walk miles each day to carry back pitchers of water that is possibly dirty and harmful to drink. The chronic water shortages that hit parts of the South of England in the summer drought of 2006 provoked a positive response from customers to the requests to save water. This was almost certainly because the threat of water standpipes in the roads was seen as a real possibility that would affect us all directly and make our lives quite difficult.

The same principles could equally apply to any of the other resources that we hold dear to us or take totally for granted, such as food, fuel, power. I feel sure that we would be far more interested in being frugal with such commodities if we could only fully comprehend the real risk of us losing them by our inappropriate actions.

Do we need celebrities to make television programs or videos with shock tactics about every aspect of our lives before we will act responsibly as individuals? I hope not! Change needs to come from a change of heart, a sense of love and compassion, rather than by the use of shock tactics.

Inaction or 'taking a stand'

We need to remind ourselves that inaction can be as irresponsible as inappropriate action. It can be important that we should take a stand. 'The world is a dangerous place, not because of those who do evil, but because of those who look on and do nothing.'[31]

Can it be so very difficult for us to make responsible consumer choices, as in the food we buy? But one often has to be courageous to speak up about something that is important to us. It is not always easy to try to paddle against the tide. It is much easier to go with the flow. As Voltaire once remarked, 'No snowflake in an avalanche ever feels responsible.' Sometimes we do not stand up for what we know to be right through fear, as my own experiences in committees have shown me vividly.

I once compromised my own career by speaking out against a superior's inappropriate behavior. I then became a victim of redundancy in the middle of a UK recession. Jobs were impossible to find so I started to build up my own accountancy and tax practice. To find my first clients I used to attend all kinds of free professional seminars, set up by large accountancy and law firms for their own self-promotion. My ambitions were just more modest! I remember clearly one such event. The speaking lawyer had introduced a tax avoidance scheme that to me was doubtful on technical but more importantly on ethical and moral grounds. I challenged him in the final time for questions. I am not sure how I found the courage, I'm quite timid really. He was certainly embarrassed. At the end of the day a lovely elderly lady, a retired English barrister and author, hunted me out and asked if I would drive her home. There she gave me tea and appointed me as her tax adviser. She was my very first client, with whom I built up a wonderful friendship and rapport until she sadly died at a great age. Why did she choose me? Because she said she admired my courage to stand up for a principle and most importantly my honesty, in which that principle was founded. These were qualities she saw deteriorating in the world around her all those years ago. Did my outburst achieve much, apart from a new client for me? Perhaps not, but then again perhaps a small seed of ethical responsibility was sown in a professional's heart somewhere in that room.

Conclusion

We may need courage to take a stand, and we have to ensure that we are properly informed before making decisions. But surely it is now time that each and every one of us realized that we must bear our own share of responsibility in the shaping of our world, and then turn that realization into action. In his acceptance speech for the Nobel Peace Prize in 1989 His Holiness the 14th Dalai Lama emphasized that responsibility does not only lie with the leaders of our countries or with those who have been appointed or elected to do a particular job. It lies with each of us individually.[32] The next day in his Nobel Peace Prize lecture he elaborated on the theme:

> The realisation that we are all basically the same human beings, who seek happiness and try to avoid suffering, is very helpful in developing a sense of brotherhood and sisterhood; a warm feeling of love and compassion for others. This, in turn, is essential if we are to survive in this ever shrinking world we live in. For if we each selfishly pursue only what we believe to be in our own interest, without caring about the needs of others, we not only may end up harming others but also ourselves. This fact has become very clear during the course of this century. We know that to wage a nuclear war today, for example, would be a form of suicide; or that by polluting the air or the oceans, in order to achieve some short-term benefit, we are destroying the very basis for our survival. As interdependents, therefore, we have no other choice than to develop what I call a sense of universal responsibility.[33]

Most importantly, we cannot confine the scope of our responsibilities to our own country. It is a matter of global justice that we have equal concern for the conditions in which our brothers and sisters live in poor parts of the world. In December 2001 a Statement was issued by 110 Nobel Laureates on the one-hundredth anniversary of the launch of the Nobel Prize. It included a plea for us all to reassess our global obligations to one another:

> The most profound danger to world peace in the coming years will stem not from the irrational acts of states or individuals but from the legitimate demands of the world's dispossessed. Of these poor and disenfranchised the majority live a marginal existence in equatorial climates. Global warming, not of their making but originating with the wealthy few, will affect their fragile ecologies most. Their situation will be desperate, and manifestly unjust. It cannot be expected, therefore, that in all cases they will be content to await the beneficence of the rich. If, then, we permit the devastating power of modern weaponry to spread through this combustible human landscape, we invite a conflagration that can engulf both rich and poor.[34]

And it is a fact that we have the technology and productive resources to eliminate worldwide misery, poverty and injustice.

In the chapters that follow I will continue to promote the need for compassion and spirit in all our material experiences, in the context of community and our woefully fractured economy, in healthcare and in our creativity. I will look for the hopeful message of the Wounded Healer and for the spiritual gifts of love, compassion and vulnerability, in everything we do, in our companies and businesses, in our professions and our homes. Whether we are consumer, housewife, author or artist, teacher or broadcaster, health care worker or company director, I pray that we will all come to understand how in this context we can take our responsibilities further in the quest to heal our fractured world.

American eco-poet and Zen Buddhist Gary Snyder writes of 'the tiresome but tangible work of school boards, county super-visors, local foresters, local politics.' It is in all those places, he reminds us, where we find our real community, our real culture. 'Get a sense of workable territory, learn about it, and start acting point by point. On all levels, from national to local, the need to move toward steady state economy – equilibrium, dynamic balance, inner growth stressed – must be taught.' [35]

No matter whom we are and what we do in our lives, he says, 'Find your place on the planet. Dig in, and take responsibility from there.'

From company boardroom to the health professional's consulting room we are meant to show our certainty, our confidence, our assertiveness. We are urged to achieve targets, deadlines or 'success' in whatever we do, which is all too often measured in monetary gain of some sort. In this world today it seems to be too often regarded as a sign of weakness to be humble and vulnerable, to expose our own doubts and fears and inadequacies to others. But this is where real healing lies.

'Ultimately, values go back to our real interactions with others,' says Snyder. 'That's where we live, in our communities.'[36]

So in the next chapter I will look at the healing power of community, because, in the words of M S Peck:

In and through community lies the salvation of the world. [37]

Chapter 5
The Hope of Community
The Foundation of a Just Society

Community means more than the comfort of souls. It means, and has always meant, the survival of the species.
Palmer[1]

We cannot make real communities happen, warned M. Scott Peck. We 'cannot heal the mess we have made of the world...[without ourselves]...undergoing some kind of spiritual healing.'[2]

Peck wrote this in 1987 and the world is now in an even bigger mess.

Lexington Virginia sounds like a good place to live. With its tourists and students it can support a good range of small retail shops and art galleries, a flourishing food co-op and independent bookshops. It also has a farmers' market.

Its residents are kept in touch through a comprehensive website[3] with all the latest local community news, from invitations to informal gardening events to the death announcement of local residents, from birthdays and anniversaries to church meetings. Just to remind us that all is not totally utopian, it has recently launched a new emergency citizen alert system and it has its share of residents living below the poverty line. But there seems to be plenty to do for its 7000[4] citizens, and evidence everywhere of a friendliness and civic pride.

In my own village we formed a volunteer workforce to save our own small local store from closure. Small retail stores form the dynamic core of a real village community. The fact is that local stores are more than simply economic units and profit centers. They offer a place where people can meet and greet, gossip, find help and companionship, as well as buy the occasional greetings card or loaf of bread. They are part of the soul of a healthy village and a supportive community life. Sadly in many areas the large malls and the cheap hypermarkets, which we all go to for convenience and fast shopping and keen prices, are driving those small stores out of business. When local shops lose that support and are forced to close, communities suffer deep fractures. At least support for local produce in farmers' markets can go some way to redress the balance.

In this chapter I will show how we can all begin to heal or create communities and be catalysts for social change at local, national and global levels. I look at how we can all contribute to the founding of a better world for us all through community.

Fractured communities

When I was a kid in the fifties, we did not have school shootings, searches of school kids for weapons were unheard of and it would never have occurred to me to shop lift. Drugs were something we were prescribed when we were ill and we had a limited notion of what sex was all about. Even those of us who saw the artificial insemination guy come to treat the cows never made the link from cow to human, calf to baby. Sex was simply not in our language. And alcohol was not available to us. I remember the one diabetic in our school was singled out as being 'unusual' whereas Type 2 Diabetes is all too common now among children. We had certainly never heard of Attention Deficit Hyperactivity Disorder or other similar syndromes or the many allergies that now seem so prevalent. We lived simply, we owned very little of our own, we shared what few toys we had, and usually shared a bedroom with siblings. We went outside to play when the weather was fine. Only the worst weather kept us indoors when we made up our own games with dolls and train sets and painting kits and dressing up boxes. Now children are driven relentlessly around from one expensive activity to the next, to fill every non-school hour. And parents have to worry about so many things that would have been beyond the imagination of a 1950s parent. One huge difference of course was that in those days many more mothers stayed at home to look after the children, to teach them morals and ethics and religion and manners and generally to be their full time mentor and friend. Our mothers baked their own cakes and often the bread as well. Sweets were few, readymade convenience foods were unheard of. Doubtful additives in foods were not the problem that they have since become.

When a community breaks up we see aimless and marginalized children. Knife, gun and drug cultures flourish, alongside lawlessness, graffiti and a general loss of respect for one and all.

It seems clear to me that we are failing our children.

But before we look at how we can make community happen, or heal it when it is fractured, we need to understand where it has all gone wrong.

Why do communities fracture?

There are a host of reasons why communities fracture, or are simply not given the chance to exist.

We can blame new track housing or housing developments that are often built with few if any opportunities for social interaction, with no supporting infrastructure, no shops, and no communal recreation facilities.

And those bigger houses in their own grounds isolate us further, when compared with the smaller houses we used to have where we chatted over the fence with our neighbor. As someone remarked, we invite strangers onto our online social networking site or send them texts across the world, but do not know our neighbors, or the names of the kids playing on the streets. And that is at the heart of the problem of fractured community.

Children are at the heart of community and we are failing them.

Policies do not support parenting

The fact is that modern parents can have a tough time bringing up their children. One reason is that social and economic policies do not support them in their task. For example America is way behind most other wealthy countries in the provision of paid maternity and paternity leave for parents. In addition parents often find that they have to both work to afford health insurance for the children. The absence of readily affordable healthcare is a real problem for many families. The CHIP, or Child Health Insurance Program, gives free health insurance for children up to a certain level of income, but that level is woefully low. This link between healthcare and wages needs to be broken.

A further reason why many families have both parents out at work is that they find themselves on the consumer driven carousel that is twenty-first century life, and they cannot find a way to step off. Children are bombarded with images of the material world. The marketing media cynically exploits them, practically as soon as they are aware of their surroundings. As a result we have more and more material possessions, we buy bigger houses to accommodate it all, we saddle ourselves with mortgages that stretch us to the limits and we then shop at cheap hypermarkets for the lower prices. '...American parents buy into a false definition of need that leaves them addicted to a two-income lifestyle and robs children of family life. These parents are not bad, selfish, or greedy. They are simply doing what most people are doing, going along with the prevailing tide of cultural expectations.'[5] And because we are out at work to fund all these things we are not on hand at home to protect our children from these influences.

The normal working week in most of Europe is less than 40 hours. In Sweden and the Netherlands, dual-earner couples with children average two fewer workdays per week than do U.S. couples.[6]

We need to value our families and our children more.

I believe that in many instances mothers would far rather be at home with their children in those early formative years. I really didn't want to return to work and leave my babies at home with childcare, but like so many others I was driven by education and a career to think I could 'have it all'. I believe that in our hearts we all want more quality time to spend with our children, to be involved in more local activities as a family, rather than ferrying our kids off to expensive entertainments all the time while we get on with our work! It has even been reported that many parents no longer have the time or energy to pursue that most wonderfully rewarding of pursuits, reading the bedtime story.

Early in 2009 and again in 2010 we had rather more snow in the UK than we are used to. It pretty much ground the country to a standstill for several days. But among the moans and wails about no gritting lorries on the streets, roads impassable and schools closed, one city man honestly admitted that for the first time in his life he was forced to stay at home with the family, spent two days making snowmen and tobogganing with them and loved every minute of it. There is certainly nothing wrong with that.

The other wonderful thing that happens when we are all snowed in is that we walk, we talk to complete strangers we meet, we have time to spare and feel happier and fitter because of that. Cars isolate us, we are cocooned from the real world outside and we fail to make important human connections in our daily lives.

We need policies that support the parent and the child. We want time to play with our families. Our children need the support of true community as much if not more than we do.

The community is responsible for its children

Our children are the fabric of our society. They mold our communities for good or ill. When we played outside all those years ago, on the pavements, in the parks and in the village and woods and fields around us, it was totally natural for any villagers around to be keeping an eye on us, to correct us as necessary and appropriate if we misbehaved. And our parents would know that we deserved it. I have recently been criticized for correcting a mischievous child being naughty in church, when she was most certainly old enough to know better. We need to build communities where again there is that strong sense of community responsibility, not just from parents, but also from everyone looking out for each other. We need communities where society supports the values of the family. We should all feel able to intervene in responsible fashion where necessary and appropriate. We are all responsible for the upbringing of the nation's children.

I think the problem is that too many of us are scared. We love the concept of John Donne's No Man is an Island poem but do not try to enact it. We are scared of political correctness, nervous of putting a foot wrong in public. We are also constantly warned by police not to become involved in crime situations where we are putting ourselves at risk. This advice absolves us from our responsibility, gives us the permission to walk by on the other side of the street, to ignore the situation. Surfing the internet, I came upon the following story:

Five shoppers at a Witchita, Kansas convenience store simply stepped over the body of 27 year-old LaShanda Calloway who lay on the floor bleeding severely. None stopped to ask if she was in need of assistance. None even bothered to call 911. Ms. Calloway died later that day at a Witchita hospital of injuries the result of a stabbing; she had been an innocent bystander, wounded in someone else's fight.[7]

Have you ever witnessed any kind of confrontational episode and done nothing to intervene? Perhaps you were on a street or in a train late at night. Do you have a continuing regret? Sadly and all too often such intervention can fuel aggression and worse. But children and youth have a right and a need to be heard and respected and understood. What sort of society have we built where an adult is scared of a child on the street, or afraid to be the Good Samaritan to someone in any kind of trouble?

We not only need to learn how to make communities and how to make them work, but we also need to understand how to heal them when they are broken. Those are the real challenges ahead for us all.

And where there are responsible citizens there is hope that we can do just that.

If we choose community and commit ourselves to work together to build it, Methodist minister David Clark writes of the positive hope that 'humankind will not only survive but will flourish.'[8] Otherwise, given the means we now have to destroy the planet, the future, he says, looks very bleak.

What is true community?
We freely talk about communities without understanding their true nature. We say we live in a community and then take a neighbor to court over a small boundary dispute; we believe that our church is a community but often know very little about what the people sitting beside us in the pew will be doing between this Sunday and the next when we see them again! Do we feel safe and comfortable in our community? Do we know our neighbors, or their children? If we answer no to any of these questions, the chances are it is not really a community at all! These are not true communities; they are clichés, along with terms such as

'community healthcare' or 'community policing'.

As Jonathan Sacks observes, 'A community is where they *know your name* and where they *miss you if you are not there* [Sacks' italics] Community is society with a human face.'[9] People do need a strong sense of their own identity and they need this to be recognized. When we talk about the 'black community', the 'white community', or other similar expressions that we drop into our conversation so freely and unthinkingly from day to day, we may make a particular group feel that it has been labeled as part of 'the problem'. This serves to make its members feel even more isolated and excluded, more defensive, even aggressive towards the rest of society. This we can see is potentially dangerous for us all.

To commune means 'to converse or talk together', usually meant in a spiritual sense. Communion is a sharing of thoughts, of feelings. As a noun it is a body with a common faith, signifying concord, fellowship and unity. The origin of the word is rooted in the Latin, where the word for gift is 'munus', and 'cum' means together, or among each other. So community literally means 'to give among each other'.

Sound communities should be happy, peaceable, supportive and relatively crime free. They should be good places in which to live. We should all be able to feel the benefits of living in a community.

Peck defined the basic community as 'a group of individuals who have learned how to communicate honestly with each other, whose relationships go deeper than their masks of composure, and who have developed some significant commitment to 'rejoice together, mourn together,' and to 'delight in each other, make others' conditions our own.'[10]This definition emphasizes the need for vulnerability among the members of a community. It sets up the conditions for healing and wholeness in an atmosphere of mutual trust.

Such a community will provide a safe place where all can

express their true selves, where we have space to become fully human.

The importance of strong communities in our lives cannot be overestimated. We need them not only to satisfy our own immediate personal needs but for our very survival, for the future of the world. Alastair McIntosh is a Scottish human ecologist, writer and campaigner. If 'humankind is to have any hope of changing the world,' he writes, 'we must constantly work to strengthen community.'[11] We will achieve this only by 'coming alive to community with one another, with the place where we live, and with soul.'[12] This, he says, recognizes 'a Celtic truth about identity, which is actually a deep human truth: a person belongs only inasmuch as they are willing to cherish and be cherished by a place and its peoples.'

Many of us truly lack this comfortable companionship, the love and safety that can be felt in a real and flourishing community. We need plenty of those local friends and acquaintances, those who are always there for each other. Deep down in our lonely hearts I believe that we all really yearn to live within a real community of this nature.

Is this one reason why social networking on the internet has such a massive following?

Not many of us could actually survive very well for very long as a total recluse. Man needs to be within loving relationships with others, to feel part of a larger whole. That is fundamental to his happiness and fulfillment. It is meaningless to talk about community in isolation from this sense of relationship.

I will develop the theme of how we heal community later, but since I continually emphasize the importance of our children in community, where better place to start than with their education? Teaching our young people in the ways of spirit and respect and love will be the world's healing force for the future.

The need for a holistic education

I visited Herm not very long ago, a very small Channel Island 'community' where life of necessity is simple. I watched the children playing outside, gloriously free and dirty and happy, using what nature has given them, the trees and bushes and grass and flowers, and their own abilities to run and hide and shout and climb trees, to be themselves. There was not an adult in sight. And I recalled the vision held by Alastair McIntosh for a spiritually rich and holistic education. He imagines a life-long curriculum of organic food and biodiversity, energy alternatives and respect for all, healing skills incorporating not only the most advanced scientific advances but also the spiritual healing principles, of poetry and story. There would be the study of conflict resolution and how to eliminate the causes of war. And the kids would have fun and play in tree houses.

McIntosh's wish list is long but the spiritual message is clear. Such an education is about 'building of *community* as right relationship between soil, soul and society, powered by the passion of the heart, steered by the reason of the head, and then applied by the skilled technique of the hand.'[13]

The Global Justice Movement, which I shall return to in the next chapter, describes the purpose of education as to 'teach people how to become life-long learners and virtuous human beings, with the capacity to adapt to change, to become masters of technology and builders of civilization through their 'leisure work,' and to pursue the highest spiritual values.'[14]

The Dalai Lama stresses that education 'constitutes one of our most powerful weapons in our quest to bring about a better, more peaceful, world.'[15] He emphasizes the need to open children's eyes to the needs and rights of others, so that their actions have a universal dimension, and they develop their 'natural feelings of empathy so that they come to have a sense of responsibility towards others.' He reminds us that traditionally it has been assumed that ethical and human values would be taught through a child's religious upbringing rather than in mainstream state education. The question of faith schools was discussed briefly in Chapter 3. With the declining influence of religion and faith in family life this vital part of a child's education has become neglected. The Dalai Lama proffers three guidelines for the education of our children. First, he says, we need to awaken their consciousness to basic human values by showing them how these are relevant to their future survival, rather than presenting them as solely an ethical or faith issue. Then we must teach them how to discuss and debate, to understand the value of dialogue rather than violence for resolving conflict. Finally there is the urgent need to teach children that differences of race, faith, culture, while important to preserve, are nevertheless secondary to the equal rights of us all from whatever background to be happy. And of course this is best done in the security of a close loving family unit.

Regrettably the purpose of education as seen in most of our traditional schools is to train people for jobs, rather than to be the rounded and spiritually grounded citizens of tomorrow. As a result the system becomes shackled by the needs of exams and syllabuses and league tables. May it come to pass sooner rather than later that many more of our schools come to be judged not only on their position in academic league tables but on how successfully they turn out well rounded, happy, respectful, empathic and spiritual citizens.

Happily there are schools that are bucking the trend. Rudolf Steiner may be best remembered for his views on education, as practiced in the Waldorf schools.[16] There are more than 900 of these schools operating today worldwide, in 83 countries, with more than 162 in the US, and the organization is growing fast. Some of Steiner's ideas are certainly controversial. But to his credit he correctly saw the danger of education being driven more by the economic needs of society than the interests of the child. He believed strongly in an education to develop the child's intellectual, creative and moral wellbeing, in an atmosphere of co-operation and love rather than competition.

But it is not only our kids who would benefit from a holistic education.

David Clark's vision of community building embraces the need for a continuing education as a shared holistic journey of spiritual discovery and growth, a development of body, mind and spirit as we all learn how to become fully human. We need to fulfill each person's possibilities, he writes. We need to understand the 'infinite value and ultimate worth of every person: young or old, rich or poor, upright or devious, in a position of power or socially marginalized'[17] and embrace the whole of that person's needs in life, whatever those needs may be. This imparts a sense of significance to each individual, an essential component of Clark's vision of successful community.

I will trace in Chapter 8 how holistic training is percolating into the mainstream curriculum of an increasing number of medical schools that are recognizing the importance of healing in the true holistic sense of the word.

So many respected people and organizations are promoting the need for a more holistic and spiritual education. This need becomes ever more urgent: we must give them all the encouragement and support possible.

How do we heal fractured community?

McIntosh's own tools for developing and healing community are shamanic in nature. We need healing, he observes, at individual and cultural level, if we are to achieve healed community.[18] He calls this process cultural psychotherapy. The difficult part of community making is in this healing. It involves 'allowing natural human conflict to surface, revealing it, addressing it – continuously naming, unmasking, engaging.'[19]

McIntosh sees community in its most holistic sense as 'a living spirituality connecting soil, soul and society.'[20] This is the

Celtic triple union of community 'with one another, with nature and with God.'[21]

First, McIntosh explains, there is a need for community with the soil, a reverence of the earth. We have to understand our fragile place within the living ecosystem of the planet earth, find our souls again, and find our own inner healing and wholeness. Only then will we behave appropriately in a sustainable manner within that system and not fight against it. In other words we must lessen our individual footprints. Secondly McIntosh refers to our need for community with human society, the need for the empathy (of the Wounded Healer) and of respect for each other. Finally we need a community with ourselves, with our souls. 'Whatever our religion or lack of one, we need spaces,' says McIntosh, 'where we can take rest, compose and compost our inner stuff, and become more deeply present to the aliveness of life...' And this means we must 'keep one eye to the ground and the other to the stars.'[22] Michael Mayne described this as a need to be re-enchanted by nature, to venerate our natural world once more.

Peck tells us of a participant in one of his community building workshops who observed, 'The greatest gift we can give each other is our own woundedness.' Only the wounded, says Peck, can heal community. His community-making principles of true honesty and openness require us to be vulnerable, to have a willingness to be wounded. In his book on community, *The Different Drum*, he wrote at length on this vulnerability in community building. The danger of invulnerability, he warns, of acting as a 'cool cat', is that psychological defenses are put up between the two parties, and the relationship between them becomes nothing more than 'two empty tanks bumping against each other in the night.' He talks of a 'peace through weakness' strategy to build community, at all levels. 'For the reality is that...there can be no community without vulnerability; and there can be no peace – ultimately no life – without community.'[23]

And this involves taking the risk of showing our vulnerability.

McIntosh recalls how Tom Forsyth, a crofter from the Scottish West Highland community of Scoraig, would say: 'it's not good enough to do your community-development only at the grass roots. So much of the grassroots are just at the level of spectator sport, television, cigarettes, drink and consumer culture. No, you've got to get down to the taproots...that are rooted in the 'ancient spiritual bedrock.'[24] This is where change has to start.

A young man murdered a teenager in a South London suburb in an unthinking moment of unprovoked aggression. This man has been sentenced to life imprisonment, and two families each lose a son. One was much loved. Nothing will fill the hole in his parents' hearts. What about the other? In summing up the case on the steps of the Law Courts the police said that these two young people came from different worlds in the same city. One was a decent and loving child. One, he said, was a yob. We must all do everything in our power to heal the damaged communities in our midst that can harbor these disaffected and dangerous people.

In 2006 David Cameron expressed his view that kids guilty of anti social behavior needed compassion and kindness from those who worked with them. The press distorted his remarks. Go out and 'hug a hoodie' or 'love a lout', they proclaimed. His comments were ridiculed.

In fact there is a serious and real truth hidden behind this media scorn!

As the UK Conservative Party leader at that time Cameron was speaking to the Centre for Social Justice on the link between social injustices and crime, particularly among the young. The point he actually made in a thoughtful and balanced speech was that long-term answers to anti-social behavior would be found in a 'pro-social' society. We have to get to grips, he said, with the causes of crime. We must understand the social circumstances that so often create the environment for the anti-social behavior in the first place. Of course we need tough sanctions and a sense of justice and boundaries. But if the police stand for sanctions and penalties, then all those who work with the kids must stand for love. Not, Cameron assured us, a soppy love, but a love that is all about relationships and emotional development in an atmosphere of security and trust.

There are plenty of examples of good work quietly going on beyond the public gaze, where kids are being helped to develop a sense of worth and belonging, a sense of purpose. There are places where families are supported in local networks, where children are made to feel loved and wanted rather than part of a 'problem'. In the longer term the most effective initiatives will be those that cut across the 'them and us' divide, avoid any kind of social exclusion and foster a broad inclusiveness for all.

I know of one man who devotes all his spare time to coaching a football team comprised of youngsters from a 'tough' area. Nothing special about that, you will say, except that these kids are disabled and fully able bodied, black and white, Muslim and Christian and Hindu, privileged and marginalized. The team is not in any way exclusive. The players share a common passion that crosses all social, cultural, and educational and faith divides. This is one of the first fundamental principles of true community and we can most certainly all contribute to such a noble and worthwhile effort in some way.

These stories and many more that we read and hear of in our local media are all about building what Robert Putnam calls 'social capital', through social networks and mutual assistance. In the hopeful book, *Better Together: Restoring the American Community,* [25] Robert Putnam and Lewis Feldstein tell the stories of twelve such initiatives, from neighborhood groups to a Fortune 500 company, from a church to a website, but all in their unique ways helping to build real community that has lasted and is respected as such.

What can I do?

In 1997 twenty indigenous Hebrideans on the Isle of Eigg in the Scottish Western Isles set up a Trust to take on the threat of 'landlordism'. They became the first Scottish community to displace the absentee laird and achieve community land ownership of their 7400 acres. The islanders had nothing to start with except hope and a belief that 'Life's capacity to heal outstrips the potential for hurt.' Their success gave them the security and responsibility that comes with a strong sense of belonging. The story illustrates the cohesive and enabling power that even a tiny community can have in the face of seemingly insurmountable opposition.[26] 11 years later in 2008 the island switched into its own electricity grid fed entirely from sustainable wind, hydro and solar power. The islanders have at last replaced their unreliable diesel electricity generator and can enjoy so many of the domestic conveniences that most of us take for granted and on a totally sustainable basis. This community clearly thrives. It is an inspiration to show us all how so much can be achieved by so few with the enablement of real community.

We must not underestimate the task. Community building needs leadership as well as our individual participation. It will involve a continual learning process for us all, and I believe this learning process must encompass the pursuit of spiritual growth, so fundamental to our healing process.

But first we need to be better informed so that we can understand more clearly the paths available towards real community building.

There are many secular and faith organizations that work in their different ways to promote good community and that welcome practical or monetary support. They all have comprehensive websites and details of a few to start with are included in the final Appendix for follow up as appropriate.

Start by looking at the 'communities' where you live.

Consider your church, your kids' school and your neighborhood. We can all add to that list our own places of work and leisure. How many real community characteristics are evident? How holistic is your child's education? Do we have the opportunity, as governor, teacher or parent, to guide towards a more holistic education?

And start building! If we cannot even build and maintain real community at local level what serious implications does this have for the world? Since we have it within our capability to steer the course of our own evolution, we certainly need to take action to ensure that we are not engineering our own extinction!

It is customary for the Christian to give up something for the season of Lent in the Church calendar, representing the 40 days and 40 nights that Jesus fasted in the wilderness. It is a time when we reflect on our faults and try to overcome them, a time to give up luxuries and practice self-discipline. It is a time to let God more fully into our lives.

Popular sacrifices are wine and chocolate, a comment if ever one was needed of our twenty-first century lifestyles! Last year our priest urged us to 'take up' something for Lent instead. This would be something, however small, that could really make a difference.

We do not need to be a Christian or indeed wait for a Lent season to start making a difference to the world around us. It would be good if we all tried that little bit harder throughout the year to seek out the vulnerable and lost persons in our midst and work towards re-establishing true community. What holds us back?

We need to embrace change

It is very easy to campaign. It is very much more difficult for me or for you to change. None of us readily accept change. It is a very natural reaction as it can threaten the comfortable security we feel within the familiar. But change we must if we are to progress in the most positive sense of the word.

I hope I have now persuaded you that real change has to start with the individual. Those of us with a few more grey hairs most certainly cannot afford to spend time wallowing in nostalgia. We have to support necessary change. Experiences and memories can be good or bad and we develop wisdom and learning from them. The youth of today have the energy and drive and so much to live for. Combining the skills of young and old creates a powerful partnership to make change happen.

There also can be resistance to any change even when it is clearly proving to be successful. This is human nature!

It is difficult to write of community building without some overlap with what I have written previously about faith. This is simply indicative of the fact that so many of our community building initiatives do indeed have their origins within the well-structured network of our organized religions.

One of our most fundamental initiatives in my local church was to make changes to our style of worship in some services to engage with the younger families. The previous style of the 'family service' that I still see being followed in many churches can exclude the interests of the more mature worshipper, or the lonely. Our Christian Gospel message is one of inclusiveness. We have therefore substituted an 'All-Age' worship that embraces the interests of everyone. We are on a steep learning curve although early reaction is promising. We already attract more to that service than to any other. But oh dear! What a resistance from some. 'Yes it was fine but I hope we don't do that too often,' is the kind of remark one hears in the coffee group afterwards from our devout elderly!

In his meditative book *The Enduring Melody*, Michael Mayne recognizes the role of the church in defining the true meaning of community. We need, he says, to celebrate the natural kindness and goodness of human nature, 'affirming human beings in their aloneness and pointing to the God who not only understands and shares their times of darkness but also lies on the other side of the dark.' And this entails 'a gathered community where *believing implies belonging,* [his italics]...It will always be full of frail human beings struggling to live in harmony.'[27]

While understanding the yearnings for the old and familiar rich prose and poetry of the 1662 Book of Common Prayer, or even the earlier 1549 version, Mayne welcomes 'the new insights of scholars and liturgies – some of which are very fine - that more realistically meet the need of our time.'[28]

The attempts of my own church to build an inclusive framework across 'all ages' is further enhanced by the interaction between congregation and the rest of the village in social events that are open to all, through our thriving allotments and in the regular village working parties to maintain our flowerbeds, green spaces, our local stream and our churchyard. And of course we also try to involve the local schools in many of these activities. All this is happening in a relatively privileged area and I am aware that this makes the task in some ways easier. But how very much more powerful and enabling could such initiatives prove in areas of greater deprivation and social division. I am sure that we still need to cast our own net further. I am confident that we can continue building our social capital from this base.

Teilhard de Chardin's vision for community is of a human development that 'bestows value on human action, not only large-scale action at national and global levels, but also on the humblest action, in the right direction, of every person...it is up to us to direct [evolution] towards a future that is in line with what it had achieved up to now. This is the grand but critical life-and-death option before us...to rise to higher levels of person and spirit – a level of personalized, communitarian globalisation.'[29]

The trap of false communities
With the advent of the World Wide Web and helped by clever marketing and cynical exploitation, some of the so-called

'community' organizations that can readily be found in a Google search are most certainly not communities. While some strive to build their own idea of communities within and across geographical boundaries, in fact by bringing together those with a common interest they can actually create a harmful exclusivity: they can cut directly across true communities. As soon as there is an underlying agenda, where those from one culture or faith form their own exclusive grouping across otherwise healthy inclusive community boundaries, there is the potential for a dangerous totalitarian divide, rather than an essential pluralism.

Other groups may claim to have altruistic intentions for saving the world that do not stand up to closer scrutiny. They often fail to see the overall global vision and lose sight of the true purpose and value of community.

There are other organizations that can be suspected of being false communities as soon as they start talking about maximizing individual potential. Many are actually commercially driven and accentuate the worst egoistic aspects of the 'Me-Culture' deplored previously. Techniques for improving personal wealth and success, based on empowerment and personal development, are unlikely to be spiritually healing processes. They should be treated with caution.

It is fashionable these days to say that we have been empowered to act in some way. But this implies 'power over' and in the sense of the vulnerability and healing power of the Wounded Healer I feel it is inappropriate. The real power in true community is in the power of powerlessness, where the Wounded Healer will come to the fore to heal and reconcile and enable. On the other hand enablement is about identifying, restoring, enhancing and exciting the self-confidence and influence that each individual brings to a community.[30] I think it is a better word to use.

Community and conflict

We saw in Chapter 4 the concept of the 'organ of consciousness' or 'noosphere' introduced by Pierre Teilhard de Chardin. De Chardin was both fearful and excited by the implications for mankind that could ensue from the resultant global convergence across all boundaries, social, cultural, economic and political that this would entail.

Surely we could expect this convergence or interaction between separate cultures, nations, faiths and other groups across global communication channels to be a positive development in our quest for a peaceful world. It can be if used responsibly. But if we sense that our boundaries are being threatened, it is also a natural human reaction to feel insecure or suspicious. We are afraid that our identities may be lost. Fear can breed violence and aggression, rather than the openness and cooperation that might be expected. It then becomes a real obstacle to any attempts at community building. And this applies as much to the inclusive faith group or the national culture as it does on the faceless and impersonal track housing or housing estate we have created, or in the inner cities. When barriers are in any way dissolved, it is important to ensure that individual and group identities continue to be preserved and respected in their overall unity. The one great melting pot that we dreamed of in the 'swinging sixties' where all differences are watered down and identities are lost will never work. And why should we want to bring all colors and cultures and faiths and backgrounds into one homogeneous mush anyway? We have to learn to celebrate all our differences of faith and creed and culture in a spirit of respect and understanding and indeed joy. Judaism has a set of principles known as Darkhei Shalom, meaning 'how to live graciously with people whose beliefs and way of life are incompatible [with the Jewish faith]. Despite profound differences, we must engage in common citizenship, contributing to the welfare of other communities as well as our own,'[31] writes Sacks.

This needs real community. It needs community at all levels, local, national and international, if we are all to learn to live together in perfect harmony. 'Beware above all of everything that isolates, that refuses to accept and that divides,' Teilhard warns. 'Each along your own line, let your thought and action be 'universal' which is to say 'total'. And tomorrow may be you will find to your surprise that all opposition has disappeared and you can love one another.'[32]

We should remember that most of the war and conflict in the world today is defensive rather than aggressive; 'defensive of rights to human dignity, freedom, property and land, to justice, or conversely, [to liberate] from oppression, exploitation etc.'[33] Much of the violence and pain we see around us has been interpreted in the context of Teilhard's theories, as being the result of our failures to adapt and evolve alongside the move we have so rapidly made towards global convergence. This suffering has been likened to the pathological birth pangs of a new world order, a world in need of healing. 'Man has to learn...not to give up security, which is psychologically impossible, but to trade in the old security of fences, boundaries, guns and bombs, for the new security of openness and trust in bonds of relationship, mutual support, brotherhood and love.'[34] That means real community.

Of course the worth or otherwise of a visionary's words can only be tested by the passage of time, but Teilhard's visions seem to be attracting ever more followers as we struggle to understand our seemingly precarious future in this twenty first century.

Bonds of mutual support, brotherhood and love seem far removed from the gated private roads, the houses surrounded by overtly secure and impenetrable security gates, the intercom devices to gain entry. Such exclusiveness continues to isolate and divide. It is misguided and harmful to achieving any real community. It removes us from being a part of the spirit and soul of a place. And it is not in accord with the teaching of any of the great faiths.

The challenge facing humankind is that of communalizing those who are in conflict. That is a large problem. It is the problem of carrying over the ideal of the primary or face-to-face group which is most easily communalized, to the larger group, and ultimately to nations and international action. What is needed is a return to the ideals of the primary group in such a shape and so adjusted as to be capable of application to cosmopolitan conditions. Otherwise, a sort of return to the communal womb is being urged, a nostalgia for the infantile.[35]

The sociologist George Simpson wrote this in 1937, just before the onset of the Second World War. Fifty years and a World War later, against the background of the Arms Race and the threat of nuclear holocaust, Peck emphasized that 'peacemaking – community-making - ultimately must begin at a grass-roots level. It begins with *you*,' [my emphasis]. [36]

We note that so many well- respected authors of their time have predicted in different ways the problems we now face. They were all visionary and perceptive. Our shame is that we do not listen to and act on these wisdoms. We have allowed our 'civilization' to overtake us.

We have the first responsibility to make change. Governments with their laws and regulations can only provide the supportive framework within which we make these changes. Governments can fight the injustices of low minimum wages, non-existent healthcare for so many, lack of security in sickness and retirement, and the huge divide between the richest and the poorest of our society. They can make the tax codes which support the status of marriage and family, that either help parents stay at home with children or force them back into the workplace.

But we need spiritual politicians who are compassionate, indeed empathic to the needs of the populace. In fact we need spirituality, compassion, empathy, and good old-fashioned moral responsibility all round. And we need changes of heart and mind in us all.

Utopia doomed by greed

Island, the last novel that Aldous Huxley wrote in 1962, is set on Pala, an imaginary island community in the Indian Ocean. The peaceful and truly content inhabitants have developed an idyllic society by committing themselves to personal spiritual growth based broadly on Shivaite Buddhism, along with some Hindu, Tao and Confucius influence. In addition they steer clear of the three pillars of Western prosperity: armaments, universal debt and planned obsolescence, the depreciation that is purposefully built into so many of our manufactured goods to encourage continual and wasteful replacement. The Palanese have equality without loss of individual initiative, empathy for all living beings and respect for the environment. And they hold an overriding belief that God is all pervading or immanent, and man is potentially transcendent, constantly seeking to find the Nirvana or Enlightenment of the ancient Eastern wisdoms.

Sadly the earthly paradise of the island is doomed. It is overtaken by the greed and militarism of an adjoining country, triggered when an English sailor shipwrecked on Pala becomes caught up in a world take-over bid for the island's oil.

I hope that this chapter gives some food for thought and indeed action. If we are to build spiritual and relational values in our own communities, there is much work to do. Sound and healed communities at all levels of society give the promise of world happiness and peace. It is imperative that we all do something towards achieving that goal. Because, in the words of Mark Twain: 'The universal brotherhood of man is our most precious possession.'

But true community is not always supported by economic policies, which can compromise even the most noble of efforts.

And that can mean, for example, the policies that do not support family values, those that encourage the formation of corporate institutions that are impersonal, competitive and driven by greed for profit. We seem to be trapped within an unjust monetary system that is fundamentally flawed. Are we doomed like Pala? I believe we could be unless urgent action is taken.

The next chapter will therefore look at those possible flaws in our monetary system. It will expose the 'money delusion!' It will look at some of the solutions, often so simple, that are being proposed and developed and indeed some that are already in successful operation.

By failing to understand links between community and economy we fail to cherish Twain's 'universal brotherhood of man', and that is at our own peril.

Chapter 6
The Hope of a Healed Economy
In Pursuit of Social Justice

When the last tree is cut, the last river poisoned, and the last fish dead, we will discover that we can't eat money...
Greenpeace message on one of their longest banners. [1]

This notion of spiritless existence can be described as materialism. All is matter; land, forests, food, water, labour, literature and art are commodities to be bought and sold in the marketplace - the world market, the stockmarket, the so-called free market... Business without spirit, trade without compassion, industry without ecology, finance without fairness, economics without equity can only bring the breakdown of society and destruction of the natural world. Only when spirit and business work together can humanity find coherent purpose.
Satish Kumar, "Spiritual Imperative," *Resurgence*[2]

In 1976 an economics professor Dr Muhammad Yunus conducted an experiment. He gave the equivalent of $26 to each of 42 workers. From this they all bought materials, spent a day weaving chairs or making pots and were able to sell their wares and repay the loans. Thus was born the concept of microcredit.

Microcredit refers to small loans of less than a few hundred dollars, with no collateral, at nil or no more than commercial interest rates, made to help the poorest of the poor in the third world to start up small enterprises. This enables them to spread their productive capacity and gain some measure of independence and a better standard of living. For Yunus' subsequent work with Grameen Bank, which was founded to foster this use of microcredit, the 2006 Nobel Peace Prize was awarded to them both in equal shares, for 'their efforts to create economic and social development from below', while improving the lives of millions of people in Yunus' native Bangladesh.

As a young child I won a ten-bob note. That was a considerable prize in those days. I was so excited. I could buy another nature book to add to my collection! How did I win this? For spotting the deliberate error in an article in our village church magazine, which misquoted the Bible as saying money is the root of all evil. Much to my dismay my mother suggested I should immediately volunteer to return this prize to the church. I still vividly remember having the collecting box held under my nose in the vestry by the priest and putting the note very reluctantly back through the slot under my mother's watchful gaze.

The lesson I had to learn was a hard one and it obviously made a deep impression! As a Christian I should be generous to those more in need than myself. But the ethics of the situation were lost on an eight year old. I had always been told we could not afford those things that my best schoolmates enjoyed, such as a pony or dancing lessons, perhaps a new bike. I was quite discouraged from entering similar competitions again. And I certainly learnt the meaning of voluntary compulsion!

In fact as with so many Biblical references the saying is taken out of context and is not complete. The full quotation reads: 'For the love of money is the root of all evils; it is through this craving that some have wandered away from the faith and pierced their hearts with many pangs.'[3]

So I believe the lesson of the ten bob note was more profound than my mother may have realized. I was learning the hard way that I had to avoid any love of money for its own sake: that there is so much more to being human in this world than striving for the accumulation of monetary wealth and possessions.

Real wealth is not about money: it is about spiritual wellbeing. It seems that we have largely lost sight of the spirit that is in all matter. As the human ecologist Alastair McIntosh observes in his inspirational book Soil and Soul, 'We are materially richer than ever before and yet suffer a spiritual poverty...we live, but suffer spiritual death. Our very accomplishments cut us off further from the soul.'[4] Real security and happiness that we all seek, consciously or unconsciously, will be found in spiritual wealth, for which we have a great hunger.

And how powerful this human soul can become against the seeming odds of the twenty first century when it is sufficiently aroused. We should not underestimate that power, even in the context of our economy! McIntosh tells the tale[5] of how in the last decade of the twentieth century the might of a great corporation was broken by spirituality and theology. Scientific and economic values clashed head on with spirituality. Against what seemed like overwhelming opposition the soul in the end prevailed.

The Community of the Isle of Harris, in the Western Isles of Scotland, was threatened by the development in their midst of a devastating super quarry, a wound and scar of massive proportions. With the assistance of a Native American Warrior Chief Sulian Stone Eagle Herney and what was said to be the first ever theological submission put before a public enquiry the islanders were able to prevent a large corporation (Redland Aggregates Plc) from going ahead with their plans. Overnight the share price of the company on the London Stock exchange fell a massive 8% or £160million pounds! [6] If the project had gone ahead who would have gained from the cruel ravages inflicted on a finely balanced community such as Harris?

The flaws of human nature

Some while ago a series of bank advertisements on the management of wealth appeared in the glossy weekend media. One of these featured a lone and pretty girl cantering away on a lovely white stallion into the beautiful and totally unblemished distance. 'What...[is wealth]...to you?' the headline asked. 'It's being able to tell the world to get lost.'

How can any single one of us afford to turn our back on the world in this way in any sense. How can any of us ride away to an unblemished horizon while so many basic human rights are not available to so many? That surely diminishes us as human beings. But someone, indeed a team of people, wrote that advertisement.

In our materially rich Western society it is too easy to be wooed by the power of marketing and advertising. Psychological insights developed to help us understand the healing needs of our souls are instead cynically used for marketing purposes. The advertisers play on our feelings of guilt or fear and our need for love and comfort, which often reflect in some of the worst aspects of human behavior, our insecurity, envy and discontent. These traits fuel our over-consumption and greed for material possessions.

If we would only understand our behavioral faults and allow them to be healed rather than exploited, there may yet be hope for the plight of our global brothers and sisters who through accident of birth are far less privileged than ourselves. Then we can hope to build an economy that is globally just and contributes to a healing world.

Before looking at ways we can all act to help our world towards some monetary justice, let's look at our current situation.

The current world situation

The divide between the materially wealthy and the hungry poor is massive and the gap is apparently widening. Statistics from the

World Bank tell us that in 2005 26% of the developing world was living below US$1.25 a day, representing 1.4 billion people. If we look at the number living on less than $2 a day, that represented 48% of the world population, or around 2.5 billion men, women and children, a massive testament to human suffering.[7]

At the same time we have the 'super rich', to be found among the celebrities of sport, television and movie, the top bankers, investment fund managers, lawyers and doctors. It is true that many on the 'rich-list' are extremely generous in giving their time, talent and wealth for the global good. Microsoft founder Bill Gates is particularly keen to stamp out the world's worst diseases that afflict and kill millions each year, most often the young and the poor. He has pledged $25 million to buy 100 million oral polio vaccines for Nigeria, and announced in 2009 that he was giving £115 million towards developing a vaccine for Malaria, which kills up to 2.7 million people a year, 75% of them African children. Bono, the Irish lead singer of U2, best known perhaps for his key involvement with the Make Poverty History campaign, uses his celebrity status to fight for social justice worldwide.

There are others whose lavish life-styles breed an envy and greed, particularly it would seem among the young who are being taught by example that material wealth and celebrity status are the measure of 'success'. And in the developing world others are attracted to our consumer life style and aspire to similar 'wealth'. Meanwhile the poor of the world continue to struggle for survival.

The truth is that we have forgotten how to live simply and sustainably with totally unselfish regard for those around us. We have lost the ability to generously share, to ensure that everyone in the same household has had their fill before going ourselves for second helpings.

Consider also that we have an obesity epidemic in the developed western world. Indeed obesity is the second leading cause of preventable death in the USA. An estimated 65% of U.S. adults, aged 20 years and older, and 15% of children and adolescents are overweight or obese. Around 34% of adults are obese. That amounts to c. 59 million people! [8] The figures elsewhere are not much better. In 2006 24% of the adult English population were obese, and in children up to 15 years of age the figure was 16%. And both figures are increasing.[9]

We need to find ways to adapt to sustainable living in a world where we can be sure that our good fortune is shared, where everyone has their basic human needs met, where both extremes of wealth and poverty do indeed become history.

We need to build our economy on principles of sustainability and justice for all. Only then can we hope to heal the world.

We must never lose sight of our part as individual players in the world economy. Whether we like it or not, we are all involved as consumers and as investors. Even if we believe we are doing all we can to help, by maximizing our recycling, curbing our expenditure, avoiding waste, and investing ethically, we are still unknowingly or blindly fuelling a wounded economy that is perpetuating the world's injustices. The responsibility is ours.

This chapter is concerned with showing how we have the knowledge that enables us to work towards justice for all through seeking healing policies in our monetary and economic systems. It includes guidelines and suggests resources to help us all to address these issues within the context of our own backgrounds and abilities.

What is money?

What is money? It is difficult to define. We have ingrained within our deepest psyche a sense that our monetary wealth reflects our success and affects our happiness.

But we know from studies that once a certain and fairly modest standard of living has been achieved any further increase in wealth does not improve our happiness. It is then influenced more by our status in society, the quality of our personal relationships and our physical health.[10] And status emphatically does not mean celebrity status. It means being valued for our own unique gifts and qualities, whatever those may be.

And if we still think that an accumulation of wealth can give us longer-term security we are deluded. Monetary wealth is a very poor long-term investment. It cannot guarantee long-term security and no investment is totally risk free. We saw this only too clearly during the global banking crisis that began in 2007 with problems in the United States over 'sub-prime' loans. The effect was soon felt in the UK as they reeled from the Northern Rock building society debacle, the first 'run' on a bank in that country for 141 years. As I write this global stock markets move dizzily up and down fuelled mostly, it would seem, by alternating cycles of fear and greed, and the longer-term effects of this financial tsunami remain uncertain.

Why do we need money?

The Greek philosopher and scientist Aristotle explained in his Politics in c 330BC why money had been invented. The art of acquisition, he said, for which a currency was required, arose out of the simple barter of goods, and he saw this as quite natural and healthy. But when 'The supply of men's needs came to depend on more foreign sources, as men began to import for themselves what they lacked, and to export what they had in superabundance: …in this way the use of a money currency was inevitably instituted.'[11]

But Aristotle made the distinction, between essential and therefore laudable expenditure for the daily needs of food, shelter and clothing, and the acquisition of money for acquisition's sake by profit associated with retail trade. The latter he censured, because the gain in which it results is not naturally made, but is made at the expense of other men. The trade of the petty usurer is hated with most reason: it makes a profit from currency itself, instead of making it from the process which currency was meant to serve. Currency came into existence merely as a means of exchange; usury tries to make it increase.[12]

Aristotle did not trust money because he could see that it could feed an insatiable desire way beyond what was necessary for our needs and he saw this as unethical.

In addition to life's basic survival necessities of warmth, clean air, medicine, clean water, food and housing, all human beings worldwide have a need and a human right to be free, to be respected as equals, able to choose their own destiny and to fulfill their full emotional, intellectual and spiritual potential. We are all entitled to the five basic human justices, of monetary and social justice, economic and environmental justice and of the right to peace.[13]

I believe that to really achieve such justice in our world we need to allow the healing qualities of compassion and vulnerability and spirituality to infuse our lives and our actions in our financial housekeeping.

First I shall look at where our present economy is flawed.

Humans are not valued

A very large number of people in our society are presently undervalued or not valued at all in monetary terms. These include the old and the young, the infirm and the disabled, the housewives and the many community and charity volunteers without whom many organizations would simply not survive. All of these people outside the conventional workforce often work very much harder and longer hours than many in full time employment. But they gain no financial independence or recognition within the economic framework from their toil. I know of a wife who for two decades has selflessly cared full time for an increasingly and profoundly disabled husband. Or I think of the mother who takes a career break to raise her own children. These women both lead enormously valuable lives, but feel undervalued.

We measure a 'healthy' economy in terms of the material wealth or prosperity that is created by and for its working citizens, expressed in terms such as the gross domestic product (GDP), gross domestic income (GDI) or gross national product (GNP). Whichever measure is used, they all put a zero valuation on the environment, on healthy citizens, social cohesion and cultural values![14] As Robert Kennedy said:

> ...the (Gross National Product) does not allow for the health of our children, the quality of their education, or the joy of their play. It does not include the beauty of our poetry or the strength of our marriages... It measures neither our wit nor our courage, neither our wisdom nor our learning, neither our compassion nor our devotion to our country, it measures everything, in short, except that which makes life worthwhile. And it tells us everything about America except why we are proud that we are Americans.[15]

We cannot sustain our present financial systems

There is massive wastage in our consumer society, both from personal consumption and in our industrial processes. Alarming statistics can be found of physical waste:

> Americans waste or cause to be wasted nearly 1 million pounds of materials per person per year...[and] this does not account for wastes generated overseas on [their] behalf...the amount of waste generated to make a laptop computer is close to 4000 times its weight.[16]

There is a beautifully sustainable cycle within nature. Dead bodies provide food for living creatures, plants photosynthesize and produce oxygen from carbon dioxide and animals use that oxygen in their respiration of which the by-product is carbon dioxide. At school we learnt all about this and called it the Carbon Cycle, little suspecting that 50 years later this would have such a fundamental significance for the future of the world!

If we can see the Earth as a single living entity involving complex interrelationships and a finely tuned balance of all life, as envisioned for example by James Lovelock, should it not be logical for a sustainable economy to mimic that natural world, indeed be a part of that world, where everything is recycled, everything has a further use elsewhere. We would then be able to build a system that is totally cyclical and sustainable and environmentally sound.

Evolution biologist and futurist Elisabet Sahtouris[17] once posed the question: doesn't it seem crazy and so obviously illogical that our household finances and the study of how we make a living (or economy) should be so totally divorced from the study of how other species make a living (or ecology)?

This seems so simple and obvious but we cannot see it!

Loans for interest are made out of fiat money

Neither a borrower nor a lender be;
For loan oft loses both itself and friend,
And borrowing dulls the edge of husbandry.[18]

Money can be created out of nothing.[19] This happens when it is created by bank debt against the payment of interest. It is fiat money. This is not widely understood by the general public outside the banking world and usually comes as a surprise. A Canadian journalist has estimated that only one person in a thousand really understands how money is made![20] It is certainly not something that is widely publicized. What is more each bank also has what it calls its Reserve Ratio. This means the proportion of cash invested into its bank deposit accounts that the bank estimates it needs to retain in case the customer wishes to withdraw again against their deposit. If for example £1000 is put on deposit with the bank and they calculate their Reserve Ratio to be 10%, then they reserve £100 and the remaining 90% of the deposit or £900 is available for the bank to lend on. And it does. The bank sets up a loan of £900 to another customer for interest, neatly increasing the supply of money available in the economy by a simple accounting entry in its books. The bank has not only made money out of nothing but it is also making an interest profit on that money that it has created out of nothing. And the bank almost certainly charged a fee for arranging the loan as well. The more times the same money can be recycled and recreated in this way the greater the arrangement fees and the interest profit that the bank can make, all from the creation of illusory money out of nothing. What is more, the amount borrowed by the customer is likely to be placed on deposit again elsewhere and the creation of further debt out of nothing can continue in another bank. The multiplier effect of this exponential increase in debt is astounding and very dangerous. Money has to continue to grow to maintain this system and to avoid financial collapse, even though actual standards of living may remain stagnant. With consumer spending the lifeblood of the economy and a personal consumption now nearing 75% of GDP, which truthful and brave politician will urge us to spend less? It is not hard to see that such a system is unjust and unsustainable. A government can and does make money out of nothing also, but this is only to the extent of new notes and coins it issues. As long ago as 1939 American President Abraham Lincoln was clear in his warnings: 'The Government should create, issue, and circulate all the currency and credits needed to satisfy the spending power of the Government and the buying power of consumers. By the adoption of these principles, the taxpayers will be saved immense sums of interest.'[21] But fiat money is still issued by banks. I was shocked when I read that 98% of the $2 trillion changing hands in the foreign exchange markets each day is purely speculative and has nothing to do with wealth creation. Only the remaining 2% relates to real goods and services.[22] As Edward Cahn observes: 'Money has taken on a life of its own: its function is to produce for the sake of reproducing – regardless of the impact on the health of the human community… increasingly what we are witnessing in the world's money markets looks more and more like cancer.'[23] Cancer is dangerous and often fatal, requiring unpleasant treatments along the way.

In such loan systems there is an impersonal relationship between the borrower and the lender with a minimal flow of information needed between them. Such loans are therefore cheaper to administer. In addition the tax system favors such business fund raising by allowing tax relief on the related interest.

Because such loans are not linked to the success or otherwise of the business, there is no reward to the lender if the business is successful and conversely the lender can foreclose on an ailing business that can no longer afford to repay. This makes the problems of the business worse and it may need to curtail its production and make efficiencies of staff by laying-off, with all the inherent human and social consequences that then arise. This is of course harmful to the economic cycle, and means that interest based economies have exaggerated cycles of 'boom and bust'.

One of the most harmful aspects of this interest on loans is that it is almost invariably charged by compounding year on year. Typically a home 'owner' with a mortgage will pay at least 2-3 times the original loan before the mortgage is fully paid off.

Our debts on credit cards have also reached massive amounts and many regularly pay double figure interest rates on their cards each year. A significant number of college students and undergraduates have credit cards and amass debt on these as well as on their other student loans. This encourages an extravagant attitude of spending among students who no longer need to budget expenditure within their means.

When I first wrote of these imperfections in our debt system a few years ago I was saying that alarm bells should ring. I was far from alone. In 2001 Bernard Lietaer predicted a 50:50 chance of a global money meltdown within 5-10 years unless steps were taken to heal what he called the global foreign exchange casino.[24] It feels as I write this in 2009 that we have drifted perilously close to that meltdown.

Unfortunately those in charge of our finances do not appear to consider alternative economic models. They want us to spend and consume our way out of recession. The problems and dangers of debt, at personal, corporate, national and international levels, are the cause of huge social disease. Such debt involves the transfer of wealth from the poor to those who are already wealthy. The system does not reflect the skill or the labor of the participant and encourages short termism.[25] Interest based economies cause unemployment, social violence and pollution.[26]

Sabine McNeill, organizer of the Forum for Stable Currencies, and co-founder with John Courtneidge of the Campaign for Interest-Free Money, observes that 'compound interest is for the monetary system what carbon dioxide is for the earth's atmosphere: man-made and unsustainable.'[27]

Companies are driven by profit and growth not by human values

As with Cahn's analogy to cancer of the world's largely artificial money markets, so according to David Korten the publicly traded limited liability company is best described as 'a pool of money dedicated to its self replication', and likened to a cancer cell in the body growing inexorably without regard for its host or its own future. Both are destined towards destruction.[28] They must adapt or die. Companies are driven to maximize profit for the ultimate benefit of the shareholders and directors, and the shareholders and directors are disassociated from the workers. The flow of wealth is all one way, normally out of the community where the business is transacted, as shareholders will almost always live elsewhere. This bleeds the community where the business is situated.

In the large corporation the chairman can defend his company's actions by saying that they were what the shareholder wanted. In fact the directors have a legal duty to maximize profit for the shareholders! This has been called[29] 'killing from behind a desk' or 'personal aspirations suppressed by institutional arrogance', there being a clear conflict between what we actually do and what we would like others to think that we do.

Large companies lose their heart and soul

As a company grows, (and remember we have an economy where companies are driven to grow or die), it loses its heart and soul, it becomes 'a person greater than its individual participants with powers that create, interpret or rise above the law, almost at will,'[30] no less than an 'ogre striding the globe'. Peck warned of this fragmentation of conscience across a group such that it becomes less than the sum of all the individual consciences. He called it 'passing the moral buck',[31] and saw therein a great potential for evil.

I know that I am not alone in thinking that the loss of corporate heart and soul has to be corrected at grass roots level, with the individual. Many agree that we have to change our values, submit to higher principles of love and truth and put profit motive firmly in its place. How on earth do we achieve that?

As the late Anita Roddick explained, 'The huge relentless wheel that is global capitalism is driven by faceless, unaccountable bureaucrats and businessmen who seem deaf to the needs of individuals, communities, indeed whole nations. Yet it takes little imagination to see that this situation is unsustainable if we wish to have a planet that is worth living in, and not one where the developed world becomes a fortress to repel the needs of poorer nations.'[32] At the end of the day, McIntosh observes, 'It is the people that matter and can make a difference.' A large company is

> ...a mindless monster, unless people all the way through the system devote themselves to making it otherwise. Then, and only then, can it start to become more like a community with values, and maybe even something of a soul....this means ...having an ethic that serves profit but transcends mere money making. It is only human goodness that can bring this about and so humanize the otherwise inhumane world created by emergent properties of greed.[33]

With so many flaws in our existing system of finance, what should we do?

Inspiration from Ancient Wisdom
One does not have to be religious to be able to appreciate the wisdom of spiritual texts in the context of the twenty first century. The Bible teaches that money is first and foremost a tool for us to use wisely for the furtherance of the Kingdom of God. The Old Testament sets out principles of economics relating to the management of land and debt that in their essence are clearly designed to promote and maintain healthy relationships and prevent the concentration of wealth and power in the hands of a minority. That to me sounds enormously relevant for today's world!

The Jubilee Land Laws

When the Israelites entered Canaan in the fourteenth century BC the land was carved up between them per capita, and the Jubilee Land Laws were formulated.[34] No freehold sales were allowed and every fiftieth year, the Jubilee Year, the land had to revert to the original family freeholder, [35] at which time the people were to return to their own clans.[36] At this same time bonded servants or debt slaves were released. This sound albeit informal welfare system ensured that the disabled, elderly and infirm were cared for, and the extended family was kept together, maintaining personal dignity and self-reliance for all.

Then there were the laws that gave freedom from debt servitude. There was an interest ban on loans between Israelites (not applicable to refugees and immigrants) and the loan would be cancelled every seven years. This kept the wealth within a family unit and worked to keep the family together.

Lending was about helping the poor and needy through financial crises. Loans were for helping in the short term, they were not intended to cause any hardship to a borrower over the longer term.

These laws for periodic debt cancellation and the return of family property protected a family's roots and avoided wealth concentration and economic dependency. The laws underlined justice on the one hand with redistribution rules and the importance of relationships on the other, with families being rooted in their own areas. 'There is hope for your future, says the Lord, and your children shall come back to their own country.'[37]

This is quite the opposite of the global mobility encouraged today in the workforce. Such mobility brings with it the inherent disadvantages of losing family cohesion, not knowing others around you in society and not feeling part of any community. When people generally do not feel loyalty and attachment to a particular area there can be an increase in crimes against the person and an increase in violence against the environment.

Many of us believe that there is an inextricable link between religious faith and social values, between theology and sociology, between the spiritual and the political. But we must have the courage to uphold these values in our lives. If we do not do so we fail society, and we fail God.[38]

How can we build a sustainable and fair system?

Economists, philosophers, theologians and more have contributed to the debate on the way forward for our economy in the context of addressing the world's often seemingly insuperable problems. Our economic system is certainly not serving us well at the moment in its present form. Perhaps this is the opportunity to consider other options that address some of the present flaws. We do urgently need a system that promotes human justice and that stresses the importance of the long-term sustainability and protection of our planet. Where can we find this?

The Global Justice Movement and Binary Economics

One such organization that works within these parameters is The Global Justice Movement.[39] The essence of this movement's message is an inclusive justice for all. It promotes policies that will provide a new, stable, just, global monetary system that will protect the environment by its sustainability, address poverty and the present rich–poor divide, and focus on real productive economy. It starts with the idea of national bank-issued interest-free loans that have a real link to productive capacity and the spreading of that productive capacity, arising from within society. It is opposed to interest bearing loans which are created without any link to production, which have no regard as to whether the needs of society are met and which are controlled by those with no concern for society. Global justice, it believes, ends with global peace.

Binary economics[40] is a system developed in the 1990s by

Rodney Shakespeare with Robert Ashford that fits well within the aims of the Global Justice Movement. It is based on the principle that both capital and labor should physically produce wealth and that all individuals should have access to such capital, provided for them if necessary using interest free money. This could produce a secure source of income for everyone, regardless of age, ability or occupation. This new and refreshing idea has been woven into a complete re-thinking of economics and politics, expressed in a most extraordinary vision in *Seven Steps to Justice*,[41] one of the most readable and potentially and profoundly life changing books I have come across. If only people would listen to wise words.

The Jubilee Manifesto and a relational economy

The Jubilee Centre champions another vision of economic change. Born out of a dream by its founder Michael Schluter in 1983, that biblical understanding would one day become a significant influence in world affairs, the Centre has been involved since in several reform initiatives, such as the UK's Keep Sunday Special Campaign. The Jubilee Centre is first and foremost a Christian social reform organization. It is now pushing for recognition internationally and towards the end of 2008 made a presentation to staff and students at two Christian colleges in California, supported by Azusa Pacific University. *The Jubilee Manifesto*, published by the Centre in 2005, is a Christian vision for social reform, based on the contention that there are sound biblical alternatives to capitalism, socialism and other ideologies. The Manifesto looks at a model of a new finance and economy based on the principle that the goal of a country's economic policy should be healthy and enriched relationships, rather than wealth.

Psychiatrists know that many of the mental illnesses so prevalent in our material Western society today stem from an unfulfilled need for sound and supportive personal relationships in our lives. It is not helpful to have an economic system that does little to support family and community life.[42] The *Manifesto* suggests that a just and relational economy would ensure everyone has access to a means of production to give them income, through a wider distribution of assets, and land reforms, and this would preserve 'rootedness and a sense of place' for a wider population. It has been written to open up debate, as a catalyst for discussion and response, in the hope, in the words of the authors, that it 'will encourage Christians in all parts of the world, and in all walks of life, to set about the reform of public policy, their workplace and their home life with a fresh sense of purpose and renewed vision.' It is a strongly recommended read and resource for stimulation and action.

The Social Venture Network and an Earth based economy

The Social Venture Network (SVN) was founded in 1987 by Josh Mailman and Wayne Silby, as a non-profit network committed to inspiring 'a community of business and social leaders to build a just economy and sustainable planet.' In 2001 the Network published an important Collaborative Working Document, titled *The Path to Living Economies*, on the website of the People-Centered Development Forum (PCDF),[43] an organization with a similar mission. Within this document many concepts representing the life's work of an array of different authors have been brought together into a valuable summary within a framework of the perceived urgent need for a Living Economy: 'a social and economic system that is sustainable, equitable and cooperative.'[44] This would incorporate systems based on fair profit as against maximum profit and businesses described as 'not for profit living enterprises' that are 'place-based, human-scale, stakeholder-owned, democratically accountable, and life serving'; that would function as 'communities of people engaged in the business of creating just, sustainable and fulfilling livelihoods for themselves and their communities.'[45]

The basic thesis of the SVN paper should sound familiar: that a system geared entirely towards the maximizing of profit for the few at the expense of many is fundamentally flawed. Its model is based instead on the natural cycle seen in nature whereby everything is reused or recycled, everything in the cycle has a use or purpose, there is a mutual dependency where nothing is wasted and where there is a balance of cooperation and competition between organisms.

A lovely example of this mutuality is seen with the life cycle of the fig wasp and the fig fruit. Each species of fig tree relies on a particular species of wasp for the pollination of its flowers, within the fruit structure. The larvae of the wasp are then nurtured to maturity within the fig fruit.

The SVN Paper argues that to ensure the survival and fulfillment of humans we must foster again that same balance and sustainable cycle, starting with individuals and communities.

What can we do individually?

Many of us are already working hard to lessen our environmental footprint. But such efforts at sustainable and socially responsible living may be still within the framework of the fundamentally flawed current economic system.

Few of us really understand the economy and how it works, or appreciate that we could be making a difference in this sphere. Nonetheless there are millions of citizens worldwide who are already making their own practical contributions using some of the ideas described here. Perhaps you are one of those. But none of us can be complacent in the amount we do. Suppose that we all start just one more ripple? The global effect could be profound.

Out of so many initiatives being taken locally, nationally and globally, only a few are briefly mentioned below. Leads to more ideas will be found in the Appendix. I urge you the reader to please find just one initiative that you find personally appealing and support it, whether by action, funding or campaign.

No one solution is ever going to be the right one or the best one to the exclusion of all others. We must see any of these initiatives within the overall big picture and we should celebrate and build upon common features rather than dwell on differences that can stifle progress. Whatever we do should be within the spirit of cooperation.

The SVN collaborative paper is itself a model of what the authors see as essential survival strategy, involving cooperation between individuals, communities and nations.

Complementary and Community Currencies

These flourished in the United States in the Great Depression but did not survive World War II and the post war economic boom. They have been successfully resurrected and now there are thousands of schemes in the United States alone and many more worldwide.

LETS (The Local Exchange Trading System) is probably the most widely available and best-known system and is well established globally.[46] This system trades in Green Dollars, a unit invented and designed by Michael Linton and David Weston in British Colombia Canada in the 1980s.

The principle of these schemes is simple. Units issued by individuals as part of a transaction between provider and recipient of services create an instant and simultaneous debit and credit. No debt is built up with an outside agency, but there is a commitment on the part of the recipient to give service to someone else in the community. Likewise those who have accumulated credits have a commitment to give the opportunity to others in the community to balance their accounts by requesting services from them.

Some of these systems allow for both national and community money to be used, so while they do not have value outside of the particular community where they operate, they allow members to conserve national currency. In this sense they complement national currency.

At community level these schemes are proving to be extremely successful in their various forms and act as cohesive forces to bring communities together in a true spirit of trust and cooperation. They can give a sense of self worth to the poor and marginalized, the unemployed or unemployable. They recognize that everyone has an intrinsic value, has unique and individual gifts. We can all offer something of ourselves to others in such a barter arrangement.

Time Dollars represent another simple system for the provision of labor. With this, one hour is represented by one credit. Everyone is valued for their own contribution regardless of skills. This appropriates equal value to the previously unvalued non-monetary economy, including traditionally unpaid caring skills for example. As a result such systems have a profound and positive effect on a person's self value.

There are many other variations on the basic idea of the complementary currency, such as Ithaca Hours, Philadelphia-Eastern Neighborhood Exchange (The PEN Exchange) and the WIR in Switzerland that celebrated its seventy-fifth anniversary in 2009.[47]

The Cooperative Movement and Credit Unions

Credit Unions are financial cooperatives owned and run by their members to whom they offer low interest loans and accessible savings facilities.[48] They are part of a worldwide movement that plays a vital part in rebuilding local economies and therefore cementing community relations for the common good of all. There are many of these in the United States, well known examples being the cranberry juice manufacturer Ocean Spray and the large natural foods cooperative, Organic Valley. I have seen these in action for myself in islands such as La Gomera in the Canaries and in Madeira, where the banana industries have been revitalized, as well as in the Algarve region of Portugal among the fishing communities there. Before the formation of such cooperatives many smaller family businesses struggled to survive against the might of the international business.

Other local initiatives

There are many other examples of local initiatives that support the principles of a living, just and sustainable economy. There are farmers' markets, local organic farms, restaurants specializing in local organic produce, fair traded goods, socially responsible community banks, recycling centers, independent book stores that serve as community learning centers, 'buy local' campaigns, independent local media, local family businesses that take a pride in community service and many more.[49]

Happily such local initiatives are often more cost effective than their global counterparts because of the lower transportation and related fuel costs.

Where do we go from here?

This chapter has highlighted some of the enormous intellectual effort that has been and continues to be directed towards the perceived flaws in the economies of the world and how we may be able to overcome them. We now have to make our own contributions. With the worldwide web there is no shortage of informed opinion and support; some would say there is too much. The internet is an extremely powerful tool in this regard, enabling rapid dissemination of information and coordination of activities worldwide. The important role of the websites such as that of the Global Justice Movement that take on such work cannot be overestimated.

Before we take an intuitive leap into such proposals as have been outlined, before we can make positive changes in our lives, in our work and in our leisure, we need strength, hope, determination, optimism and prayer. But we also need courage, and trust and most of all love and compassion. As long as we feel driven by greed or insecurity or envy to make as much money as possible for our own material well being and to covet unnecessary possessions, we fuel consumerism and ultimately self destruction. It is too easy for our materialistic emotions to override any fleeting feelings of spiritual conscience!

Our individual responsibility and choice

But we need that conscience. In the day to day rush of our lives we quickly forget those many parts of the world where finding the basic necessities of life, warmth, clean air, medicine, clean water, food and housing is a daily and often dangerous struggle. Are we sure that how we earn, spend, save and invest our money is not in some way adversely affecting our fellow human beings in less fortunate parts of the world? And do we care?

It has been said that one of the underlying problems with money is that '...it breaks the chain of desire and effect. [It] provokes people to act, for the sake of payment, in a fashion that, if they knew how the action would turn out, they would not contemplate.'[50]

It is all too easy to 'tell the world to get lost' and at least in our dreams ride off into the distance like the beautiful lady in the advertisement. That is no solution. Escapism is no way to a clear conscience. We really do need to fight our complacency and apathy. People are suffering as you read this and actions need to be taken. Of course we have to alleviate as much suffering as possible immediately, but without at any time losing sight of the longer term plan of rescue. For those victims of war, poverty, disease and drought, life is a daily struggle for survival. Getting those people back on their feet is a much more effective long-term strategy than any amount of aid that we can give now. The story of the micro credit loans to the poor Bangladeshi women to help them establish their small businesses and give them some measure of independence is a good example.

Governing bodies are cumbersome. They move ponderously and not always in the right direction. Time delays between ideas and action can be far too long. And then policies stall as the political power base changes. Action is much more effective at local level with individual commitment. So what inhibits us?

Our money gives us 'spending power'. By choosing how we spend it, we can influence how shops stock their shelves, what goods are manufactured, the conditions in which they are manufactured. Our money can be a very powerful influence in all manner of ways that can affect our environment either directly or indirectly, for good or evil, when we have money available to spend. Supermarkets will justify their actions in stocking inappropriate products that we know to be environmentally unfriendly, or harmful in some other way, with the excuse that they are simply giving us what as consumers we demand. If we buy them they will continue to stock them. It really is that simple!

Are our spending patterns encouraging animal cruelty or slave labor in garment 'sweat shops'? Appalling working conditions, child labor and poor pay still exist and we could be encouraging these without even realizing it.

The most effective and immediate impact we can all make is through changing our spending patterns. We are all in control of how we save, invest and spend, whether we choose ethical products, buy fair-trade and Traidcraft products, or perhaps give generously to aid agencies where we can be sure our money provides rapid relief.

We can and must fight to bring ethical trading in from the bottom up. We can enquire where our goods are produced and in what conditions and avoid all unreasonably cheap goods where we suspect that unethical working practices are present. If the information is not available, demand it.

We should support local enterprise. The local farmers' markets promote respect for land and food. We could pay more for quality and eat less. Why not get back in touch with the seasons and eat foods at the right time of year when they are available locally. I am aware of the controversies over air miles versus the need to support foreign enterprise to help other communities; many of these stories must be considered on their own merits. Some of these choices may seem more expensive. But are they when balanced against the alternative predictions for our world? Does the suffering of fellow beings and the future of our planet matter so little to us that we are not prepared to change our habits today?

Many of us own company stock, some of us perhaps without even knowing it, or at least thinking about it, because it is out of sight in our pension funds (although the deep recession at the end of the first decade of the new millennium, and the turmoil on world financial markets, brought such funds sharply into focus for many). Businesses must now be more accountable for their green credentials. But what about those companies that still operate unethical work practices. Those holding pension funds delegate full powers of investment to the fund managers who will be motivated and driven by the need to maximize profits and growth for the funds in their charge. As major shareholders these funds have enormous powers and are not likely to consider the ethical views of the individual pensioners against the overall drive for growth. It may seem that the individual does not have a voice. But we can have our say; we can influence others. All it needs is knowledge and courage and the support of other like - minded people. It can be done. Have you ever questioned your pension fund managers on this?

Does the small shareholder really know or even care how the company operates as long as he receives his regular dividend income? Can he possibly understand the full implications of the company's business, how it treats its employees, how it deals with its waste, how it invests its own money. So many share-holders make their investments motivated solely by profit, without any regard for the ethical considerations. This is no less true of buying shares than buying consumer goods.

The implications of all this are enormous. As individuals we may unwittingly be helping to fuel warfare, for example, by carelessly investing or allowing our pension funds or banks or investment funds or unit trusts to invest in any company involved along the way with the production of weapons.

I pray for there to be a shift in attitude. When I was in practice as a Chartered Accountant and Independent Financial Adviser I had a particular interest in ethical investment funds for my clients. One bank without my knowledge or consultation trans-ferred the ethical funds of one of my most principled clients into its own funds, declaring in the process that they would never take ethical considerations into account in their investment choices, only investment performance. This was some time ago. I hope the bank has reviewed its policies. Individuals who would think of themselves as ethical and feel aghast at the mess we are in have had their conscience swayed by the profit promise in this way. Have you checked the ethics of your own bank? There is plenty of information now available to check this out. Do you care?

Even the employees of a company who individually may think of themselves as honest and decent can be remote from the realities of the company's business and the adverse environ-mental or social effects it may be initiating in its drive to make profits.

Do you know what your employer really does? Not just at the superficial level of your daily employment, but at grass roots? Are you absolutely comfortable with the company's trading practices, its markets and its environmental footprint? And if not, what are you doing about it?

Most important of all we need to bring the healing power of spiritual values back into the company and its boardrooms. In our businesses and economies we can choose between technologies that are 'developed for...commercial profit...that disregard natural rhythms and human aspirations' or we can adopt a technology that is 'appropriate, benign and renewable and makes a small footprint on the Earth. Such technologies work in harmony with nature, rather than attempting to dominate or conquer her.'[51]

> 'Whereas *we*,' said Dr. Robert in Huxley's *Island*, 'have always chosen to adapt our economy and technology to human beings - not our human beings to somebody else's economy and technology. We import what we can't make; but we make and import only what we can afford. And what we can afford is limited not merely by our supply of pounds and marks and dollars, but also primarily - *primarily*,' he insisted, 'by our wish to be happy, our ambition to become fully human.' [52]

A healed economy will support a global justice for all: it will give us all equal opportunities that we may flourish and become fully human. A healed economy is also an essential prerequisite for a just and affordable healthcare for all. In a later chapter I shall explain why I see a need for the healing power of spiritual values to be restored to medicine.

First I shall digress for a while in the next chapter into an overview of how the influence of the soul became lost within our healthcare systems.

Chapter 7
The History of Soul Medicine

Introduction

A full history of the Wounded Healer from its origins in Greek mythology and the indigenous shamanic tribes to the present day is a subject far beyond the scope of this book. I also believe that we need to look beyond the Wounded Healer motif to a much broader remit, in my quest for us to rediscover our own spirituality, to recognize with new eyes the spiritual in all our material experiences, to feel that spiritual awakening in our own individual consciences. In the context of medicine this means the need to de-mechanize our bodies, to consider the healing needs of soul and spirit alongside the modern and often wonderful scientific advances, to develop a truly holistic healing opportunity for the patient.

In this chapter I have attempted to give some idea as to why healing came to lose its soul within Western medicine and how it is being rediscovered, with particular reference to the Wounded Healer. Those who would appreciate a more detailed introduction could refer to the very comprehensive address on the Wounded Healer given by Stanley W. Jackson in 2000,[1] that was enormously useful in setting me off on the trail for this book. For a broader history of the soul and mind in medicine, I recommend the very readable and inspiring book *Soul Medicine*[2] by Norman Shealy and Dawson Church.

This chapter stands alone and may be skipped over without

losing the overall sense of the book if the reader has no interest in tracing any of these historical developments.

Earliest man

For earliest man physical illness was inextricably linked with the mind, with spirituality[3] and with religion. The original belief was that disease came from the gods as punishment for invoking their displeasure in some way. Amulets found alongside the remains of Paleolithic man were almost certainly used as charms for healing purposes, a recognition at that time of the importance of the mind to the cause of illness, a precursor of modern psychology long before it was known as such!

Later, but still long before the birth of medical science, man called on his religion to heal his pain and suffering. He sought wholeness of the body, a holistic approach to healing.

Medicine largely lost this holistic wisdom with the advancement of medical science, not to be rediscovered until the second half of the last century. In this new millennium I believe that in time we will come to marvel at how we could have lost this sense of the soul's healing significance for so long.

Hippocrates, Asklepios and Galen

We have already met in a previous chapter the archetype of the Wounded Healer reflected in the story of Chiron in ancient Greek mythology. We have seen the nature of the Wounded Healer in the earliest indigenous shamanic tribes, practicing a skill that survives to this day.

We pick up the story again in Ancient Greece with Hippocrates, widely and popularly regarded as the father of Western medicine as we now know it.

Hippocrates was a Greek physician born in the fifth century BC on the island of Cos. Considering that he has profoundly influenced the development of Western medicine we rather surprisingly know very little about him. The Hippocratic Oath or a modified version of it is still taken by physicians on first quali-fication at some Universities.[4] Hippocrates developed and worked with a physical model of the human being, looking for cures to physical conditions and following a rational, evidence based medicine with recourse to external agents to effect the cures, much as science is applied to medicine today. His medicine was based on observation and objectivity, placing more emphasis on the body that could be measured and described, rather than on the subjectivity of feelings and senses. The Hippocratic physicians were not very interested in the opinion of the patient and distanced themselves from any of the charms and incantations of the many traditional and 'unconventional' healing methods of the time based on magic and religion. This is why Virgil described the medicine of the day as the silent art. Indeed Hippocrates is still sometimes blamed when people today say that doctors do not communicate well with their patients. [5] Hippocrates was however said to be good at diagnosis and prognosis. Perhaps, who knows, he used his intuitive skills, that we now see in the medical intuitives such as Robert Leichtman and Caroline Myss.[6] The Hippocratic School believed that all disease had its origin in the yellow and black biles, blood and phlegm, which were the four fluids of the body. These fluids were believed to parallel the natural elements of air, earth, fire and water and their varying proportions in the body influenced the emotional or physical attributes of the patient, or their 'humors'. At that time medicine was by no means the respectable profession that we recognize today. It had no status and anyone was able to practice in whatever form they wished. Hippocrates gained respect in this environment with his more detailed methodology. That is not to say that he lost sight of the holistic approach to medicine, which he is said to have still regarded as important in the overall treatment of the person. It seems though that he believed in a natural and unknown healing power of the mind rather than a divine or spiritual healing force. Hippocrates insisted that the body could heal itself naturally and that no treatment should interfere with that healing process.

The predominant philosophy in Hippocrates' time regarding the relationship of the mind and body was that of Plato, who broadly speaking believed that humans had an external soul, linked to the physical body but existing before and after the life of the material body. Certainly the influences of the mind and emotions on physical health were recognized.

One of the less conventional methods of healing that was already well established in Greece at that time was to be found in the Asklepian Temples, named after Asklepios, the Greek God of Healing. Hippocrates was said to respect this hugely popular treatment of the day. Asklepios was the son of a union between the nymph Coronis and the great Apollo. Because Coronis had been unfaithful to Apollo, Apollo's twin sister Artemis killed her during her pregnancy. The baby Asklepios was removed from his mother's dead body on the funeral pyre, probably by his father or Hermes, and handed over to Chiron the Wounded Healer to raise him in the art of healing.

Asklepios looked towards psychological and spiritual healing, of the mind and soul, for what were otherwise regarded as incurable and chronic conditions. The Greek view of the day was that such conditions were caused by the gods and needed divine healing and that this had to come from within. The Island of Cos had an important Asklepian healing temple and would be visited by such invalids. The patients would be fasted, rested and cleansed in sacred springs under the supervision of the priests. They would then be left to sleep in special resting places, where they would dream. The essence of the healing was that this process of dreaming worked within the psyche of the patient rather than at his conscious level. In the morning the dreams would be discussed with the temple priests and the patient would then leave an offering before he went on his way.

Snakes played an important role in this healing process in the temples. It is possible that their healing power was attributed to their ability to slough their skins regularly. This would have been seen as rejuvenation, although of course we know now that this is a natural stage of the growth process. Snakes are still symbolized in the Caduceus, the international medical symbol that shows a serpent entwined around Asklepios' staff. The Caduceus has also become the popular symbol of the Wounded Healer.

It is known that Hippocrates worked in co-operation with the Asklepians and may have referred some of his patients to the temples. There was clearly some integration of these different schools of healing.

The Asklepian Temples and their healing methods had disappeared by 500AD although of all the pagan cults of the time these treatments lasted longer than any of the others into the Christian era. This was because they were enormously popular with the ordinary citizens. With the demise of these healing temples the Greek recognition of the influence of mind and spirit in the healing process was lost to Hippocratic medicine. [7]

Although aspects of the Asklepian healing method are seen again in some of the complementary and alternative therapies of today, there is widespread resistance to these 'soft' therapies among many 'mainstream' medical clinicians.

Meanwhile into that ancient Greek culture a new genre of healing literature was appearing. It was being recognized that writing about one's own afflictions could be a source of comfort for others with similar suffering. This 'consolatory ministering' flourished from around the mid fourth century BC to the Renaissance of the fifteenth century.[8]

There were few changes in the basic practice of Hippocratic medicine until in the second century AD the Greek physician and philosopher Galen came on the scene. Galen developed the theory that the heart generated the heat of the body and that air from the lungs then regulated the body temperature and stopped it overheating. His was a very theoretical physiology, in marked contrast to the objective, factual medicine of Hippocrates. He was however held in very high regard and when he later moved to Rome he was engaged as physician to the Gladiators, a privileged role. His respected theories, born more out of philosophy than from science or theology, served to stifle the further development of medicine as a science for fifteen centuries until the seventeenth century.

The early Christian church

All the time this was going on the advent and spread of Christianity with its ministry of healing and compassion was also influencing the practice of medicine of the first few centuries AD and inhibiting the advance of scientific medicine.

For a Christian Jesus Christ is seen as the greatest Wounded Healer of all time and the spirit of the Wounded Healer in Christ again sits comfortably with the latest developments in the fields of spirituality, religion and health. Christ's healing powers were manifest in many stories throughout His ministry and were carried through into the early healing missions of the Christian apostles. The methods they used included prayer, anointing with Holy Oils and the laying on of hands, methods that are being reintroduced into healing services in the twenty first century. But the influence of these healing powers in the very early Christian church diminished over time. The apostles were not Jesus and they lacked the confidence or faith to impart His very special healing gifts to the afflicted. There was a gradual reversion to the earliest religious beliefs that illness was in some way caused by man's sins, that it was mostly in his own power to heal his afflictions.[9]

Any link between the healing methods of the early church and the clinical methodology of Hippocrates were short lived. In 1215 Pope Innocent the Third condemned surgery and all priests who practiced it. Then in 1248 the dissection of the human body was declared sacrilegious and anatomy was condemned as a subject of study. A split of medicine away from the healing ministries of the church was inevitable.[10]

Science and philosophy in Western medicine
Little then changed in the development of western medicine until 400 years later in 1628 the English physician William Harvey, after nine years of painstaking research, was able to present his theories on the circulation of the blood. This proved to be the most significant medical event since Galen. It opened the way for massive advances in medical science that were fuelled further by the work of two gentlemen, another English physician Thomas Sydenham and a French philosopher, Rene Descartes.

Sydenham lived in the latter half of the seventeenth century.[11] During his career he took it upon himself to revive the Hippocratic School by beginning to catalogue all known diseases of man in extreme and objective detail. Throughout this work he stressed the importance of observation rather than theory in clinical medicine. He was not however always respected for his views. One of his quainter remedies, for 'senile decrepitude', was to have the patient share his bed with a 'vital young person'![12]

All this was happening alongside advances in the philosophical and theological debate on the nature of the body and its mind/spirit, popularly known as the mind/body problem. This huge and complex philosophical issue is still debated today, but with exciting developments, as we shall see in the next chapter. By the time that Thomas Sydenham had written his *Observationes Medicae,* the French Philosopher Rene Descartes, usually regarded as the father of Modern Philosophy, had set out his own philosophical theory on the duality of the mind and the body. In his *Meditations* Descartes developed the basic philosophy of Plato regarding the dual nature of the mind and body, into what has become known as Cartesian dualism. While

Descartes saw the brain as the seat of intelligence, he regarded the body and brain together as simply a machine, quite separate from the soul or mind that Descartes saw as non- physical in nature. He did though believe that the body and soul in some way influence one another, in a way not yet understood.

This was the excuse needed by Western medical scientists to divorce themselves totally from the mystic element of the life forces. It enabled them to pursue their medical researches in the context of the body alone, aided immeasurably by Harvey's legacy. The mind and soul could now be left entirely to the cure of the church, which was also losing its grip on the healing nature of its ministry. The scientific study of medicine was able to advance without having to worry about the possible influences of mind and soul that were intangible and not scientifically measurable. Thus in the excitement of scientific discovery, medicine lost sight of any causal links between mind and body, let alone soul or spirit and any essence of healing, as opposed to caring and curing. The possible values of holistic medicine had been all but lost sight of in the scientific gold rush.

There were many great medical scientists of the ensuing centuries in Western Europe, for example Louis Pasteur and Joseph Lister (the fathers of bacteriology and antiseptics respectively), Simpson (anesthetics) and Robert Koch who discovered the Tubercle and Cholera bacilli. The physiology of medicine was being inexorably pursued but alas this was largely at the expense of any attention to the mind or souls of patients. Their bodies came to be regarded simply as a mechanism to be cured, much as a mechanic might fix the engine of a faulty car. This attitude was made even worse by the development of cellular biology by the German pathologist Rudolf Virchow, who showed that disease was something that invaded the healthy cell. The physiology of the disease was triumphing over the care of the whole person.

Throughout this period the health of the Western European population was improving dramatically. This however was in spite of rather than because of the dramatic increase of medical knowledge. The reasons were more attributable to the prevention of the main diseases of the day, for which no cures were yet known. Thus for example, smallpox, cholera and tuberculosis were actually eliminated or drastically reduced by the improvements in social conditions such as sanitation, housing and water supplies in the late nineteenth century.

The mid 1800s up to the mid 1950s saw the significant development of clinical medicine, when doctors wanted nothing but the predictability and precision provided by scientific advances. Medicine became wholly science based and drugs, surgical procedures, radiation and other technical treatments were dominant. It was not until the discovery of the sulphonamides in the 1930s that real advances were made in the ability of a physician to cure disease. Ironically the improved health of the British population during the 1939-45 Second World War has been attributed more to the better nutrition of the nation, as a result of shortages of unhealthy sweet products, than to medical advances. [13]

What was happening in the more recent history of North American medicine? Spirituality and healthcare had a strong connection here from the mid eighteenth century until the late nineteenth century, when the medical profession began to be more formalized. Then in 1910 the Flexner Report was published, requiring the complete overhaul of the profession and suggesting that its medical schools needed organizing on a strictly scientific basis. With these changes any link between medicine and spirituality was largely abandoned, at least for the time being. The soul had been disregarded.

The Wounded Healer

Where was the Wounded Healer in all of this? We saw the idea that a person's own suffering or woundedness could be a source of healing for others reflected in the consolatory ministry with its accompanying literature from Ancient Greece onwards. By the seventeenth and eighteenth century in Western Europe the idea was well established in pastoral healing, mostly among the clergy of the time, but also in use by some physicians.[14] Men such as George Fox, who founded the Society of Friends (or Quakers), George Trosse and Timothy Rogers, both Nonconformist English clergy of the seventeenth century and the English Physician George Cheyne, these and more used their own personal stories of suffering in their successful healing ministries. They were all reflecting the power of the Wounded Healer to heal others.

But it was only with the development of the modern psychological schools of Freud, Adler and Jung, picking up the threads of pre Hippocratic holistic care, that the concept was first articulated, by Carl Gustav Jung (1875 – 1961), as a recognized healing archetype.

Research papers and specialist textbooks on the concept of the Wounded Healer are plentiful, but these are mostly within the realms of analytical psychology. Both Jung and Sigmund Freud (1856 – 1939) [15] were at certain periods of their lives deeply disturbed psychologically. By submitting themselves to their own styles of self-analysis, they both came to understand their own sufferings more clearly and were able to appreciate and treat their patients more effectively.

Jung introduced extensive self-analysis as an essential part of the training of a psychotherapist, to be followed up by continuing clinical supervision, because, he said,

The patient's treatment begins with the doctor...in any ongoing analysis the whole personality of both patient and doctor is called into play. There are many cases that the doctor cannot cure without committing himself. When important matters are at stake, it makes all the difference whether the doctor sees himself as a part of the drama, or cloaks himself in his authority. In the great crises of life, in the supreme moments when to be or not to be is the question, little tricks of suggestion do not help. Then the whole being of the doctor is challenged…the Doctor is effective only when he himself is affected…'the wounded physician heals.' But when the doctor wears his personality like a coat of armour, he has no effect. [16]

Elsewhere Jung wrote:

Without too much exaggeration a good half of every treatment that probes at all deeply consists in the doctor examining himself, for only what he can put right in himself can he hope to put right in the patient…It is his own hurt that gives the measure of his power to heal. This, and nothing else, is the meaning of the Greek myth of the wounded physician.[17]

Jung's followers proceeded to give the term special significance in their work and thinking and it was Jungian analysts who apparently started referring to the Wounded Healer Archetype as a recognized tool in the healing process.

Jung's ideas were specifically developed in the context of the doctor and his patient in psychotherapy, but his wisdom articulated in these passages should surely be recognized to be just as relevant today within the context of the general medical practitioner's relationship with his patient.

It was the Dutch priest and successful spiritual writer Henri Nouwen who did so much to popularize the use of the term Wounded Healer in his own works in the context of pastoral healing. In the introduction to his book *The Wounded Healer* he wrote; 'nothing can be written about ministry without a deeper understanding of the ways in which the minister can make his own wounds available as a source of healing.'[18] This gem of writing was a bestseller of its time and is still in print 20 years later.

Like Carl Jung, Alfred Adler (1870 – 1937), a pioneer Austrian psychiatrist, was a prominent member of Freud's psychological group, before they both broke away from Freud to develop their own psychological theories. Jung developed a more analytical psychology, introducing the concept of the introvert and extrovert and the Collective Unconscious, with a description of the various archetypes of man's basic and inherent psychic nature. Adler on the other hand developed his own 'individual psychology' theory, and introduced the concept of the 'inferiority complex'. 'The method of Individual Psychology begins and ends with the problem of inferiority,' he wrote.[19] Adler believed that all human motivation was power induced, for example by the drive to be superior or the drive to control others.

So what were the attitudes of these three pioneering psychologists towards religion and spirituality? While Jung's interpretations of Christianity were controversial, (he would often quip to close friends that he would have been burnt as a heretic in the Middle Ages),[20] he was nevertheless a clear advocate of the importance of religion and more so the need for spirituality within the psychological treatment process. He regarded spirituality as an instinct and he had a great knowledge of and respect for the diversity of different religious traditions. It seems that he could accept that a person could be healed in the sense of being free of symptoms without the assistance of any religious conviction. On the other hand, he clearly felt that for a person to be truly healed in the context of being made whole in body, mind and spirit, a communion of the spirit with God was essential. Freud on the other hand had no time for religion and could see no place for it in the healing process, it being rather a crutch, he said, for the immature adult, a neurosis in its own right.

Little is known about Adler's attitude to religion. He was born a Jew but early in life became a Christian, although in his practice it seems that he saw no place for God. He believed that man is in charge of his own soul and that any healing must come from the attitude of the mind, with no spiritual intervention. He did though once say of clergy and ministers that they could best spread his ideas:

> because their profession is already one of goodwill...the clergy are the chief practitioners of social interest by profession, and also, which specially appeals to me, they need not take money from their patients. I have always felt this to be a real disadvantage to psychologists who practice character training. It would be far better not to have a question of money between them and their patients...they could treat their patients' psychological difficulties without any question of personal interest arising between them.[21]

But these psychological theories and the treatments arising from them were developing apart from rather than in cooperation with clinical medical practice. Indeed in many medical circles the new psychologies were viewed with suspicion and regarded as nothing more than 'quackery'. Science was coming to be regarded as the supreme truth: that nothing could be real unless scientifically proven. The scientists thought that there was no room for an intangible global value to exist alongside the material and capitalist values that were reigning supreme. Indeed in many academic circles today the writings of Freud and Jung are still regarded with scorn, on the basis that their theories are too anecdotal and can therefore be of little value to any furtherance of understanding of the human condition and the mind/body problem.

Why do I mention these psychologists here? It seems to me that the ideas of Carl Jung in particular are very much in line with modern developments of thought in the fields of consciousness and intuition, ideas which we shall see in the next chapter are gaining credibility and significance in modern medicine.

Healing versus curing

I do not wish to imply that throughout this period there were no physicians who understood in their practices the importance of a sympathetic interaction, a sensitivity of feeling between the doctor and the patient. Of course there were many, but not, I feel, enough. One such American physician, Eric J. Cassell, had a mission in the 1970s to help physicians understand the difference between curing and healing in the relief of suffering. We could acknowledge,[22] he wrote, that diseases of the body require a cure, to be found within the medical abilities of the latest technologies available, coupled with the diagnostic and treatment skills, alongside the knowledge and experience of the medical personnel involved with the patient. This is the practice of medicine as a science. But this, he went on to say, is by no means the whole story. This scientific approach does not address the overall illness of the patient, the need for the patient to be made whole, the need to address all the other complex interrelated factors affecting the patient's overall well being and the all important need, the ultimate purpose of all medicine, to relieve the patient's suffering.

By the 1990s Cassell had developed this theme into a new book and lamented that in his view modern medicine was generally still failing to relieve suffering. He said that we could recognize the obvious, in pain and breathing difficulties for example, but suffering involved much more than that. 'Bodies do not suffer,' he wrote, 'persons suffer.' [23]

Furthermore, he claimed that the profession was failing even to understand the nature of suffering. He felt that in spite of two generations during which solutions had been sought, books had been written and innovative changes had been made in training methods, improvements were isolated and seen as 'islands of excellence ... separated from the mainland.' [24] He regretted the fact that a real remedy had still not been found for the dehumanization and impersonalizing of medicine. He saw that there was still a need to understand the person as well as the body (the latter of course now being wonderfully well understood due to science and technological advances). In other words we were still failing to recognize medicine as an Art alongside the prevailing practice of Medicine as a Science.

Cassell's work on the nature of suffering was born out of research at the Hastings Center, founded in 1969 as the Institute of Society, Ethics and the Life Sciences. He became involved there from 1971 on The Task Force on Dying, an experience, he claimed, which was life changing for him. The organization continues to 'address fundamental ethical issues in the areas of health, medicine, and the environment as they affect individuals, communities, and societies.'[25]

A second edition of his book *The Nature of Suffering* appeared in 2004 when Cassell still had to note with regret[26] that sickness and suffering had not gone away. If anything physicians were less skilled at working towards healing the whole person, in spite of the advances in the knowledge and understanding of suffering. In this later edition Cassell also makes his own contribution to the mind/body debate, writing at length on the importance of the integration of mind and body in medicine. Cassell's aim in his book was to motivate a change in attitude, before, he says, we can hope for institutional change, and a lasting and real effect through training on future medical practice. The physician should be the master of science and technology, not its servant, he wrote. The person must be central to the healing process, not the disease within the patient. But this cannot be changed all at once. As much because of resource limitations as attitudinal resistances, he acknowledged that any such program of change must of necessity be rolled out gradually.

Throughout his work Cassell has emphasized that mind, body and soul or spirit are one and cannot be viewed in isolation. 'We are of a piece,' he writes. 'Virtually nothing happens to one part that does not affect the others.' [27] For this reason it is essential to understand the interrelationships between physical, social and psychological influences on the patient and the integration with the experiences of the physician. We have to accept, he says, that the practice of medicine is an inseparable triad of patient/experience/physician and that we have to educate the physician accordingly. 'Better health care requires physicians who can be healers; who have the skills and knowledge to provide services that are appropriate for sick and well persons within their life contexts' [28] building on his view that 'only another person can empathetically experience the experience of a person.'[29] Cassell apparently does not make the connection, but this surely shadows the role of the Wounded Healer in medical practice.

Twenty years earlier than Cassell, in London in the 1950s, an extremely popular, if sometimes controversial, English Methodist Minister and legendary preacher Leslie D. Weatherhead was writing an important thesis on the links between psychology, religion and healing. This was a subject that had come to intrigue him immensely. In this thesis he wrote eloquently and in much detail of a perceived new era in medicine, when faith and soul would again be widely recognized as a vital part of the mainstream medical practice.

Weatherhead had developed a keen interest as a young man of the early 1900s in the developing Jungian and Freudian 'new psychologies' and was one of the first to recognize the importance to the clergy of these new insights into the workings of the mind. He saw the limitations of the average medical doctor, in terms of time constraints and training, for healing more than the physiological body. In relation to patients for whom he thought the illness was rooted in the mind or the soul, he wrote: 'the ordinary doctor is usually of little use in such cases. He tends to interpret physical symptoms only in terms of physical origins. He works on what I have described as the 'garage level'. He is skilled to repair the machine. It is no disparagement of the general practitioner to say that he has not the time or, often, the skill, to interpret physical symptoms in terms of psychological, let alone spiritual, disharmony. If he had, in the latter case at least, he usually would not know what to do about it.'[30] Seeing the potential for using the combined skills of the psychologist, doctor and pastor in the healing process, by 1935 he had established the City Temple Psychological Clinic in the heart of London, where these principles were successfully put into practice.

Weatherhead wrote extensively of the spiritual and religious aspects of medicine as foreseen in Jung's work. Although certainly controversial in his preaching and healing, he was also widely regarded and respected[31] for much of his work and insight. But he was of course trying to reintroduce the soul into mainline medical practice in the broadly secular climate of that time and his work failed to capture the combined and co-operative imaginations of the public, the pastor and the doctor. After his death in 1976 he seemed to all but disappear from public awareness and his thesis of the integration of psychology, religion and healing was largely forgotten, or so it seemed, in the continuing inexorable march of scientific knowledge.

When I started researching for this book information on Weatherhead was not so easy to come by and I had to satisfy myself with a very old secondhand copy of the revised 1955 version of his thesis, which I treasure as being an important influence from which much of my early research progressed.

It is surely a positive sign of change in our attitudes towards spirituality and a resurgence of interest in the links between spirituality and medicine that Weatherhead's thesis has been made available again as a reprint in 2008.[32]

Forty years later, Larry Dossey looked back and saw the development of mind/body medicine by physicians such as Eric Cassell from the 1950s as an important advance beyond the mechanical medicine of the previous 100 years or so. Dossey has called these two phases in the history of scientific medicine Era I and Era II. As with Weatherhead previously, Dossey also foresaw and hoped for the start of a new era, when the importance of the soul would properly be recognized and even the field of 'non local' approaches to healing, such as prayer, would also be seen as a respectable further therapy within mainstream medicine.[33] I shall describe in the next chapter this third era of Dossey's classification, as Dossey expands on and develops his theme.

Weatherhead was not only a renowned preacher who regularly packed the church with up to 1000 people who came just to hear him. He was also a true visionary, with ideas ahead of his time, exploring as he did the mind/body aspects of healthcare within the spiritual paradigm.

At the time those who supported such ideas must have felt like voices lost in the wilderness of the inexorable march of scientific progress and medical positivism.

We pick up the story again at the end of the twentieth century.

In its 1990 definition of palliative care, the World Health Organization said that the 'control of ... psychological, social and spiritual problems is paramount' in the total care package of those with incurable disease.

At the same time, Michael Kearney, clearly not sharing the optimism of Dossey or the WHO, was predicting that the holistic focus in palliative care (let alone in the wider medical field) was in danger of being lost under the weight of the biomedical model of medicine [34] and the narrow mindedness of those who paid attention only to physical symptoms, whom he called 'symptomologists'. His concerns were justified. Only a few years later in a paper in *Progress in Palliative Care* a leader in the field, Sam Ahmedzai, wrote in his editorial:

The view now, within palliative medicine, is that it is okay to be symptomologists, and proud of it …Ultimately, suffering from losses, lack of love, existential doubts as well as from poverty and cruelty are not medical issues, and the response to them is not necessarily the responsibility of any healthcare discipline.[35]

Surely those who have argued for the exclusion of psychological concerns from the field of medicine, let alone spiritual elements, must be mistaken.[36]

Many have campaigned over the years for a greater understanding of suffering and holistic healing in a medical context. This first assumed some recognition in the UK within the field of cancer and other terminal illness care, where an understanding was developed within the hospice movement, founded in 1967 on the ideas of Dame Cicely Saunders. The first hospice established by Cicely Saunders was the St. Christopher's Hospice in South London. An American nurse Florence Wald was one of the first staff members at St. Christopher's Hospice and is credited with introducing the hospice movement to the United States. Some credit is also due to the Canadian physician Dr Balfour Mount. After visiting this establishment and seeing for himself the treatments and care offered, he was inspired to take the philosophy over to the Royal Victoria Hospital in Montreal where he established its own hospice unit and introduced the term 'palliative care' into the medical vocabulary.

The spiritual theme of medical care is also picked up by Michael Lerner who has a special interest in mind/body health in the care of cancer patients. In his book, *Choices in Healing*, [37] he explores the very diverse range of mainstream and complementary treatments available to the cancer patient. These include for example the practice of Yoga and the power of prayer, in addition to shamanism, all clearly understanding the importance of the inner life of the mind and spirit to the overall well being of a patient in the context of a terminal illness. Some of this is inevitably out of date in a fast changing world but Lerner's book is still available as a valuable overview of the wealth of ideas and treatments available. The book is well illustrated from literary sources that delightfully complement the consideration of the technical aspects of treatments.

Michael Kearney, palliative care consultant and former medical director of palliative care at Our Lady's Hospice in Dublin, Ireland, has also long campaigned for medical practitioners to pay more attention to the interactions of body, mind and spirit in healthcare. [38] He writes of the 'deep' as well as the 'surface' elements of suffering, and the patient's 'soul pain' that must be acknowledged in addition to the physical pain.[39] He suggested that the principles of Asklepian healing should be taught alongside the traditional and well-established Hippocratic style training almost universally taught in medical schools today, so that they can again work together as happened in Hippocrates' day. Healing, he says, needs to be given the environment in which the natural human psyche can be given the space to take over and do its own healing work.

The overriding problem in healthcare today seems to be that too often our doctors are 'Techno-doctors' [40]and 'Super Specialists' in a system that reduces patients to paper statistics and doctors to slaves of machinery, forgetting the importance of the personal, the subjective and the social aspects of care. 'By their very nature doctors deal with bits and pieces – microbes, hormone deficiencies or tumours – while patients experience illness as the disorders, disruption and possible disintegration of their ordinary lives...Every healing art sees illness in its own terms. Patients need to remember that the illness is theirs and theirs alone.'[41]And physicians need to remember this also.

Apart from the palliative care available for patients at the end of life, it still seems that the different forms of spiritual and religious healthcare (S/RH), complementary and alternative medicine (CAMs) and conventional allopathic clinical practice are not working together as well as they could and should. Many of the CAMs are gaining credibility within mainstream traditional healthcare but the influence of S/RH lags woefully behind.

There may be several factors holding back the progress of the spiritual and religious aspects of healthcare within the American medical framework. Hufford[42] explains that any progress in this area has largely been driven from a Protestant Christian perspective, the quasi- theological language of which may make acceptance more difficult for atheists and agnostics. There are of course contentions between the different religions in terms of understanding the meaning of spirituality, spirit and soul, for example. Hufford also believes that Quality of Life studies are still not receiving the attention they deserve and he wonders that Parish Nursing[43] and chaplaincies are surprisingly under used to develop research initiatives, given the information they must surely be able to supply. Chaplaincies in particular, he notes, have been subject to financial pressures and dwindling support. If we also include among these objections the general lack of tested and tried research instruments in this field that can be trusted as empirically sound it is surely no wonder that this type of work is still met so often with a general cynicism and skepticism among many of us, scientist and layman alike.

If we can overcome these difficulties and transcend the objections, the social significance of such fundamental changes to our conventionally accepted wisdoms will become ever more apparent.

What now?
'It's time we heed the symptoms indicating that our medical system is dangerously out of balance,' says Joan Borysenko. 'Modern technology is marvelous and lifesaving, and if we can integrate it with the deep wisdom of the past then we can birth a medicine that exalts and nurtures rather than one that is predi-

cated on the fear of death.'[44]

We are indeed seeing the dawning of a new paradigm in the history of medicine: we are entering an era where the spiritual healing needs of the patient can be met alongside both alternative and complementary therapies and the very best of the latest clinical medicine. There are certainly pockets of excellence across the healthcare establishments, for example the Integrative Medical Clinic[45] of Santa Rosa, California, is at the very forefront of this exciting new world of enlightened healthcare. As in so many fields the UK will in due course follow the lead of America in the full recognition of truly holistic healthcare that is available for all. But much work needs to be done.

At the beginning of this new millennium the American Association of Medical Colleges challenged all North American medical schools to update the teaching of their clinical medicine curricula.[46]

What progress have we seen a decade later? We shall discover in the next chapter.

Chapter 8
The Hope of Soul Medicine

Future generations, looking back, will regard conventional medicine during the twentieth century as being as limited as five-finger arithmetic. A new medicine is arising; one which embraces spirituality and consciousness as emphatically as conventional medicine has dismissed them.
Larry Dossey, M.D.[1]

This chapter is a celebration. It was the first chapter I researched when I was putting together ideas for the structure of the book. Where better to start, I thought, than with exploring the Wounded Healer and its social significance where it was best understood, in the medical and pastoral fields? Time has passed and the progress within the medical profession within those few years has been so rapid that of necessity my parameters have broadened. As a result it felt better to split what I wanted to say into two chapters, putting the historical aspects into a separate chapter. At the same time this chapter has needed a complete overhaul as I have also come to recognize the significance of the wounded healer motif itself as part of a wider spiritual paradigm.

We have cause to celebrate. Because the future of an integrated healthcare available to all looks considerably more certain than it did only a few years ago. By integrated healthcare I mean a system that considers not only the interaction of the mind and body, but also the influence of the soul and spirit, in a holistic approach to healing.

Of course there are those who are not ready to accept such developments into their lives. This is in spite of the increasing evidence and support for the power of unseen forces within the holistic healing experience. Some even become aggressive in their denial of any hint of such spirituality, soul, Higher Being, or God. That is their great loss. But it is also a loss to the world.

I really believe that only by experiencing the transcendent in our lives, submitting ourselves to this new consciousness and spirituality that is all around us, infusing our lives with spirit, will we achieve a personal level of real health, wholeness and wellbeing never before seen in the history of scientific clinical medicine. Not only that, but the social significance of some of these changes could be immense. This fractured world would be healed in so many ways, with increased potential for us all to enjoy a life of wellbeing, global justice, love and peace. The cost savings could also be significant, relieving the healthcare profession from its present almost unbelievable financial burden. Indeed medicine could be leading the way for us all in this spiritual journey.

The doctor as shaman

'To be a good doctor you have to be a compassionate chameleon, a shape shifter, a shaman.' So wrote Cecil Helman, family doctor, medical anthropologist, poet, traveler and observer of health systems worldwide, in his book *Suburban Shaman*.[2] From fascinating anecdotes of consultations with traditional South African shamans or Sangomas to the curative trance dances in the Brazilian favelas, he reflects on how western Doctors can learn much from the folk wisdom and shrewd knowledge of human nature as demonstrated by these indigenous Wounded Healers.

In the midst of the poverty, illiteracy and appalling living conditions of the shanty - towns of Southern Brazil, a Brazilian doctor, Carlos Grossman, has developed an innovative Community Health Program. The 'social doctors' who work in such areas not only provide the primary health care for their patients but also devote as much as half of their time to community development, to health education, to campaigning for improved conditions and generally engaging with the underlying social conditions of those patients in their care. This, says Helman, is 'real' medicine.

The shantytown conditions of Brazil or the indigenous medicine man may seem far removed both culturally and geographically from our own Western experience. But the healing methods of indigenous tribes are found in the culture of the Native Americans, in the Ayurveda of native Indian, in Chinese Oriental medicine and in many other cultures worldwide. These traditions go back thousands of years. Nevertheless I would suggest that the importance of the personal, subjective and social elements of patient care are no less relevant in mainstream healthcare provision in the USA or the UK than they are in the favelas of Brazil.

The World Health Organization (WHO) first recognized the value of these traditional shamanic healers as long ago as 1978, as being especially relevant in areas where there were few conventional doctors. The shamans, the WHO said, should be allies of conventional healthcare, not opponents, as they had the holistic advantage of 'viewing man in his totality within a wide ecological spectrum, and of emphasizing ...that ill health or disease is brought about by an imbalance...of man in his total ecological system...'[3] The shaman could work cooperatively alongside conventional physicians in helping to combat AIDs, to promote family planning, child health and mental illness for example, as 'social workers.'

Unfortunately the genuine holistic healing skills of the true indigenous shaman are too often today confused with the fads and abuses introduced by some of those unscrupulous 'medicine men' and 'faith healers' in our twenty first century culture, who are driven more by monetary gain than by any altruistic motive. This insults true shamanism and its origins.

Visions of a better healthcare

This chapter is about the healing of suffering. It is also about healing the individual, healing the medical profession and about the contribution that the healthcare profession can make towards healing the world. It is not only about finding the Wounded Healer in our healthcare system; it is also about infusing that healthcare with spirit. Indeed an understanding of the former should assist a greater appreciation of the latter.

I wrote of the new era of spiritual awakening in the context of pastoral care. Medicine is also at the dawn of a new understanding of consciousness. While such changes are for the moment only evident in a few pockets of holistic excellence across America, even less in the UK, progress in this interesting and exciting field is being fuelled by the much more rapid dissemination of information now possible through that most wonderful of tools when used responsibly and with selective discernment, the worldwide web!

Such exciting developments are yet to be embraced universally in spite of the growing mass of empirical evidence in their support. I also understand that some may find it difficult to share this excitement when 47 million American do not have access to free healthcare, when so many physicians are disillusioned with their work and when morale within the profession is probably at an all time low. When people are preoccupied not with the state of medical advances but with how they can possibly afford to pay for even basic treatment, perhaps urgent treatment for a sick child, it may seem hopelessly inappropriate to suggest that existing healthcare needs to regain its soul, to suggest that a new spirituality needs to infuse the healthcare profession.

As I watched President Obama make his inaugural speech to the

American nation early in 2009, I was concerned. 'We will restore science to its rightful place,' he said, 'and wield technology's wonders to raise health care's quality and lower its costs.'

With the emphasis on technology there was no recognition of the need to support an integrated healthcare. Perhaps that was neither the appropriate time nor occasion to raise such issues. But it may be that Obama's two aims for healthcare are incompatible. Ever more complex drug regimes and technological advances are alone unlikely to lower the costs of healthcare. Also hurling more money at the present healthcare system seems to me like handing out more pills to deal with the side effect of a prescribed drug, rather than looking for a more appropriate initial treatment without that unwanted reaction.

Let me stress, by contrast, that the healing power of the spirit is free and wholesome, with no unwanted side effects.

We know that the new American president understands the compassion and empathy of the Wounded Healer.[4] He also understands that government policies cannot work alone, but require changes in our own hearts and minds.[5] I hope that healthcare professionals enlightened in the latest advances in integrated healthcare are involved in any discussions on reform and that Obama's own empathic sentiments will spill over into America's healthcare system as soon as possible.

Healthcare is certainly not a commodity to take or leave. The quality of its provision should not depend on the wealth of an individual. It is a matter of religious compassion and social justice that a basic healthcare should be freely available for all as a human right, not only for fellow citizens but also for all populations across the world. I hope that, as we surely work towards a more integrated and less expensive health system, the money saved could be redirected to help to provide basic medical needs across the globe in the fight to combat malaria, AIDS and the other crippling health concerns of so many who are very much less fortunate than ourselves.

Healing needs a soul

For far too many of us, the soul is nowhere to be found in the clinical medicine setting. The modern physician is able to draw upon a vast wealth of advanced techniques that may be available, whether drugs or surgery or radiation or other interventions that he deems to be suitable from his scientific knowledge, training and experience. With the amazing march of scientific progress and the significant development of clinical medicine, physicians have welcomed the predictability and precision provided by these advances. They have become increasingly trained and skilled in clinical excellence, curing disease, with some wonderful achievements to record.

With the increasing demands of the twenty first century, the work related stress, the bombardment with bad news, relationship problems, even chemical imbalances in the brain, the patient often presents himself at the surgery with mind related disorders. These may include mental disturbances or psychosomatic illness or simply an indefinable need, perhaps even subconscious, to be made whole in some intangible way. The physician is often not prepared or adequately trained for this modern need.

We may be cured clinically, as far as is possible within the capacity of the available treatments; but what have we cured, the illness or the disease? Are we healed?

It is often said that the physician used to be able to cure rarely but care always. Now it seems that the reverse is the case: he can cure very often but somehow it seems that there is often little room for the caring and the healing.

The fact is that millions of times a day our health professionals in our surgeries and hospitals come face to face with patients in search of curing, but in need of healing. And that basic need is so often not being met.

The physician can feel frustrated and wounded, even sense that in some way he has failed his patient. There is often an equally frustrated patient who remains wounded and who is likely to be back before too long with another physical complaint requiring some 'listening' treatment. Although the patient may not fully comprehend his own need to achieve wholeness, to be healed, he certainly recognizes that the consultation has been unsatisfactory in some way.

It is surely because so many of us do not receive the healing for which we yearn on the visit to the physician that we join the ever increasing number of people who seek complementary and alternative therapies (CAMs) elsewhere, often without our physician's knowledge and with varying degrees of success. It is no coincidence that the number of practitioners trained in such therapies has mushroomed. This is also one of the reasons for the increasing interest in faiths and religions, a trend noticed in the chapter on pastoral care. Doctors have even sometimes been deserted in favor of spiritual retreats and similar events, but the help that these can offer may often be limited by time constraints and lack of suitable training. Pastoral Counselors are another important resource but of course they do not have the clinical medical training.

Because our woundedness remains, we may even resort to dealing with those wounds in other ways, through retail therapy,[6] with drug abuse (including alcoholism) and with smoking. These habits may alleviate our problems in the short term but at the same time are harmful to ourselves, to the environment, or indeed to both.

This all raises a serious and fundamental question. Should healthcare be seen as a problem of cost, or an opportunity for growth? It should be neither! It should be a dynamic and readily affordable system that continually strives to integrate its conventional allopathic disciplines with the various and increasingly popular complementary and alternative medicines, including spiritual and religious healing methods. These should all work alongside one another in a spirit of full cooperation and mutual respect. This is truly integrated medicine at its very best.[7]

It has been recognized for many years that:

> doctors are not merely biological repair men, people who know how we work and people who can twiddle knobs or replace faulty parts when they threaten to go wrong. A doctor must be a healer in the fullest, most spiritual sense, someone who accepts that human beings are congenitally lonely and dissatisfied but who may be able to reconcile them to the difficulties of their condition...to share the journey [of pain or anxiety or grief] with the patient.[8]

The renowned Austrian Psychiatrist Viktor E Frankl survived four different concentration camps, including Auschwitz, during the holocaust. 'Man lives in three dimensions,' he wrote, 'the somatic, the mental and the spiritual. The spiritual dimension cannot be ignored, for it is what makes us human.'[9]

We saw in the last chapter that the early links between spirituality and healthcare in the history of American medicine were just about abandoned entirely with the Flexner Report of 1910. It was not until the 1960s that any links between spirituality, religion and healthcare began to re-emerge, primarily it would seem driven by the charismatic movement and the neo Pentecostalism churches. As we also saw in the previous chapter, the movement to bring the soul back into medicine had started in the 1950s with psychiatrists such as Jung and Rogers, together with the work of Methodist Minister Leslie Weatherhead.

Real growth in this field really only came about in the late 1980s and the 1990s and started with what is probably the most famous experiment of all on the healing power of prayer. In 1988 Byrd, a cardiologist at the San Francisco General Hospital and also a devout Christian was struck by a conversation with a colleague about a terminally ill cancer patient. All medical avenues had been exhausted and the physicians really did not know what else they could do for the patient. We could try prayer, said Byrd.[10] Thus began the prayer study that has inspired so many subsequent experiments into non -local healing phenomena. The scientifically designed and double blind trials produced more positive responses in those groups of patients who were prayed for, when compared with the control groups. Although the sample was small and the statistical interpretation of the results controversial, there have been many more studies since then that have corroborated in different ways the principal of that pioneer experiment; non local intervention such as prayer can give a positive outcome. Byrd's work certainly proved to be a catalyst for physicians such as Dossey who was interested in exploring the spiritual questions of medicine within wider parameters beyond the known interaction of mind and body.

In a paper published by the Fetzer Institute in 1993 David Aldridge noted the need to 'recognize that patience, grace, prayer, meditation, hope, forgiveness and fellowship are as important to many of our health initiatives as medication, hospitalization, incarceration or surgery.'[11]

Michael Mayne, busy parish priest who subsequently became Dean of Westminster Abbey within the Anglican Communion, was well qualified to write about the patient's perception of healthcare. In his book *A Year Lost and Found* he describes his experiences and struggle with a debilitating episode of ME, or Myalgic Encephalomyelitis, the post-viral fatigue syndrome. Of all the various treatments and advice he received for a condition that is still very little understood, he significantly gives special credit to a certain Dr D, whose particular efficacy in helping him cope with his condition is attributed to

his grasp of the inter-relatedness of body and spirit...he talked and he tested or massaged parts of my body. Sometimes he just talked. He had the great gift of encouragement. He understood that the question 'How are you?' is at root a metaphysical question, which is not sufficiently answered with clinical lists and data ...but goes to the deepest part of ourselves as the complex and uniquely precious beings we are.[12]

Mayne tragically died from cancer in 2006, but not before heroically putting the finishing touches to his final book *The Enduring Melody*. This started as a meditation of his life, but when the cancer struck it became his daily meditations interwoven into an autobiography of his final year. The book is a brave and very thoughtful journal through those last ten months. It culminates in a reflective essay on illness and healing, and the need for a holistic approach. 'To treat a disease,' he said:

is to inhibit it and hopefully help the body to destroy it or control it: to treat a patient is to observe, foster, nurture and listen to a life...In an ideal [health service] it would be good if every doctor and nurse in training would reflect on the mystery of the human being with both the learning of the scientist and the observation and sympathy of the novelist or the poet.[13]

He was writing of the United Kingdom's National Health Service but his thoughts are equally relevant in the United States, which is actually ahead of the UK in recognizing the importance of spirituality in healthcare.

Mayne understood only too well that chasm that is so often evident between what the patient actually receives from a short medical consultation and what he is really looking for.

Of course credit should be given for the advances that are being made in medical science, the technological achievements, the surgical and clinical skills, the development of ever more efficacious drugs and the efforts of the very many health care professionals working competently and tirelessly using best knowledge, experience and facilities for the benefit of the patient.

Perhaps more doctors than we realize do understand and practice the philosophy of holistic health care, with due regard to the full impact of body, mind and spirit in considering the 'wellness' of the person. Even so it is unlikely that this can often be realistically achieved within the normal time constraints of a busy practice. Nevertheless there is an opportunity here that should not be ignored; indeed we may not be able to ignore it for much longer.

The incredible reinvention of medicine

A few years ago I picked up in our local library a very battered secondhand copy of *Healing Words: The Power of Prayer and the Practice of Medicine*[14] by Larry Dossey. I was intrigued by the book's title. Now I realize that Dossey[15] has been in the vanguard of mind body healing for some time and is even sometimes credited with being the father of this genre of medicine with which so many are still uncomfortable. His influence was perhaps first felt in the 1990s with *Healing Words.* Upon reading further, I was immediately fascinated by Dossey's division of the history of medicine, from when it first became scientific in the mid 1800s, into three Eras. The first 100 years or so from around the time of the American Civil War of Independence up until around 1950 he calls Era I, the rise of 'mechanical medicine', because, he says, 'of its adherence to classical, mechanical physics.' Era II from then until the first publication of his book in 1993 and still developing to this day he described as the age of mind/body medicine. During that period there was an increasing recognition that the state of a person's mind, their thoughts and emotions can affect the physical body and cause what is usually described as psychosomatic illness. Such illnesses are often unfairly misrepresented, by being thought of as imaginary, or 'all in the mind', a misnomer that is unhelpful to the further study of this important phenomenon. Dossey now says that he prefers to look at this concept the other way around: that it is better to show how positive feelings keep us healthy, or whole. Both Era I and Era II medicine remain, he says, 'wholly devoted to the tenets of classical science as an explanation for all events, including the actions of the mind.'

The predicted reinvention of medicine arises from the dawning of Dossey's latest phase of medical history, that he calls Era III. This is the era of non-local mind medicine. Some of the most exciting work to emerge over the last few years has been that of Dossey himself as he works to show to the world the ability of a mind that is 'unconfined to the brain and body, mind spread infinitely throughout space and time,' a concept introduced in his 1989 book *Recovering the Soul*.[16] 'This is the first era of scientific medicine that acknowledges that our thoughts may affect not only our own body, (Era II), but the body of a distant individual, without the mediation of any known physical energy or force, and without diminution by spatial separation,' he writes. 'Non-local healing phenomena appear almost always to involve consciousness; the empathic, loving intent of one individual to help another,'[17] influences that of course reflect the healing power of the Wounded Healer.

Perhaps at this stage you are still skeptical. However building on Byrd's earlier and famous research the increasing numbers of empirical and scientifically measurable studies on spiritual tools such as prayer intercessions, intuition, dreams and stories of coincidence provide a sound foundation for those who believe that medicine can be imbued with spirit. In his book *Reinventing Medicine* Dossey relates stories of experiments conducted on subjects as diverse as barley seeds and yeast cells, mice and human tissue cultures, to see the effect of prayer or other healing intention, often using conditions and analyses as stringent as any employed in traditional drug trials. In one such experiment, for example, mice were measured for their ability to heal from a deliberate wound made on their backs. The subjects were divided into three groups. The group that was exposed to the attentions of a healer showed a statistically significant healing rate above that of the group looked after by inexperienced medical students with no interest in healing, or by the control group. Similarly, it has been shown that yeast cells respond with an increased growth rate to the attentions of spiritual healers when compared with the attention of those disinterested students. It has to be assumed that mice and yeast cells are incapable of giving a bias to the experiments through their own positive thinking, or by praying for themselves or for those in one of the other groups. This answers some of the cynicism often displayed around prayer experiments on human beings. We do not need to understand why these experiments give the results they do. As Dossey points out, we still don't understand gravity but we have come to accept it! If we are prepared to accept these profound findings medicine certainly will require reinvention.[18]

Inspired by his belief in faith's healing power, and by personal experience Harold G. Koenig[19] has also has spent many years studying the impact of people's religious life on their physical and emotional health. He shows how prayer can very definitely help people come through serious afflictions and improve the outcome of many illnesses. He relates many such stories of hope and inspiration in *The Healing Power of Faith,* [20] which he later followed up with *The Healing Connection: The Story of a Physician's Search for the Link Between Faith and Health.*[21]

Of course these aspects of medicine seen in the three Eras will all operate concurrently in the ideal treatment center. They are definitely not mutually exclusive.

And this idea of non-local medicine is not new. What is new is the recognition that it can be used as a part of the conventional medicine's toolkit for the healing process. There are still plenty of skeptics. Indeed as with any suggestion of the existence, let alone the power, of spirit and soul, some views can be at best intolerant, at worst aggressive. This reaction from so many is in some ways valuable. It encourages a scientific rigor to the experiments; it ensures the most stringent tests are conducted, to support the credibility of the experiments. This is surely the best way to meet the resistance of the cynic.

While recent growth in medical research into spiritual and religious healthcare has been dramatic, this knowledge is not always as well represented within the consultation room and hospital, in spite of the best efforts of those physicians who hold a particular interest in this field. Why are these truths still being so widely ignored or are at least taking so long to be more widely appreciated?

What is holding us back?

Some explanations for the slow growth of the spiritual and religious aspects of healthcare within the American medical framework have been offered in the previous chapter.[22]

The whole idea of any link between spirituality, soul and health is still beyond the comfort zone of many practitioners. Many find it difficult if not impossible to acknowledge the importance of the emotional, the spiritual and the relational dimensions of the human body, let alone the impact of global consciousness, in the diagnosis and treatment of disease and the cultivation of general wellbeing.

It seems that anything to do with the holistic approach of medicine in general and with the balance of body with mind and spirit in particular is still regarded in many circles as being too vague and not capable of being quantitatively measured, in spite of the alternative evidence.

Jon Kabat-Zinn points out that while we cannot know the value of any therapy until it has been tested experimentally according to the strict standards of scientific scrutiny, at the same time he says we must acknowledge that within that scrutiny the possible psychological, social, nutritional, environmental and possibly even spiritual factors cannot be ignored, as these might significantly influence the health and disease process.[23]

Knowledge that does not fall within already accepted parameters can often be ignored as if it does not exist in spite of scientific evidence to the contrary. 'Scientists, including physicians, can have blind spots in their vision.' [24] They can have what Dossey calls 'immense intellectual indigestion'[25] so that they dismiss results with disparagement.

Ignaz Semmelweis was a young Hungarian doctor who worked in the obstetrical ward of Vienna General Hospital in the late 1840s. He was dismayed at the mortality rate for the women in his ward during childbirth, compared with those in an adjoining ward looked after by midwifery students. When one of his colleagues cut himself in the autopsy room and suffered symptoms of the childbed fever similar to that seen in the ward, Semmelweis thought he knew the answer. He introduced to his staff the idea of careful hand washing between patients. To his delight the mortality rate plummeted. But his ideas were treated with hostility, even derision, by the medical profession. As a result, he suffered a mental breakdown and in 1865 he died in a mental hospital.

Sometimes there is prejudice or simply antagonism to new ideas through lack of information or understanding. It can be difficult to gain acceptance of new ideas even in scientific circles where all the evidence is presented in respectable technical journals. As far as the general public is concerned, the non-scientific media may even distort the knowledge for sensation and effect, if they pick it up at all.

We saw in the chapter on faith the prevalent attitude among many scientists and philosophers that everything must have scientific reason and meaning, that all things will ultimately be explained and that there can be no room within science for any kind of ethereal being, soul, or God.

By continually striving to find scientific explanations for

everything we also take away the sense of awe, of wonder, of the unfathomable in our lives, and make no room for any kind of spiritual dimension whatsoever.[26]

None of this resistance is helped along by the use of inappropriate language when introducing new ideas to a skeptical audience. A new discipline also needs a new universal language if there is to be any meaningful progress in dialogue between the spiritual and the clinical interests in medicine. It is not helpful to be stifled by a terminology that seems increasingly to espouse the modern values of a secular and positivist clinical medical approach. Dossey tells the story of a restaurant in a small town in the Ozark Mountains of northern Arkansas. One day they introduced a new item onto the menu, Beef Stroganoff. It was a dismal failure. Then someone had the bright idea to rename it Beef with Noodles, and they could not make enough of it to satisfy the demand! Dossey calls this the Beef Stroganoff Principle; 'If you want to sell it be careful what you call it.'[27]

Pastoral Counselor J.J. Means has written at some length on the dangerous trend in mental health circles towards adopting business orientated words such as 'products' and 'value-added' in relation to their profession or calling patients the 'consumer' or 'client'. How, he argues, could these terms be sympathetic to the total acceptance and furtherance of a discipline that seeks above all else to help to relieve personal suffering? As a pastoral counselor this is even less appropriate and the gulf even wider, given the contrast between 'consumer' and 'child of God'.[28]

Dossey has also spoken out against the inappropriate and careless use of 'energy' as a metaphor in the description of some long distance healing methods that actually are not fully understood. We know, he agrees, that there are energetic healing forces within our own bodies and that they can be triggered in others at a distance by unknown forces between. But he is adamant that the energy itself does not travel in some way between the two and to use careless and unscientific language simply undermines any credibility for the healing powers that are demonstrably in force. Any new idea will not even get past the first post towards acceptance if the language used is inappropriate to the audience being wooed.[29]

The Ontario Multifaith Council on Spiritual and Religious Care recognized these difficulties in interpretation and the problems they can cause. The Council saw that existing medical vocabulary had built up around and was relevant to clinical and scientific aspects of healthcare but that this language did not recognize the spiritual aspects of healing. This made communications and integration difficult between the disciplines. A working party was therefore set up to draw up suggested definitions of basic concepts, to aid meaningful communication and to hopefully assist the integration of the spiritual and subjective into mainstream medical practice. This Working Group of acknowledged experts in integrated care came up with the following concept of suffering: 'a state of anguish or pain. It is subjective and personal. It is experienced by whole persons and is not merely somatic. It may arise in any aspect of the individual. Suffering occurs with a perceived threat to one's sense of personal integrity and ends when the threat passes, or when integrity is restored in another way.'[30] The Group defined healing[31] as entailing a 'movement toward integration, integrity, and wholeness. It may or may not involve a return to physical health. It is possible to die 'healed', in the sense of having moved toward a previously unattained sense of wholeness.'

The social significance of healing

For the moment let's assume that healthcare professionals recognize their fundamental role in the relief of suffering. There seems to be less understanding of the social significance of true healing, as opposed to curing. Carl Jung and Scott Peck, Carl Rogers and Aldous Huxley, have all written in their time of the social impact of wounded behavior and the significance of individual healing within this context. This we saw in a previous chapter. [32]

Psychiatric and mental health nurse Conti O'Hare has a vision for the importance of nursing in the healing of society in the twenty first century. Writing about the nursing profession in the USA she urges nurses to understand the wounded healer concept in their profession, stressing how important it is for them to heal themselves properly before they can generate true healing in their patients and in their profession. Conti-O'Hare reflects on the ills of the world, such as terrorism, addiction and violence on our streets, that she recognizes as symptomatic of our inner woundedness. Nurses, she says, have the potential not only to heal their own profession but to foster healing in the world. 'We can only wonder,' she says, 'if people with serious emotional disorders will seek healing solutions or continue to inflict woundedness on others by their antisocial and unacceptable behavior...What a glorious expectation for nurses to be armed with the knowledge that they are Wounded Healers who have participated in transforming their own health and that of others.'[33]

O'Hare has developed what she calls the Q.U.E.S.T. Model[34] for Self-Transcendence to help nurses and other health professionals to heal themselves and their professions, as an aid for them to transform and transcend wounds to become true Wounded Healers. This transformation (from walking wounded to Wounded Healer), she believes, 'will have a positive impact on the health care system, society and the nursing profession as a whole.'[35]

While O'Hare merely hints in her book at the profound responsibilities of the nursing profession as Wounded Healers to the world, we have seen that J. J. Means, a pastoral counselor at the Des Moines Pastoral Counseling Center, Iowa USA, is more certain of his wider healing role in society.[36] I have also considered the healing power of forgiveness in a pastoral context, to reach the psychological and spiritual roots of the world's critical issues, a mission of the Fetzer Institute.[37] The medical and caring professions are in similarly privileged and indeed socially responsible positions to reach those psychological and spiritual roots of social strategy, within the domain of the nation's healthcare and soul care. And while the ills of the world at first sight may seem to be far removed from the day-to-day practice of medicine, in fact I hope I have shown that they are issues that are inextricably linked. These professions have a profound responsibility to recognize their role as healers to the world. North America is taking the lead in this for other countries no doubt to follow.

The way forward

If we suppress or ignore these important advances in the knowledge of the forces behind holistic healthcare, many patients will continue to live in a culture of pill popping and technological domination, of retail therapy and addictions, of dissatisfaction and unrest within the community. And many will still have a deep sense of something missing in their lives.

An organization called Physicians for Social Responsibility[38] was founded in 1961, as a network of medical and health professionals including students at medical and public health schools and concerned citizens and activists. It is a unique nationwide organization 'committed to a safe and healthy world.' Originally dedicated to halting the dangerous proliferation of nuclear weapons, the network now extends its mission into any aspects of life on this planet that threaten our health and survival, such as issues of climate change, violence and pollution. 'Guided by the values and expertise of medicine and public health,' its vision 'is a healthy, just and peaceful world for present and future generations.'

While this successful and socially responsible organization is of enormous value it is not addressing the social healing that I see as a vision in the context of this book. My idea of social responsibility transcends those boundaries. I am looking for the wider social significance of being a whole person, of being healed in the entire holistic sense, of reaching and healing those psychological and spiritual roots. I am interested in what implications this has for healing the world beyond our own individual bodies, and I invite readers' comments on this.

Medicine needs to nurture its own Wounded Healers. It needs to recover its soul and its spirit. Fortunately there is an increasing number of initiatives that are recognizing and supporting the furtherance of these needs, that are working towards a better world for all.

I closed the previous chapter with the challenge made in 2000 by the American Association of Medical Colleges (AAMC) to all North American medical schools, including the 17 in Canada, to update the teaching of their clinical medicine curricula.[39]

The Faculty of Medicine at the McGill University in Quebec, Canada prides itself on curriculum innovation. The McGill Programs in Integrated Whole Person Care [40] were instituted in February 1999 on the initiative of Dean Abraham Fuks and Dr. Balfour Mount to address the need for a greater recognition of the subjective elements, including the power of spirituality, in the healing process and to improve the way in which they integrated these into the mainstream. They were therefore in good shape to meet this challenge of the AAMC.

What McGill found was that the terms 'healing' or 'to heal' apparently did not appear once in their formal teaching objectives. Building on the advice of a task force of medical experts that included such acknowledged experts in their field as Balfour Mount, Eric Cassell and Michael Kearney, the Faculty started rolling out a revised curriculum that emphasizes the importance of the physician as healer. This will take time to have any positive impact on future doctors and the healthcare they offer, but will hopefully ensure their position in the forefront of medical education.[41]

The George Washington Institute for Spirituality and Health (GWish) was founded in May 2001, with a mission: 'to foster more compassionate and caring healthcare systems and restore the heart and humanity to healthcare.' To this end they provide all the practical skills and tools to help healthcare professionals 'to more fully integrate spirituality in their professional work with patients,' and to help clinicians 'bring spirituality to the bedside.'[42]

The Institute of Noetic Sciences is 'a nonprofit membership organization located in Northern California that conducts and sponsors leading-edge research into the potentials and powers of consciousness, including perceptions, beliefs, attention, intention, and intuition. The Institute explores phenomena that do not necessarily fit conventional scientific models, while maintaining a commitment to scientific rigor.'[43] It is conducting its own studies on distance healing and the relationship between consciousness and healing. [44]

These are just a sample of the many initiatives that will transform the face of medicine. We see plenty of signs of hope as a wider understanding is emerging within the medical profession of the opportunities for healing a patient's suffering within a spiritual context. A survey of medical teaching curricula carried out for Gwish[45] in 2001 found that of the 144 medical and osteopathic schools in the United States at that time 101 schools had courses, classes, and topics (required and elective) in spirituality and health.

When his book *Healing Words*[46] was first published in 1993 Dossey tells us that only three U.S. medical schools had courses devoted to exploring the role of religious practice and prayer in health. Clearly there has been considerable progress in the last few years, but there is plenty still to do. The availability of training does not of course guarantee a good take up rate or wider acceptance once the rigors of teaching are left behind for the harsh realities of practice.

While soul medicine is at a new dawn, art therapy within the healthcare system has been widely used for many years and most certainly draws upon the spiritual and transcendent for its efficacy.

Psychologist, psychotherapist and art therapist Natalie Rogers set herself a mission in the 1980s to bring creativity, soul, and spirit into our lives, 'to empower us as activists in this troubled world.' She discovered that 'using a combination of visual art, movement, sound and writing enhances the client's journey and facilitates communication between client and therapist.' Continuing the work of her father Carl Rogers, she founded in 1984 the Person-Centered Expressive Therapy Institute based upon his values and philosophy that 'each individual has worth, dignity and the capacity for self-direction if given an empathic, non-judgmental, supportive environment.' [47] In the next chapter I shall look at the potential for creativity to heal and the capacity of creativity to hurt in the context of the Wounded Healer, because 'Life beats down and crushes the soul and art reminds you that you have one.'[48]

Chapter 9
Healing Creativity

Through Art we can see deep truths that are otherwise invisible. In great works of art we feel the deepest yearnings of our Heart and glimpse the shimmering revelations of our Spirit.
Dana Lynne Andersen [1]

Creating a work of art is not a harmless thing. It always is a powerful medium. Art is extraordinarily powerful and important. It challenges people's lives.
Chögyam Trungpa [2]

There is nothing neutral about creative force. We can use it as a source of inspiration and healing for ourselves and for those around us. Or it has the power to hurt or corrupt, to disturb or destroy. We cannot escape its impact; creativity is an integral part of our lives.

Creativity to heal
Henri Nouwen described the effect on him of viewing for the first time a poster of Rembrandt's painting, The Return of the Prodigal Son. He had recently returned to France to spend time as a pastor for people with development or learning disabilities at L'Arche[3] community in Trosly-Breuil. Nouwen had spent a grueling lecture tour in the USA, which had left him exhausted physically and emotionally. The sight of this poster, he says,

made his heart leap, and 'set in motion a long spiritual adventure that brought me to a new understanding of my vocation and new strength to live it.'[4] Nouwen was later given the opportunity to study the original painting in depth, where it hangs in the Hermitage in St Petersburg. He described how moved he was by the depth of compassion in the father's hands on the shoulders of the repentant son kneeling before him in worn out cloak and sandals. Over the months and years that followed, 'Rembrandt's embrace remained imprinted on my soul far more profoundly than any temporary expression of emotional support,' he writes. 'It had brought me into touch with something within me that lies far beyond the ups and downs of a busy life, something that represents the ongoing yearning of the human spirit, the yearning for a final return, an unambiguous sense of safety, a lasting home.'[5]

Rembrandt was close to his death when he completed this painting in 1669, after a life of some success and wealth but also personal tragedies and grief. By this time he was a poor and lonely man. Nouwen senses in the painting an expression of the deep understanding that Rembrandt held of his own spiritual homecoming. Nouwen struggled throughout his own life with much mental anguish, with anxiety and with insecurity, but his pastoral abilities were undoubted. He gave spiritual support to many through his priestly ministry and through his books, many of which, including *The Return of the Prodigal Son: A Story of Homecoming*, are still bestsellers today. Something beautiful and life affirming was speaking to Nouwen from the picture and his ability to convey that on to his reader is very powerful indeed.

Creativity to hurt
Creativity however can hurt as well as heal.

Many share my dismay at the almost unbelievably violent computer games sold to children, but how many have the courage to take a stand against such things? Patience Wheatcroft in The Times[6] wrote: 'Whatever previous research has deter-mined, it is hard to believe that prolonged exposure to such horrors does not breed some nasty ideas in the more impres-sionable of minds.' She went on to say: 'The instances in which youngsters have gone out and committed murders akin to those they have watched are mercifully rare, although there have been a few notorious cases. But instinct suggests that bloodlust culti-vated on a computer screen might at least have a desensitising effect, even if it does not drive the player to go out and...[copy that violence.]' She quotes research from the University of Missouri-Columbia that shows that 'regular players of violent games suffer reduction in a type of brain activity called the P300 response, which reflects the emotional impact of an image on the viewer. The reaction of gamers to violent images was muted, suggesting that they were desensitised to brutality. They were also found more likely to behave aggressively...'[7] Even without the benefit of scientific evidence, common sense tells us that the emotions provoked by such violence can hardly be healing. We are healed by beauty, sensitivity and spirituality, not by ugly brutality. Studies such as these are always controversial and science rarely proves anything, it simply offers balances of probability. Nonetheless those who create such horror for the retail trade seem to be allowing their own wounds to crush them. They certainly have a responsibility for the potential negative effects of their work; for the harm it possibly inflicts on the minds of others. We know that people who are subjected to too much gratuitous violence put up a barrier of defense and they become desensitized, a process sometimes known as 'psychic numbing'. It is not hard to see that the longer-term effects of such material on the general behavior of the human race could be far reaching.

Arun Gandhi travels the world trying to keep alive his grand-father Mahatma Gandhi's philosophy of non-violence, based on the principles of love and truth. A young teacher in one of Arun's lectures raised the question of 'the corrupting effect of violent movies, TV shows and obscene and violent music on the young people in America.' Should they avoid such things, she asked. This, he replied, placed the cart before the horse. Those who live a life of practicing 'truthfulness' would not want to watch or listen to any such media in the first instance.[8] But such a noble life is not so easy for many of us to achieve.

When I was a very young girl we had an illustrated nature book at home. Among the photographs was a full page spread of a family of fearsome looking gorillas. They terrified me and made me scream every time I opened the book at that page, but I still insisted on continually going back to that photo! They held a gruesome fascination for me.

Many of us have an almost ghoulish tendency to look at the evil that is around us. We are certainly not very good at protecting ourselves from harmful influences. We therefore have government and industry guidelines that protect us from ourselves! We have rules and regulations that prohibit or restrict certain creative material, such as those that may determine the content and timing of television and radio programs. Films are classified according to their perceived suitability for different audiences. Such rules are often although not exclusively designed to protect the young and vulnerable in our societies.

Of course it is difficult if not impossible for government agencies to restrict what goes on within the confines of our own homes and neither would this be desirable. But it does seem to me that the bar of acceptability is being continually and subtly lowered, but perhaps this is a sign of me getting older! Certainly yesterday's restrictions often seem to have been diluted to the extent that they become today's standards! Does it matter?

Yes it does! I make no apology for returning again to this maxim, that it is our own behavior, not government intervention, which in the end will influence our future, the future of this planet and the future for our children and grandchildren. In his

UK best seller *Heat: How We Can Stop the Planet Burning*, environmental scientist, philosopher and bestselling author George Monbiot admits to being driven to action by the birth of his own child. He is as keen to see her survive in 'a liveable world'[9] as any of us must surely be for our own children and grandchildren.

In the contrasting stories of Henri Nouwen with Rembrandt's painting of The Return of the Prodigal Son and then in the harmful effect of violent computer games, we see that creativity in all its forms can be used either to help our spiritual regeneration, or to destroy our sensitivities. With its power to hurt or heal, creativity is at the very heart of all our lives, in boardroom or kitchen, hospital or garden, at work or at leisure. We do not have to be an author or painter, musician or inventor, writer or poet. Just about all of us use our creative skills as we go about our daily lives. Creativity infuses our work and leisure activities.

And so we all have a personal choice. We can be responsible and spread healing and beauty; we can radiate a sense of the soul and the spiritual throughout our lives and our communities. Or we can nurture evil and hurt in a world that has too much of it already.

This chapter is about that healing choice.

The Wounded Healer in creativity
The Performing Arts as Healer, in Music, Drama and Dance

Music and dance have been an integral part of man's healing rituals throughout the long history and tradition of shamanism, dating back more than 30,000 years and practiced to the present day. Indeed music is very probably our original language of communication. Until man learnt to notate music in a written form, there can obviously be little evidence of much of this early musical activity, but Paleolithic cave paintings show people dancing and the bone flutes found in such caves suggest that they danced to some kind of music.[10]

One of the earliest written records of the healing power of music is surely the biblical story of King David playing on his harp (or lyre, the earliest musical instrument mentioned in the bible) to King Saul, to cure the King's madness:

Now the Spirit of the Lord departed from Saul, and an evil spirit from the Lord tormented him...And whenever the evil spirit from God was upon Saul, David took the lyre and played it with his hand; So Saul was refreshed, and was well, and the evil spirit departed from him.[11]

Many examples of music with this healing quality are to be found among the works of the great classical composers. Amid poverty, a developing deafness and consequent depression and despair leading to suicidal thoughts Beethoven desperately sought cures from herbs, hydrotherapy and even galvanism,[12] but found none of them relieved his distress. Determined to commit himself to his art to overcome this depression, he put his heart and mind into writing some of the most beautifully sublime music ever. He found meaning through his disability. Those who listen to Beethoven's music will hear something of this torment and healing coming through in his compositions, for example in his Eroica or Pastoral Symphony.[13] To the Chief Rabbi Sir Jonathan Sacks, Beethoven's quartets are 'little less than the sound of heaven itself.'[14] His Goldberg Variations for Harpsichord were written in the mid-eighteenth century as a balm for sleep inducement, at the request of Count Kaiserling via his emissary Johann Goldberg. 'Needless to say they have been soothing troubled minds and bodies ever since.'[15]

Sacks describes several other examples of music transcending suffering. He writes of the healing capacity found among the work of other famous composers such as Chopin, and Joaquin Rodrigo, who was blind from the age of three. 'Happiness, these lives seem to say, is not the absence of suffering but the ability to take its fractured discords and turn them into music that rescues from the darkest regions of the soul a haunting yet humanizing beauty; surely the supreme achievement down here on earth.'[16] That beauty found through great music is clearly recognized by many as one of the ways in which the soul may be healed.

Anthony Storr, consultant psychiatrist and author, writes: 'I am subjectively certain that my involvement with Bach, Beethoven, Mozart, Haydn, Sibelius, Brahms, Bartok, Stravinsky, Wagner and many other great composers has not only brought me pleasure but has deepened my appreciation of life, and I am not alone in feeling this.'[17] The English composer and international conductor John Rutter claims to be not a particularly religious man. However his beautiful spiritual music is surely capable of softening the hardest heart.

The effect of music on our wellbeing may not be obvious but can be very real. In the late 1960s Texan musician Don Campbell[18] was called in to advise on the depression and general listlessness that had overcome a community of Benedictine monks in the South of France. On further enquiry Campbell found that until recently they had been used to singing Gregorian chants in their worship throughout the day, but that this practice had been discontinued following proposals that initiated out of the Second Vatican Council.[19] On reinstating the chants into their worship, health was restored to the monks! They had benefited apparently from the physiological effects of the chanting and their deprivation made them ill. [20]

Campbell has a particular interest in the therapeutic or healing properties of sound, in related educational programs and in the contemporary and indigenous spiritual traditions. In his lectures and books he has been influenced by the research of Fr Physician Alfred Tomatis who in the second half of the twentieth century established his theories on the healing and creative power of music and sound, in particular through what became known as The Mozart Effect. Tomatis found again and again that as compared with many other musical geniuses, it was the music of Mozart that 'calmed listeners, improved spatial perception, and allowed them to express themselves more clearly – communicating with both heart and mind.' Mozart, explains Campbell, 'is at once deeply mysterious and accessible, and above all without guile. His wit, charm, and simplicity allow us to locate a deeper wisdom in ourselves.'[21] Campbell and his work is not without its critics, but of course ideas such as these perhaps receive more than their fair share of controversy, for being 'fluffy' and subjective rather than empirically proven.

There is however a darker side to music.

The psychiatrist Anthony Storr discusses the evil powers of music in his book *Music and the Mind*,[22] citing as one example the music used by the campaigning Hitler to heighten the emotions of the crowd.

Is black metal and death metal music written from wounds and hurts? Is this destructive to the listener? Or does it satisfy some need? Does it in some way harmlessly channel such wounds during a healing process? Storr is confident that 'Plato and Aristotle were right. Music is a powerful instrument of education which can be used for good or ill,' and we should, he says, 'ensure that everyone in our society is given the opportunity of participating in a wide range of different kinds of music.'[23] He refers to Allan Bloom, who expressed an anxiety in his own best selling albeit controversial book *The Closing of the American Mind* [24] that the popularity of rock music among students was banishing 'any interest in, or feeling of need for, any other kind of music.' This is serious, Bloom says, because great music is 'powerfully educative.'

Campbell looks forward to new knowledge on the use of music in therapy and healing and his hope is that such information 'may also influence musical performance, composition, and listening tastes, contributing to the development of individuals and fostering a world community more attuned to the healthful and peaceful rhythms of life.' This he says would indeed be a 'joyous revolution.'[25] It certainly would be, but sadly most 'popular' musicians of today seem to be motivated to write and perform what they think will sell rather than what will be a healing force for good in the world. And we provide the demand!

Of course music is also used to accompany dance in its many different styles. The choreographer Arlene Phillips once said of dance that it engages the brain, the heart, the body and the soul. Shamanic healing rituals certainly involve dance. I can find watching a beautiful ballet an uplifting and spiritual experience. The theme of Michael Mayne's book *Learning to Dance* is 'the dance of life; the dance of the cosmos, of the natural world and of the tiniest particle of matter; the dance of music and paint and words, whereby artists may make journeys into the unknown in order to recapture lost parts of themselves for our mutual healing.'[26]

Painting

The same early cave paintings that show us how long music and dance have been around also reflect the importance of pictures among prehistoric man. We see this same significance right up to the present day in the story of Henri Nouwen and his experience with Rembrandt's The Return of the Prodigal Son. Thus may great paintings not only arise out of a realm of pain: they may also impart a spirituality that has a profound effect on the observer's soul. As Basil Hallward suggests in Oscar Wilde's novel, *The Picture of Dorian Gray;* 'Every portrait that is painted with feeling is a portrait of the artist, not of the sitter.'[27]

Visionary and spiritual artist Alex Grey sees art 'as a covenant relationship between spirit, the art, and the viewer. And so the artist,' Grey explains, 'if he or she gets lucky and has some kind of inspiring spiritual experience, has a responsibility to translate and transmit it as closely as possible so as to evoke a similar experience in the viewer.' Artists, according to Grey,

> want to translate their experience clearly enough so that if the
> viewers can trust the work they are able to let go of their own
> ego identity and merge with the inspiring moment that the
> artist was able to capture. At that point, they will stand in the
> same relationship to the transcendental that was the initial gift
> given to the artist. So the artist becomes a transparent medium
> through which a person is able to reconnect with his or her
> own deeper nature. [28]

It is well known that Winston Churchill suffered from serious
bouts of depression. He used to call them his 'black dog', after
Samuel Johnson who described his own bouts of depression that
he suffered as 'his walk with the black dog.'

Churchill found solace and healing in his own painting hobby,
admitting that this helped him after the personal depressive crisis
he suffered following the mayhem of the year long unsuccessful
Dardanelles campaign in the First World War. Many of
Churchill's paintings were inspired in the picturesque fishing
village of Camara de Lobos in Madeira, where he spent holidays
at the island's famous Reid's Palace Hotel. Some of his works can
be seen in his studio at Chartwell, his English country home in
Kent. Although he had no formal training in the art, his paintings
are widely acclaimed. I am not sure whether they can be credited
with their own healing powers in the same sense as the
Rembrandt painting that moved Nouwen so deeply. They do
though in their own way give one a transitory sense of enjoyment
or well being such as can be experienced from any object of
beauty. 'I know of nothing which, without exhausting the body,
more entirely occupies the mind,' Churchill wrote of his pastime
that absorbed him so much during the last 40 years of his life.[29]

Poetry and prose

'Words are weapons, often the most dangerous types of weapons...in the end we assure ourselves, the truth will prevail. But what about in the meantime?'[30] Conyers Read's words remind us, if ever a reminder was needed, that words can wound, and deeply so.

Words can also heal. The recognition of the healing power of the Wounded Healer within creativity has a long history, nowhere more so perhaps than in the realms of poetry and prose.

Some of the earliest examples of this healing power are found in the psalms of the Old Testament, written during the 1000 years or so leading up to the birth of Christ. People throughout the world still turn to these psalms to seek guidance, comfort and solace when they have to face difficult times in their life. There are many who feel that the psalms speak to them in the torment of their human condition, that they express their innermost anguishes that they cannot voice. As Sacks observes, 'some of the greatest psalms come from this realm of pain.'[31]

There was another form of healing prose emerging during that period, in the consolatory literature of the ancient Greeks. Perhaps the earliest example of this was *On Grief*, written by the Greek academic and philosopher Crantor in the mid fourth century BC. This type of consolation was offered on the occasion of any human misfortune, but seems to have been used particularly to console or heal following the death of a loved one, often a child. The consolatory ministry was built around the belief that by writing about one's own suffering the author is not only helping himself through his own difficulties but can be in a better position to help others in a similar situation. The soul or spirit was often implicated in this healing process. It reflected the healing vulnerability of the Wounded Healer.

There were many examples of this genre of literature, which developed well into the European Renaissance period of the fourteenth to seventeenth centuries. By that time there was 'a growing recognition of sorrow, misery, and misfortune as matters for sympathetic appreciation rather than as stemming from sinfulness,'[32] the prevailing attitude up until that time. Francesco Petrarca, or Petrarch, who lived in the fourteenth century, was well known for his self- care and self -analysis. 'No one's solace,' he wrote, 'penetrates a saddened mind more than that of a fellow sufferer, and therefore the most effective words to strengthen the spirits of the bystanders are those which emerge from the actual torments.' He quoted from Virgil: 'Being acquainted with grief, I learn to succor the wretched (Aen. 2.630).'[33]

The consolatory genre surely survives to the present day in the spiritual works of Henri Nouwen and perhaps Michael Mayne, for example. It was only when I read Michael Mayne's *Learning to Dance* that I discovered that he had been deeply wounded as a child, when at the age of three his father, with no warning, committed suicide and left his wife and son homeless and very poor. This, Mayne said, left 'an immense emptiness' in his life.[34] He was writing a meditation on his life of faith when he learnt that he had cancer. As he struggled with his terminal and painful illness, he completed *Enduring Melody*, [35] which became his own beautifully written and moving epitaph. In an addition to Mayne's obituary in the Times[36] in November 2006, Canon Chris Chivers wrote of Mayne: 'The letter he wrote to me...was full of down-to-earth wisdom, mixed with deep prayerfulness, and an all-too-rare ability to put himself in the shoes and soul of another. This will surely be the enduring melody of his richly sacrificial ministry.' Mayne's meditational books are steeped in wonderful imagery that helps us understand more clearly the ineffable, the God immanent but unknowable. In his vocation as priest he was clearly the very essence of the Wounded Healer to those who received his ministry.

Books such as those of Nouwen and Mayne should never be confused with the abundance of 'misery memoirs' that feed our voyeuristic tendencies while they fill the bookshop and supermarket shelves. These have been described as often sordid, sometimes even pornographic in the detail they provide. Sadly they often become best sellers. Sadly too we are drawn to such books rather than to the beauty and healing in poetry and spiritual or meditative prose, so much of which expresses our own blocked emotions in a way that can become part of our own deep healing process. The publishers, of course, are merely supplying the demand! But 'for publishers to claim a moral high ground about books whose contents would be better off kept between client and therapist is disingenuous. It is all about profits.'[37]

This observation applies no less to the media in all its forms, with its own hidden agendas. 'In our times,' writes Helen Moore, self-styled eco-poet and environmental author:

the freedom of the media is subtly challenged by the fact that it's ultimately beholden to corporate interest...Like all employees, journalists are recruited to maximise profits. In essence their job is to sell wealthy audiences to the all-important advertisers, on whom the average broadsheet depends for fully 75% of its revenue. The hidden agenda, undiscussed, often unconscious, is to report the truth in an interesting, entertaining way that does not alienate these advertisers, or wealthy media owners, or parent companies or governments...[38]

The media, writes George Monbiot, 'driven by fear and advertising, are hopelessly biased towards the consumer economy and against the biosphere.'[39]

The media is so invasive into our consciousness, so easy to tap into in film or internet, YouTube and blog, so difficult to avoid and yet so powerful and far reaching in its influence. The creative forces at work in the media that relentlessly bring so many images into our lives, the writers, editors, journalists, photographers and all the myriad of support staff we see listed for example in the credits at the end of any film, bear an awesome responsibility.

As with other creativity, those working in the media can use their talents to help heal the world and nourish our souls, or to assist in the destruction of both. The choice is theirs.

Jam and Jerusalem: Other forms of creativity

So far I have written only of the healing creativity to be found within the performing arts, painting, prose and poetry.

The humanist psychologist Abraham Maslow said that his clients taught him that: 'a first-rate soup is more creative than a second rate painting, and that, generally, cooking or parenthood or making a home could be creative while poetry need not be...'[40]

'The action,' wrote Carl Rogers, 'of the child inventing a new game with his playmates; Einstein formulating a theory of relativity; the housewife devising a new sauce for the meat; a young author writing his first novel; all of these are...creative...there is no attempt to set them in some order of more or less...'[41]

I am the verger at our local Anglican church. Recently I was on duty at an inspiring funeral. It was actually more of a celebration, for a lady who gave her life to bringing up her children and supporting her grandchildren and great grandchildren. She lived to a great age and had clearly led a wholly fulfilled and happy life. What a contrast, I thought, to the clearly stressed and self-important businessman who came late to the service with his bulging briefcase and laptop. As we sang the next hymn my mind drifted. How do we measure success and fulfillment? From his demeanor and the cut of his suit he seemed wealthy. But was he truly happy and fulfilled? How much did he see of his family? And did he, I wondered, achieve his gains without the exploitation in any way of people or resources? Was his work tarnished with unethical trading, sweatshops and child labor?

That lady left a legacy worth far more than any monetary wealth, however acquired. She was obviously loved by her extended family and clearly proud of them all.

I acknowledge that most of us have to earn a living, that we may be forced by circumstance to make arduous daily commutes, with mortgages and healthcare costs to pay and families to support.

Surely we need to foster a society that appreciates the value and healing properties of domestic creativity, of baking bread and cakes, of making jams and preserves, of preparing family meals and general home making. These are almost a forgotten art in many households. But they can all be therapeutic occupations for the whole family and ultimately prove vital for the well being of our world.

How many of us I wonder find the real fulfillment and contentment of the lady we buried that day?

Art and the young

I am told that Venezuela is a stunning country, with its Andean peaks, its Caribbean coastline, its tranquil offshore islands, its wetlands teeming with life, the steamy Amazon and its rolling savanna towered over by the flat-topped mountains called tepuis. But perhaps it has more than its fair share of unemployment, slums, poverty and a youth in need of a focus away from the temptations of crime and drugs.

Venezuelan Jose Antonia Abreo is a trained economist. He is also a talented pianist and a visionary activist. In 1975 he founded an educational system for the youth of Venezuela based on the teaching of music as a basis for intellectual growth. This innovative idea was to use music as the focus of education, provide children with free musical instruments and teach them to play in an orchestra. Abreo saw this as a way to give children of all ages a meaningful purpose and self esteem, a means for social and intellectual improvement that would rescue them from the harmful alternatives around them in their otherwise deprived lives. His organization is now known as El Sistema.

The vision and energy of this one man has improved the lives of hundreds of thousands of deprived children. The flagship orchestra of El Sistema, the Simon Bolivar Youth Orchestra, has played in Carnegie Hall, at the London Proms and elsewhere, always to widespread acclaim. The idea has been so successful that it is finding outlets across the world, for example in other Latin American countries, in Spain and across the United States. The concept is also being developed in England and in Stirling, Scotland, where youth disaffection is seen to be a real problem.

In his acceptance speech for the B'nai B'rith Human Rights Award in 2008, Abreu succinctly summarized the goal of El Sistema and of his life's work by saying; 'In the struggle for Human Rights, let us vigorously incorporate children's sublime right to music, in whose bosom shines Beingness in its splendor and its ineffable mystery. Let us reveal to our children the beauty of music and music shall reveal to our children the beauty of life.'[42]

It seems so obvious to remind ourselves yet again that our children and our youth are our future. How many of us outside the realms of school and family, however, spend any time by example or action to encourage their positive and wholesome development through the medium of music?

The social significance of creativity

Throughout the previous chapters I hope I have conveyed something of the social significance, the importance to the future of this world, of finding our own spiritual healing. And creativity most certainly plays a vital part.

Helen Moore has come to firmly believe that the artist now has a duty to resist the pressures of corporate profit, the fear of upsetting a status quo, of offending vested financial interests, a responsibility 'for at least considering the effect on the wider community of the kind of work that he or she puts into the world.' Of her own work she continues:

> the new awareness of my interdependence with all beings fills me with awe and wonder. No longer can I take anything for granted, and I feel humbled as never before. And whilst it's true that I can never know what listening I'm speaking into, I now want to scrutinize the intention that lies behind the work I release into the world. Do I want to contribute to more violence or despair? Or do I want to help people envision a sustainable future for our species on this planet?[43]

Moore is far from being the only artist to recognize our burgeoning responsibilities in this world. She is supported by the work of poets such as Mary Oliver, Gary Snyder and others.

Neither is she introducing a new idea. In his essay in 1961 '*Towards a Theory of Creativity*'[44] Carl Rogers wrote of the urgent social need for the fostering of creativity. He predicted that a 'passive and culture bound' people could not cope with the fantastic advances in both creative and destructive technology.

> Unless individuals, groups, and nations can imagine, construct, and creatively revise new ways of relating to these complex changes, the lights will go out. Unless man can make new and original adaptations to his environment as rapidly as his science can change the environment, our culture will perish. Not only individual maladjustment and group tensions, but international annihilation will be the price we pay for a lack of creativity.[45]

The Shakespearean scholar Jonathan Bate in his *Song of the Earth* has written of the links between literature and the environment. He is convinced that in our technological world poetry is becoming ever more important to reconnect us to our natural roots. 'The earth may only be healed,' he writes, 'if the human mind becomes a mansion for all lovely forms instead of an engine-house for the invention of an infinity of devices by which we might enjoy, without any effort, the fruits of the earth and all its commodities.'[46]

The evolution of creativity

I think it was probably Graham Wallas who first put forward the idea that the progress of human creativity may follow the Darwinian laws of natural selection,[47] that creativity has a part to play, for good or ill, in our evolution, in determining the future of the human race on this planet.

Dean Keith Simonton, professor of psychology at the University of California at Davis, provides an updated perspective on Wallas in his book, *Origins of Genius: Darwinian Perspectives on Creativity*,[48] where he further explores this idea and agrees that 'creative genius, or the ability to produce highly original ideas with staying power, is a fundamentally Darwinian process that enhances the adaptive fitness of the individual and the human species.' In other words, creativity 'can be understood as a process akin to natural selection that leads to the survival of those ideas that prove their hardiness.'[49]

At the same time Hungarian psychology professor and leading researcher on positive psychology Mihaly Csikszentmihalyi was in 1996 linking creativity to biological evolution. His view is that units of information or memes, (the word coined by Richard Dawkins in *The Selfish Gene*, in 1976), are passed down through generations by learning. Cultures develop over time by creative people changing these memes and if the changes are seen as useful to a developing culture so they will continue to be handed on to new generations and become entrenched.

Because of this, Csikzentmihalyi argues that we have taken over from God as the creator in this world and it would help, he warns, 'if we realized the awesome responsibility of this new role...' He continues:

> Whether this transformation will help the human race or cause its downfall is not yet clear...The gods of the ancients, like Shiva, like Yehova, were both builders and destroyers. The universe endured in a precarious balance between their mercy and their wrath...The world we inhabit today...teeters between becoming either the lovely garden or the barren desert that our contrary impulses strive to bring about. The desert is likely to prevail if we ignore the potential for destruction our stewardship implies and go on abusing blindly our new-won powers. [50]

Responsible use of our own creative skills

'Art first heals the artist and subsequently helps heal others,'[51] writes Kay Jamieson, psychiatrist and herself a manic-depressive, who has made the connection between personal wounds and creativity and explores the link in some detail in her book *Touched With Fire*.

All the creative therapies tap into this healing power, whether as art, music, poetry or dance. As Edward Adamson, one time artistic director at a psychiatric hospital in Southern England, explains: 'The artist is also on familiar terms with the inner self, and therefore is a little closer to those who are obliged to wrestle with its problems. The hospital artist's main role is to be a catalyst who allows the healing art to emerge.'[52]

But the work produced in such therapy sessions can become more if the patient has his own artistic talent. It then 'transforms other people's lives in its representation, and majesty, in its depiction of the human condition reaching towards the sublime... Van Gogh wrote to his brother Theo: 'Either shut me up right away in a madhouse or else let me work with all my strength.''[53]

I can personally testify to the healing power of creativity. As I struggled to climb out of the black depression of my own serious breakdown, it was therapy in the art room, with the imaginative use of collage, clay, paint and loads of paper both of the drawing and tissue kind (!), that helped me as well as many others to unblock so much that was otherwise too painful to speak about. My own creations sadly showed none of the flair of Van Gogh. Nonetheless it is only following such release that true healing of mind and spirit can really begin, just as a foreign body or infection must be cleared from a wound before the skin will properly heal over it.

We must however look beyond the caring professions and embrace healing creativity as a guiding principle for us all if we are to live sustainably, responsibly and peaceably together.

Within all our communities people are dedicating much of their spare time to selflessly bring purpose and hope and healing to many where there was previously disharmony and ugliness. Drama and dance can turn feral youth into young responsible adults. Football can unite otherwise divided communities. Nature rambles can introduce children to a further dimension in their lives. Beautiful nature films are produced to inspire us all.

We will find examples all around us if we attune ourselves to the healing needs of the world.

In Chapter 1, I made a plea for us to find a more spiritual connection with the earth, to respect it and love it, in the context of the damage we persist in inflicting on it. We saw the significant part that the world's religions play in healing God's Creation, but I also wrote of the need for us all of any faith or none, to heal ourselves, in a holistic spiritual sense, to heal our wounded behavior, before we can hope to heal what is around us, animate and inanimate.

I have ended by linking this need with the healing power of our own creativity. We can all be a part of that healing process. We can all allow the beauty of creation in its many forms to come into our lives. We can be receptive to its spiritually healing qualities. Whether this happens through a great work of art from one of the Old Masters, or from a poem, an inspiring book, a symphony or our own creative efforts, it may indeed be the Wounded Healer at work. We can then pass that healing on to others.

It is not only those who call themselves artists who have this serious responsibility as agents for social change: creativity is not only about painting and music, poetry and the media. We are all artists: whether as parent or homemaker, businessman or scientist, whether we are in one of the caring or pastoral professions or in education and training, we will all knowingly or perhaps unwittingly put our creative powers and talents to either good or evil use.

Art is an essential feature of sustainable living and as responsible human beings we have a choice as to how we use this for the future of our earth. We can choose 'celebrity and commercial art, that is disengaged from the concerns of the world... isolationistic and egotistic...[which] has little to do with the ecological spiritual or social challenges of our time.' Alternatively we can encourage and produce 'art with integrity; art that inspires, uplifts and serves the greater purpose of life.'[54]

We can heal or hurt with our creativity. The choice is ultimately ours and ours alone, as is the responsibility.

"Art is the symbol of the two noblest human efforts; to construct and to refrain from destruction." Simone Weil.

May we be wise with those choices.

Conclusion

This brings my exploration of the Wounded Healer in our lives to a close. I have tried to offer a broad perspective of the issues that I believe to be relevant to saving ourselves on this planet. Whether you are happier and more comfortable joining in with collective efforts, or shared initiatives, or whether you are leaders, willing to take the first steps, I hope that in what I have written you will find plenty of material to support and inspire. There is more information in the Notes, References and Appendix that follow. It is also my hope that these resources will help us all to examine our own consciences and recognize our responsibilities, will prompt us to think about how our actions affect those around us, will inspire us to ponder on whether we allow our own wounds to infect those around us, both near and far away, or whether we take it upon ourselves to heal our behavior and heal the world.

Remember this. There is always someone who is responsible, someone who signs the final authority, provides the funding, owns the original idea, helps in the manufacture, draws up the accounts, prepares the legal papers or supports a project in some way, or simply just allows something to happen. There is always a person somewhere behind a good or bad decision, behind all the good and evil in the world. We ultimately encourage or condone such decisions by our action or inaction.

In our culture today vulnerability is too often regarded as a weakness, whereas of course it is really a great strength. A shift in attitude is needed, and courage. And it only needs one person at a time!

Whatever our faith or none, we need to feel and find and heal our wounds, become more sensitive and vulnerable, restore spiritual values within our lives, look for the spirit in all matter and cast healing ripples of hope out into a world that yearns for equality, health, happiness and peace for us all.

I pray this may be so!

Dorset 2009

Appendix
Journey of Hope – Words into Action

Never doubt that a small group of committed people can change the world – indeed it's the only thing that ever has.
American cultural anthropologist Margaret Mead

There is an old story of a man who was walking along the surf at the edge of the sea. Every now and then he knelt down to pick up one of many hundreds of starfish left stranded by the tide, and threw it back into the water. 'Why are you doing that?' asked his friend. 'How can that make any difference?' 'It makes a difference,' came the reply, 'to that one.'

I can hear some at this stage, having read the book, being highly critical of what must seem an impossibly unrealistic dream, a romantic idealism. But perhaps we need to remember this story.

We have to keep alive that hope, the hope of making a difference, however small that difference may be. How can we afford not to take action? Action may not always be as simple as stooping down to throw a starfish back into the sea. It may require courage, open mindedness and a huge leap of faith, but a leap of faith that is fundamental to accepting and taking on the role of healers to a wounded world. How we shape the future of that world for our children is in our own hands.

Full acknowledgements of books and websites consulted and quoted in writing this book are in the Notes and References.

Between them they form a huge resource. The following selective and annotated collection of organizations and their websites, with a few additional books also noted, is meant to complement those resources and the chapters that have gone before, to inspire and enable response and action; I have drawn them up as a further tool to help the reader become involved with something that will make a difference.

With so many ideas from which to choose, surely we must all be able to find something we can do to help. That is why I have spent so much time and energy completing this book, with such a wealth of information included. To inform is to enable.

First I briefly want to sketch my own journey of hope and inspiration that led to this book.

My journey
Once the idea for this book emerged, one of my earliest inspirations was then undoubtedly *Soil and Soul, People versus Corporate Power,* the wonderfully spiritual book by the Scottish human ecologist, writer and campaigner Alastair McIntosh, (Aurum Press 2004). Here I found the stories of the Scottish Western Isles of Eigg and Harris and how in both places a few local islanders overcame the might of 'landlordism' and corporate might respectively to protect their community and their land. I urge the reader not only to read this book but also to visit McIntosh's website, (http://www.alastairmcintosh.com/) for the many initiatives with which he is involved. His later book, *Rekindling Community: Connecting People, Environment and Spirituality* (Schumacher Briefing, Green Books 2008) I can also strongly recommend, with practical examples of community building at work; real life stories that have happened, and can happen again, and can make such a difference to the world around us.

Another early influence came from the work of Satish Kumar, editor of *Resurgence,* the magazine that is at the heart of earth, art and spirit, dedicated 'to the service of soil, soul and society.' I recommend his article, 'Spiritual Imperative,' in that publication, Issue 229, March/April 2005 at (http://www.resurgence.org/2005/kumarspirit229.htm), and more recently his beautiful book, based on the Indian Ayurvedic tradition as applied to our work and our environment, *Spiritual Compass: The Three Qualities of Life* (Green Books, 1st edition 2007). All matter, he says, is imbued with spirit, and spirit manifests through matter.

I then found in a secondhand bookshop the first edition, from 1993, of Larry Dossey's *Healing Words, The Power of Prayer and the Practice of Medicine.* (HarperCollins; new edition 2007) and Leslie Weatherhead's *Psychology Religion and Healing* (revised reprint 1955) now reprinted in Paperback by Stewart Press, 2007). I took these away on a yoga retreat to Mallorca, was inspired by their work and as a scientist I have followed Dossey's ideas since with increasing interest. Dossey is a prolific author. His latest book is *The Science of Premonitions: How Knowing the Future Can Help Us Avoid Danger, Maximize Opportunities, and Create a Better Life* (Plume, paperback due May, 2010)

During those early years of research I was introduced to The Scientific and Medical Network. This network for science and medical professionals (http://www.scimednet.org/aims.htm), was founded in 1973 to explore the frontiers of science, medicine, spirituality and human experience. It counts many eminent scientists among its members, and its aims are not only 'to provide a safe forum for the critical and open minded discussion of ideas that go beyond conventional paradigms in science, medicine and philosophy,' but also to 'integrate intuitive insights with rational analysis in…investigations, to encourage a respect for Earth and community which emphasizes a spiritual and holistic approach and to challenge the adequacy of 'scientific materialism' as an exclusive basis for knowledge and values,' while maintaining the highest standards of scientific scrutiny and objective principles.

Other global networks and organizations

Many organizations are mentioned throughout the book which need our support. Below is a short list of some others of importance that didn't make it into the text, with stated missions copied from their own websites, and with a few additional books to track down and read:

The Micah Challenge 'is a global coalition of Christians holding governments to account for their promise to halve extreme poverty by 2015,' whose aim is 'to encourage Christians worldwide to deepen their commitment to the poor and to speak out to leaders to act with justice' (http://www.micahchallenge. org/) 'Around the world Micah Challenge seeks to ignite and fuel a global movement of Christians from the South and the North - Christians who are united in seeking dramatic reductions in poverty, and in speaking out against its injustices with a single, formidable voice.' They want this to be 'a movement that is truly inclusive, engaging Christians of contrasting denominations in a way that stays true to a clear, shared Christian identity.'

See also Micah Challenge International Director Joel Edwards' book *An Agenda for Change: a Global Call for Spiritual Transformation.* (Michigan: Zondervan, 2008).

Sojourners. Their mission 'is to articulate the biblical call to social justice, inspiring hope and building a movement to transform individuals, communities, the church, and the world.' They believe that 'unity in diversity is not only desirable, but *essential* to fulfilling God's ultimate desire for God's people, as expressed in scripture (Acts 2, Revelation 7:9), and thus an essential element of seeking God's will on earth as it is in heaven...' (www.sojo.net) Also visit their *God's Politics* Blog, the blog of Jim Wallis, author of *The Great Awakening; Seven Ways to Change the World,* (HarperOne; Reprint edition, 2009), and *Rediscovering*

Values: On Wall Street, Main Street, and Your Street, (Howard Books, 2010).

Stop Climate Chaos Coalition (http://www.stopclimatechaos .org/) is a large and powerful coalition which includes Christian Ecology Link among its many corporate and institutional members. Its site has useful links to many other organizations with green credentials, and many actions to support.

The Tony Blair Faith Foundation. This foundation 'aims to promote respect and understanding about the world's major religions and show how faith is a powerful force for good in the modern world...using the full power of modern communications to support and step up efforts at every level to educate, inform and develop understanding about the different faiths and between them.' (http://tonyblairfaithfoundation.org/)

Further discussion and explanation of the flaws in our money system, together with ideas for change to support community and sustainability, can be found in an interview with Bernard Lietaer, Summer 1997: 'Money: Print Your Own! Beyond Greed and Scarcity,' in *YES! A Journal of Positive Futures,* (http://www.yesmagazine.org/issues/money-print-your-own/beyond-greed-and-scarcity).

The Jubilee Centre was mentioned in Chapter 6 in connection with its vision for a relational economy based on biblical principles. But its work goes far beyond that. It is a Christian social reform organization, that believes that 'the Bible describes a coherent vision for society that has enduring relevance for Britain and the world in the twenty-first century' and that 'there is and ought to be a constructive relationship between social reform and the advance of the gospel.' The Jubilee Centre 'is fully committed to the proclamation of the 'good news' of salvation through faith in

Christ for the forgiveness of sins leading to new life in the power of the Holy Spirit.' Their *Jubilee Manifesto* was written to 'encourage Christians in all parts of the world, and in all walks of life, to set about the reform of public policy, their workplace and their home life with a fresh sense of purpose and renewed vision.' But one does not have to be a Christian to respond to the challenges set in the Manifesto. The ideas are appropriate for all. The Centre regularly publishes up to the minute books on social issues. See for example their *Christianity, Climate Change and Sustainable Living,* by Nick Spencer, and Robert White (London: SPCK, 2007).

Among the hundreds and thousands of relevant blogs and sites on the parlous state of our planet and what to do about it, I like David Alexander's Website *Planet Thoughts*, which 'provides focused environment information with positive energy and insight, for individuals around the world...[because] clear information is the first step, toward creating a population of citizen leaders in improving the world's environment.' (www.planet-thoughts.org)

There are of course many other sites that a discerning Googler will find!

What is immediately obvious from the list above is the vast wealth of effort now being expended by so many institutes and organizations in developing and promoting their ideas within this new era of consciousness, spirituality and healing. There are so many pockets of activity and influence, and new similarly motivated organizations continue to appear. There must be plenty of overlap and too much duplicated effort. There is a clear need for an umbrella organization, a network, to coordinate all this effort, for joined up thinking. The faith organizations have the International Interfaith Organisations Network. But what is otherwise available?

The Scientific and Medical Network has recognized this need to bring together initiatives, to pool resources, to make the most of the many different efforts being made to heal our world, but most importantly the need to promote action. In the 100th issue of their journal, *Network Review*, Summer 2009, p. 3, Oliver Robinson, John Clark and David Lorimer have launched their own program of action for the Network, seeking to bring ideas together into a planned book, *Crisis as Opportunity: Seizing the Moment for a New Renaissance*. This will underpin and develop their campaign.

My preoccupation has always been with the need to act, with not intellectualizing too much. We all need to promote real action. I hope this SMN initiative is a positive step in the right direction.

If you have read this far, I implore you to explore the sites and read the books that most interest you, discuss and debate the ideas in your own social or church groups, or with colleagues, and reach a consensus on possible ways forward. Then make sure the ideas are converted into action: in other words make things happen!

Then there may be hope, and we have to retain that hope, that between us we can heal this wounded Earth.

Endnotes

Preface

1. Henri J. M. Nouwen, 1994.
2. Michael Ford, 1999.
3. A term embracing those of us 'having religious faith and honesty of intention as well as those who may lack the religious faith but still have the honesty of intention.' I am indebted to Peter Challen and Rodney Shakespeare who use this phrase in their book *Seven Steps to Justice* (London: New European Publications, 2002) p. 1.

Introduction

1. Larry Dossey, 2000, p. 12.
2. see note 3 to Preface.
3. From a 2007 YouGov survey commissioned for the UK charity the Mental Health Foundation
4. Riane Eisler, quoted at http://www.saiv.net/about.htm website of The Spiritual Alliance to Stop Intimate Violence, recognized as the training ground for war, terrorism, political repression and crime. 'In her germinal book *The Chalice & The Blade* and her award-winning *The Power of Partnership*, Riane Eisler shows that throughout history, and cross culturally, the most violently despotic and warlike cultures have been those where violence in homes is culturally condoned. We see this connection in Hitler's Germany and Stalin's Soviet Union. We see it in the Taliban, and other cultures that feed terrorism and war today. Logic

alone tells us that early training to accept violence as a means of imposing one's will on others is useful to violent and repressive regimes.' Sourced 25 November 2009.

5.   From Greenpeace website.

6.   Cecil Helman, 2006, p. 77.

Chapter 1

1.   Christian Aid Report, May 2006.

2.   Aldous Huxley, *Island* 1976, pp. 247, 248.

3.   Belden C. Lane, 1998, p. 216.

4.   http://www.clintoncommunitygarden.org/   sourced   27 January 2009

5.   *San Francisco Chronicle Editorial*: Tuesday 6 February 2007. The earlier IPCC report in 2001 concluded that it was 'likely' that observed global warming in the previous 50 years was due to increased greenhouse gases. That in scientific terms means a chance of 66% or more. The scientific odds have increased substantially from 66% to 90% now, and the finger of guilt in the later report has been pointed specifically at man and his activities. This is a significant shift of emphasis over 6 years. See also the site of the Intergovernmental Panel on Climate Change, http://www.ipcc.ch/press_information/ press_information_fact_sheet1.htm sourced 23 November 2009.

6.   Alastair McIntosh, 2004, p. 128.

7.   A fuller explanation of the Wounded Healer is in the next chapter.

8.   James Lovelock, 2006, p. 162.

9.   The Earth System Science Partnership (ESSP) comprises the four arms of global environmental change science, namely the International Geosphere-Biosphere Programme (IGBP), the International Human Dimensions Programme on Global Environmental Change (IHDP), the World Climate Research Programme (WCRP) and the international biodiversity

programme (DIVERSITAS). See
http://216.239.59.132/search?q=cache:uFwAGbtOz1YJ:
www.igbp.kva.se/page.php%3Fpid%3D415+
Amsterdam+Statement+2001+Earth+System+Science&
hl=en&ct=clnk&cd=7 sourced December 2008.

10. James Lovelock, 2006 pp. 5 and 25.

11. Ibid., p.138.

12. Dr Francis Rose, taken from a plaque at Wakehurst Place, West Sussex, UK. Francis Rose was a celebrated and author-itative field botanist and naturalist, researcher, teacher and author, with a lifelong passion for plant ecology and conser-vation. He died in 2006. The Francis Rose Reserve named in his memory at Wakehurst comprises a collection of Mosses, lichens, liverworts and filmy ferns in a natural valley setting.

13. Biographical information for James Lovelock is at his website, http://www.ecolo.org/lovelock/lovedeten.htm sourced December 2008.

14. Friends of the Earth International at http://www.foei.org/en/campaigns sourced December 2008. See also http://www.foe.org/

15. Paul R. Erlich, *Population Bomb* (Ballantine Books: Revised edition 1971). This is out of print and with limited avail-ability but the problem of overpopulation is even worse today.

16. Al Gore 9 November 2008 The Climate for Change at http://www.planetthoughts.org/?pg=pt/Whole&qid=2569&sc=t sourced January 2009

17. Upton Beall Sinclair, 1994, p. 109.

18. RSV, Ecclesiastes 1.9 probably written by Solomon in his old age c. 950 BC but could be later.

19. Professor Paul Slovic University of Oregon: Report to Conference of American Association for the Advancement of Science. Reported in The Times 17 February 2007.

20. Latest figures available, for 2007, at

http://www.eia.doe.gov/cneaf/electricity/epa/epat1p1.html sourced 19 February 2009.

21. James Lovelock, 2006 pp. 25, 26.

22. James Lovelock, 2009.

23. Sir Nicholas Stern UK Government Chief Economist: 2006 and 2007

24. Teilhard de Chardin, 1969, p. 49 cited in Violence and the Rising Tide of Globalisation – a Teilhardian Perspective; lecture on de Chardin work by Dr Mervyn Fernando Founder-Director of the Teilhard de Chardin Centre for Science, Spirituality and the Future – Subodhi Institute, Piliyandala, Sri Lanka

http://home.worldonline.nl/~sttdc/violence.htm

25. Elisabet Sahtouris, 1999

26. Martin Palmer with Victoria Finlay, 2003. I owe much of the material in this chapter on the different world faiths, and specifically their creeds relating to their care of creation, to the statements compiled specifically by those faiths for the Alliance of Religions and Conservation (ARC) and included in this book by Palmer and Finlay. The statements are freely quoted with the explicit permission of all parties involved in their production. As the authors point out, no one owns the wisdom of the faiths any more than we can own creation itself. I do acknowledge with thanks the use of all such material. I have deliberately quoted largely intact those parts of the faith statements that I have chosen specifically to illustrate my theme, as I wish to preserve as far as possible their integrity of doctrine and theology without wishing to impose a further layer of interpretation. The information is available in full on the ARC website and generally on the individual faith websites, as well as in the book *Faith in Conservation*. I also acknowledge the authors of each faith statement as appropriate in these endnotes.

27. Ibid., p. 3.

28. The Qur'an 007.031.

29. Palmer and Finlay 2003. The statement on Christianity in *Faith in Conservation* 2003 was compiled and endorsed by the Ecumenical Patriarchate of Constantinople, the World Council of Churches, and the Vatican Franciscan Center of Environmental Studies. Quotations from pp. 83-85.

30. Ibid.

31. Professor Nahum Rakover, an Orthodox legalist and Torah/Talmud scholar, was appointed by the World Jewish Congress to write a very extensive and comprehensive statement on ecology in Judaism for *Faith in Conservation*, 2003, from which these extracts have been taken. Also at http://www.arcworld.org/faiths.asp?pageID=81

32. Hyder Ihsan Mahasneh is a biologist and Islamic scholar and was the first African head of the Kenya National Parks Service. He was appointed by the Muslim World League to compile this paper for *Faith in Conservation*, 2003. Also at http://www.arcworld.org/faiths.asp?pageID=75

33. From the Sikh faith statement compiled by Sri Akhal Takhat Sahib under the guidance of Sri Singh Sahib Manjit Singh, the Jathedar of Anandapur, for *Faith in Conservation*: 2003, pp. 132 and 134.

34. From the Hindu faith statement written for *Faith in Conservation*, 2003, which consists of three distinct sections reflecting the major strands within Vedic (Hindu) thought – these quotations are from the statement based on the comments by: Swami Vibudhesha Teertha, Acharya of Madhvacarya Vaishnavas, Udupi, Central Advisory Committee Member of the Visva Hindu Parishad.
    From *Faith in Conservation*: 2003, pp. 91 and 93, also at http://www.arcworld.org/faiths.asp?pageID=77 sourced 21 February 2009.

35. The Buddhist faith statement for the ARC was prepared by Kevin Fossey, Buddhist educator and representative of

Engaged Buddhism in Europe; Somdech Preah Maha Ghosananda, Patriarch of Cambodian Buddhism; His Excellency Sri Kushok Bakula, 20th Reincarnation of the Buddha's Disciple Bakula, head of Ladakhi Buddhism, and initial rebuilder of Mongolian Buddhism; and Venerable Nhem Kim Teng, Patriarch of Vietnamese Buddhism: From *Faith in Conservation*: 2003, pp.77, 78. Also at http://www.arcworld.org/faiths.asp?pageID=66

36. From the statement compiled under the guidance of Sri Singh Sahib Manjit Singh, the Jathedar of Anandapur, who is one of the five spiritual and temporal heads of Sikhism; and Sri Akhal Takhat Sahib, his deputy. From *Faith in Conservation* 2003, p.141 and at
http://www.arcworld.org/faiths.asp?pageID=73

37. Alliance of Religions and Conservation, (ARC), vision and strategy at http://www.arcworld.org/about.asp?pageID=4 8 December 2008

38. Rowan Williams Archbishop of Canterbury, cited at website of the Shri Venkateswara(Balaji) Temple of UK

39. Alliance of Religions and Conservation,
http://www.arcworld.org/news.asp?pageID=146#top 23 November 2009

40. James Lovelock, 2006, p. 146.

41. Barry Cottrell, 2008, p107.

42. James Lovelock, 2006, p. 8.

43. Colin Tudge, 2004.

44. The Food Programme BBC Radio 4 18 February 2007 Colin Tudge.

45. The most Revd. and Rt. Hon. Dr. John Sentamu 97th Archbishop for York and Primate of England sermon on inauguration as Archbishop of York, 2005, York Minster http://www.dioceseofyork.org.uk/files/adminandinfo393-1.doc sourced 6 April 2009.

Chapter 2

1. Petrusca Clarkson, 2002, p 236 cited by Penelope Hill 2006. Petrusca Clarkson was an eminent psychotherapist and writer of recommended textbooks who took her own life in Amsterdam in May 2006 age 58.
2. Jonathan Sacks, 2005, p. 273.
3. For consistency the Greek spellings are used throughout, the Roman equivalents often having a different spelling e.g. Cheiron.
4. Michael Lerner, 1998, p.123.
5. The interested reader is referred for follow up to the work of such experts in the field as Micrea Eliade and Michael Harner.
6. Remen, May, Young, and Berland, (1985), 5 (1) pp. 84-93.
7. Although I believe that the situation was actually no better then: there was simply less media exposure.
8. 'Briefing Paper, Hunger on the Rise: Soaring Prices add 75 Million People to Global Hunger Rolls,' Food and Agriculture Organization 17 September 2008, cited at http://www.bread.org/learn/hunger-basics/hunger-facts-international.html sourced 17 February 2009
9. Black, Robert, Morris, Saul, & Jennifer Bryce, (2003), vol. 361: pp. 2226-2234. 2003.
10. http://nobelprize.org/nobel_prizes/peace/laureates/1989/lama-acceptance.html
Sourced 19 February 2009
11. Nick Clegg in *Guardian Unlimited*, 2006. 'Queen's speech: legislation as a proxy for governing; we are facing a sixth immigration bill, an eighth terrorism bill and a 23rd justice bill. This is frenzied law-making.'He went on to say: 'Since 1997, the Labor government has passed over 114,000 pages of legislation, and...[the November 2006 Queen's Speech]...offered thousands of pages more.' At http://commentisfree.guardian.co.uk/nick_clegg/2006/11/po

st_641.html sourced 17 February 2009. As to which country is the safest in the world it really does depend on what criteria are used to measure 'safety.' Googling will bring up many different answers more amusing than useful!!

12. Senator Barack Obama, 2006.
13. American natural historian and philosopher, essayist and poet.
14. Henri Nouwen, 1994, p. 83.
15. Malcolm Langford, 2000. Langford draws much of his inspiration from Henri Nouwen.
16. Ian McEwan, 2001.
17. Jonathan Sacks, *The Times,* 5 January 2008, Count your Blessings and Begin to Change your Life.
18. The theory of memes is a scientific theory in its infancy and quite unproven, unlike the scientific knowledge about genes and how they affect inheritance that is now well researched and understood. The meme, a term attributed to Richard Dawkins the evolutionary biologist, may be defined as a unit of cultural information that, the theory goes, can be transferred from one mind to another, its survival through generations depending at least partly on its appeal to human psychology and basic human needs. It is said that by a process of unconscious evolution this process can shape the progress of a culture. But see Iain McGilchrist, *The Master and his Emissary,* (Newhaven and London: Yale University Press, 2009) Chapter 7, 'Imitation and the Evolution of Culture' for a critical discussion on memes.
19. Judith Thompson and James O'Dea, 2005.
20. Alastair McIntosh, 2004, p. 183.
21. Anne Frank, 1993.
22. Anthony de Mello, 1992, p.182.
23. Thomas Merton, 1972
24. Senator Barack Obama, 2006.
25. Anthony de Mello, 'A visualization prayer / meditation, An

Excerpt from *Contact with God: Retreat Conferences,'*
http://www.katinkahesselink.net/christianity/Anthony-de-
mello-prayer.html sourced 19 February 2009.

26. Alastair V Campbell, 1986 p. 38.

27. Henri J. M. Nouwen, 1994, pp. 88, 89.

28. Adherents.com for National & World Religion statistics -
Church Statistics - World Religions at
http://www.adherents.com/ for national and world religion
statistics, 23 November 2009.

29. Peter Challen and Rodney Shakespeare 2002, see Note 3 in
Preface.

30. Martin Luther King Jnr., Nobel Peace Prize Acceptance
Speech 10th December 1964 http://nobelprize.org/nobel_
prizes/peace/laureates/1964/king-acceptance.html
sourced 19 February 2009.

31. Martin Luther King Jnr., Nobel Peace Prize lecture December
11 1964

32. Holy Bible, RSV, 1 Corinthians 13:4-8.

33. cited by Satish Kumar 2005.

34. Patanjali is a pseudonym, and the name may belong to
several individuals. The yoga sutras are considered to be the
product of several writers over a period of several centuries.

35. Arun Gandhi with his wife Sunanda founded The Gandhi
Institute for Non-Violence in 1991 through which they keep
his grandfather's traditions alive. See Consul B. John Zavrel,
'Arun Gandhi: The Pursuit of Truthfulness,' for more material
on truth and peace and love at
http://www.meaus.com/arun_gandhi.htm   sourced   19
February 2009.

36. Attributed to Charles Carver, professor of psychology at
University of Miami and a leading researcher studying the
Thriving Response, cited in http://www.intuitive-connec-
tions.net/2004/book-beethoven.htm Book Summary by
Clayton Montez, Atlantic University, of *The Beethoven Factor*

by Paul Pearsall, *The Beethoven Factor: The new Positive Psychology of Hardiness, Happiness, Healing and Hope* (Hampton Roads Publishing, 2003), sourced 19 February 2009

37. Conti O'Hare 2002, pp. 39-42.
38. David Smith, 1999 cited in O'Hare 2002 p. 41.
39. Michael Mayne, 2006), p. 13.
40. Sacks (2005) Chapter 20: On Dreams and Responsibilities.
41. Inspired by and attributed to Janine Beynus author of *Biomimicry* and Elisabet Sahtouris, in *The Path to Living Economies – A Collaborative Working Document of the Social Venture Network* page 11 of 40, from The People-Centered Development Forum, a forum 'Seeking a just, inclusive, and sustainable world that works for all,' at page 11 of 40: http://www.pcdf.org/SVN_Living_Economies.htm sourced 15 March 2009.
42. Senator Barack Obama, 2006.
http://www.sojo.net/index.cfm?action=news.display
_article&mode=C&NewsID=5454 sourced 19 February 2009.

Chapter 3

1. George Bernard Shaw
2. Barack Obama 2006.
3. See Preface note 3. Attributed to Peter Challen and Rodney Shakespeare.
4. His Holiness the Dalai Lama, 2000, p. 11.
5. Friedrich Nietzsche, used a few times through his literature, for example spoken by the madman in *The Gay Science* (Philosophical Classics) Friedrich Nietzsche with Thomas Common (Translator)(New York: Dover Publications, 2006).
6. From *The Collected Works of C G Jung,* 1970 pp304-305 as quoted in Claire Dunn: 2000 p.199.
7. Martin Luther King, Nobel Peace Prize Lecture December 11 1964

8. Alexander Pope English Writer, (1688-1744) from *Part II* of *An Essay on Criticism.*

9. Johann Christoph Arnold, 1998 pp. 16, 22, 27.

10. Desmond Tutu, January 2006, reported by Waveney Ann Moore in the St. Petersburg Times, sourced 6 April 2009 at http://www.sptimes.com/2006/01/20/news_pf/Tampabay/Tutu__Forgive_and_beg.shtml

11. Fetzer Institute, http://www.fetzer.org/ sourced 21 February 2009 (nothing at all to do with Fetzer Wines of California, but the latter do have a wonderful website and are justly proud of their sustainable and organic achievements!).

12. Friedrich Nietzsche from *Die Frohliche Wissenschaft, The Gay Science* (1882, 1887) paragraph 125 Walter Kaufmann ed. (New York: Vintage, 1974), pp.181-82, sourced http://www.fordham.edu/halsall/mod/nietzsche-madman.html 25 March 2009.

13. Holy Bible, RSV John 14.27 'Peace I leave with you; my peace I give to you; not as the world gives do I give to you.'

14. Satish Kumar, 2005.

15. John Sentamu in his inauguration sermon in November 2005.

16. Dr Mervyn Fernando, in *Violence and the Rising Tide of Globalisation – a Teilhardian Perspective;*

17. Aldous, Huxley,1970, p. vii.

18. Richard Dawkins and Steven Pinker, 1999.

19. Dawkins, Richard, 2006.

20. See for example: Anthony Flew, 2007, John C Lennox, 2007, Williams, Peter S, 2009, Alister McGrath, 2005, Alister McGrath and Joanna Collicutt McGrath, 2007.

21. His Holiness the Dalai Lama, 2000, p. 12.

22. Williams, Peter S, 2009, p. 31.

23. W.E.B. Du Bois, 2005.

24. Eboo Patel, 2007a.

25. Eboo Patel, 2007b.

26. Interfaith Youth Core www.ifyc.org sourced 6 April 2009.
27. Eboo Patel, 2007b, p. 61.
28. International Committee for the Peace Council, www.peace-council.org sourced 21 February 2009
29. Ibid.
30. International Interfaith Organisations Network at http://interfaithorganisations.net/member-organisations/ 6 April 2009.
31. The Council for a Parliament of the World's Religions (CPWR) a member of the International Interfaith Organisations Network
32. John Sentamu inauguration sermon 2005.
33. From *Sanhedrin* tractate of the Talmud cited in Henri J. M. Nouwen, 1994, p. 81.
34. A study by sociologists at Duke University and the University of Arizona, reported at http://news.softpedia.com/news/Loneliness-Is-Getting-Rampant-in-America-27518.shtml 6 April 2009, also Cited in Chuck Collins, We're in This Together, Sojourners Magazine, February 2009 (Vol. 38, No. 2, pp. 27) http://www.sojo.net/index.cfm?action=magazine.article&issue=soj0902&article=we-re-in-this-together 6 April 2009.
35. Henri Nouwen, 1994, p. 84.
36. Ibid., p. 92.
37. The United Methodist Church website
38. RSV Hebrews 13.2,
39. For more on Islamic hospitality see *Hospitality: A Worldwide Islamic Tradition* 2005.
40. Sikhnet, Sharing the Sikh Experience, http://www.sikhnet.com/news/united-sikh-association-serves-langar-nyu-students 6 April 2009.
41. Mahabharata 12.374 cited at http://hinduism.iskcon.com/lifestyle/810.htm 25 March 2009.
42. On the Move International, The Free Barbeque Ministry.

43. Martin Graham, 2006.
44. Peter Selby, 1983. The Right Reverend Dr Peter Stephen Maurice Selby retired Bishop of Worcester became the new President of the UK National Council for Independent Monitoring Boards for prisons as from January 1 2008.
45. Ibid.,1983, p.7.
46. J. J. Means, Spring 2002, Vol. 56, No. 1
47. Faith and Community Voices against Poverty, Living Wage Campaign, http://letjusticeroll.org/news/00936-churches-push-10-minimum-wage-2010 sourced 23 November 2009, responding to the challenge of the prophet Amos 5.24, RSV, "But let justice roll down like waters, and righteousness like an overflowing stream."
48. From the Hindu faith statement written for *Faith in Conservation*, p. 96. Also at http://www.arcworld.org/faiths.asp?pageID=77 sourced 21 February 2009. See also Chapter 1.
49. The Golden Rule of Zoroastrianism.
50. Jim Wallis, 2008, Chapter 12, p. 232.
51. http://news.bbc.co.uk/1/hi/special_report /1998/10/98/world_war_i/197627.stm Adapted from the book *Christmas Truce* by Malcolm Brown and Shirley Seaton sourced 6 April 2009.
52. Thomas Merton: 1972, p. 122.

Chapter 4

1. O'Dell, Larry, 2007.
2. Tony Blair, 2006.
3. William Lloyd Garrison, 1854.
4. Holy Bible, Revised Standard Version Matthew 5.6.
5. Rowan Williams, full transcript at http://www.archbishopof-canterbury.org/557
6. Barack Obama, Canongate Books, 2008, p. 67, 68.
7. Martin Luther King, Nobel Lecture 11 December 1964.

8. John Donne seventeenth century English poet died 1631. Famous words of prose taken from the final lines of his 1624 Meditation 17, from Devotions Upon Emergent Occasions.

9. Holy Bible, Revised Standard Version, 1 Corinthians 12. 25,26.

10. From Baha'u'llah's Revelation, as he enjoins his followers to develop a sense of world citizenship and a commitment to stewardship of the earth. From *Faith in Conservation*, 2003, p. 72.

11. Pierre Teilhard de Chardin, *The Phenomenon of Man* was written to understand what is happening to man and to help others understand.

12. Pierre Teilhard de Chardin, 1969.

13. Martin Luther King, Nobel Lecture 11th December 1964.

14. Viktor Frankl, 2004, p. 24.

15. Sacks, 2005, p. 3.

16. John Singleton, 2004.

17. From *The Collected Works of C G Jung, vol. 11* 1969, p. 459. as cited in Claire Dunn, 2000, p.199.

18. From *C J Jung Letters volume 2*, 1953, p. 316 cited in *Clare Dunn,* 2000, p.199.

19. Carl Rogers, 1961, p. 27.

20. http://www.itp.edu/about/carl_rogers.php sourced 25 February 2009 in site of Institute of Transpersonal Psychology, which defines Transpersonal Psychology briefly as: 'the extension of psychological studies into consciousness studies, spiritual inquiry, body-mind relationships and transformation.' Other pioneers of transpersonal psychology include: Aldous Huxley, James, Carl Jung and Maslow as well as Rogers. See also http://www.bapca.org.uk/ British Association for Person Centred Approach – and http://www.adpca.org/ site for The Association for the Development of the Person Centered Approach, an international network, both of which support and promote Carl

Rogers methodology.

21. Carl Rogers, 1980, p. 356.

22. D. Sawyer, 2002, p. 95, cited at http://www.itp.edu/about/aldous_huxley.php sourced 25 February 2009.

23. Peter Selby, 1983.

24. The use of 'in mind' for 'remembered' and 'out of mind' for 'forgotten' date back to at least the 13th century. The earliest printed citation of a link with memory and the sight of something is in John Heywood's *Woorkes. A dialogue conteynyng prouerbes and epigrammes*, 1562, as reprinted by the Spenser Society, 1867: 'Out of sight out of minde.' From http://www.phrases.org.uk/meanings/274400.html author Gary Martin sourced 26 March 2009.

25. Humane Society of the United States.

26. Farm Aid, Keep America Growing.

27. Channel 4 'Chicken Run' January 2008.

28. Channel 4 'Jamie's Fowl Dinners' January 2008

29. Brian Skoloff, 2007.

30. Presidential Candidates Avoid Talk Of Water Shortage,' 2007.

31. Of doubtful origin but attributed to Albert Einstein

32. The 14th Dalai Lama in his Acceptance Speech for the 1989 Nobel Peace Prize.

33. The 14th Dalai Lama in his Nobel Lecture December 11th 1989.

34. Statement by Nobel Laureates on the occasion of the one-hundredth anniversary of the Nobel Prize, Stockholm, December 11, 2001.

35. Gary Snyder, at http://www.tomradulovich.com/?p=55 26 March 2009.

36. Trevor Carolan, 1996.

37. M. Scott Peck, 1990a, p.17.

Chapter 5

1. P. Palmer, 1987, p.15 cited in David Clark, 2005, p. 11.
2. M. Scott Peck, 1990a, pp.19, 20.
3. http://www.lexva.com/ sourced 26 February 2009.
4. 6867 at the last census in 2000 http://factfinder.census.gov sourced 6 February 2009.
5. Danny and Polly Duncan Collum, 2006 (Vol. 35, No. 1, pp. 12-19).
6. Ibid.
7. Amital Etzioni blog 8:14 AM PDT, July 27, 2007 A Duty to assist? http://www.amazon.com/Spirit-Community-Amitai-Etzioni/dp/0671885243 sourced 25 February 2009.
8. David Clark, 2005, p. xvii. All Christian Church leaders particularly should read this important and groundbreaking Christian perspective on community.
9. Sacks, *To Heal a Fractured World,* 2005, p. 54.
10. M. Scott Peck, 1990a, p.59.
11. Alastair McIntosh, 2004, p. 284.
12. Ibid., p. 4
13. Ibid., p. 117.
14. www.globaljusticemovement.net/home/comparisons.htm 5 Jan 2007.
15. His Holiness the Dalai Lama, *Ancient Wisdom Modern World: Ethics for the New Millennium* (London: Abacus, Time Warner Books UK, 2000), p.192.
16. Association of Waldorf Schools of North America, AWSNA, http://www.whywaldorfworks.org/ sourced 24 November 2009.
17. David Clark, *Breaking the Mould of Christendom – Kingdom Community, Diaconal Church and the Liberation of the Laity* (Peterborough: Epworth, 2005) p. 38.
18. Alastair McIntosh, *Soil and Soul: People versus Corporate Power* (London: Aurum Press, 2004), p. 4.
19. Ibid., p. 146.

20. Ibid., p. 19.
21. Ibid., p. 214.
22. Ibid., p284.
23. M. Scott Peck, 1990a, Chapter XI
24. Alastair McIntosh, 2004, p.176.
25. Robert Putnam, Lewis Feldstein and Donald Cohen, 2005.
26. McIntosh, 2004, The Eigg story beginning at Part Two, Chapter 13, p. 131.
27. Michael Mayne, *The Enduring Melody* (London: Darton Longman and Todd, 2006) p. 154.
28. Ibid., p. 151.
29. Dr J. E. Mervyn Fernando, lecture, *Violence and the Rising Tide of Globalisation – a Teilhardian Perspective.*
30. I am grateful to Canon Peter Challen for his input into this debate-taken from personal dialogue with permission.
31. Jonathan Sacks, 2005, pp.108, 109.
32. Teilhard de Chardin, 1970, p.95 cited in Mervyn Fernando, *Violence and the Rising Tide of Globalisation – a Teilhardian perspective.*
33. Mervyn Fernando, *Violence and the Rising Tide of Globalisation – a Teilhardian perspective.*
34. Ibid.
35. George Simpson, 1937, cited in David Clark, 2005, p.11.
36. M. Scott Peck, 1990a, p. 325.

Chapter 6

1. Greenpeace website.
2. Satish Kumar, 2005.
3. Holy Bible, RSV, 1 Timothy 6.10
4. Alastair McIntosh, 2004, p. 4.
5. Ibid., Chapter 14 et. seq.
6. Ibid., p.161.
7. World Bank poverty statistics available for 2005 as at March 2009.

8. Center for Disease Control and Prevention, statistics at http://www.cdc.gov/obesity/data/index.html

9. Statistics on obesity, physical activity and diet: England, January 2008

10. Michael Schluter and John Ashcroft, Editors, 2005, p. 217.

11. *Aristotle Politics*, translated by Ernest Barker Revised R F Stalley 1998, 1.9 1257a 5 p.26.

12. Ibid., 1258a 35 p.30.

13. Based on the principle of global justice taken from the five principles of the Global Justice Movement at www.globaljusticemovement.net/home/principles.htm 3 March 2009.

14. Hazel Henderson, 2001, cited in *The Path to Living Economies – a collaborative Working Document of the Social Ventures Network* at http://www.pcdf.org/SVN_Living_Economies.htm

15. Robert F. Kennedy, 18 March 1968.

16. Paul Hawken and Amory and T. Hunter Lovins,1999, p. 52 cited in The Path to Living Economies – a collaborative Working Document of the Social Ventures Network at http://www.pcdf.org/SVN_Living_Economies.htm

17. Attributed to Janine Benyus at a Bioneers conference – from a Note from the Author Elisabet Sahtouris, 2000).

18. Lord Polonius in Shakespeare's *Hamlet*, 1603.

19. See for example Darryl Schoon, 2008.

20. Cited on the Forum for Stable Currencies website

21. Senate Document 23, 1939 http://www.uhuh.com/unreal/lincoln.htm 3 March 2009.

22. Bernard Lietaer, 2001.

23. Edgar S Cahn, 2000, p. 68.

24. Bernard Lietaer, 2001.

25. Bernard Lietaer, 1997.

26. The Campaign for Interest-Free Money at http://www.interestfreemoney.org/index.htm 3 March 2009.

27. http://www.monies.cc/ 3 March 2009

28. David Korten, *Living Economies for a Living Planet*.
29. Peter Challen, 2005.
30. Ibid.
31. M. Scott Peck, 1990b, p. 249.
32. Anita Roddick, 2001.
33. Alastair McIntosh, p. 280
34. Holy Bible, RSV, Joshua chapters 13 to 21
35. Ibid, Leviticus 25.
36. Ibid., Lev 25.10
37. Ibid., Jeremiah 31.17
38. The Rt. Reverend James Jones, Bishop of Liverpool, 2005, p. 11.
39. http://www.globaljusticemovement.net/admin/news.htm   3 March 2009 .
40. Robert Ashford and Rodney Shakespeare, 1999.
41. Rodney Shakespeare and Peter Challen, 2002.
42. Michael Schluter and John Ashcroft Editors, 2005, p. 207.
43. http://www.pcdf.org/SVN_Living_Economies.htm and http://www.pcdf.org/living_economies/ for David Korten essay "Living Economies for a Living Planet. With further links to extensive resources
44. Social Ventures Network - Living Economies – The Path to Living Economies
www.pcdf.org/SVN_Living_Economies.htm 28 March 2009
45. Ibid., Social Ventures Network p. 6 of 40. 15 Jan 2006.
46. http://www.lets-linkup.com/080-All%20About%20LETS.htm and
http://www.lets-linkup.com/71-USA.htm 3 March 2009.
47. See for example: Bernard Lietaer, *The Future of Money – Creating New Wealth, Work and a Wiser World*, and Thomas H. Greco, *Money:* 2001.
48. A Brief History of the Credit Union Movement, at http://www.abcul.org/lib/liDownload/317/ABCUL%20History%20Of%20Credit%20Unions.pdf 3 March 2009.

49. Korten sourced in Social Ventures Network - Living Economies – The Path to Living Economies www.pcdf.org/SVN_Living_Economies.htm 10/40 ref 15 sourced 3 March 2009.
50. James Buchan, 2001, p. 48, where he describes the painting by Rembrandt entitled Judas, Repentant, Returning the Pieces of Silver and how it captures the 'strangeness of money' and the devastating realization by Judas that for…pieces of silver he has brought about the assassination of Jesus Christ. Painted 1629 – one of Rembrandt's early paintings.
51. Canon Revd. Peter Challen, SLIM annual lecture 2005.
52. Aldous Huxley, *Island,* 1976, p.164.

Chapter 7

1. Stanley W. Jackson, 2001, pp. 1-36. Based on Presidential Address delivered at the seventy-third annual meeting of the American Association for the History of Medicine, Bethesda, Md., 19th May 2000. Dr Jackson died on 24th May 2000.
2. Norman Shealy and Dawson Church, 2008.
3. Spirituality is distinguished from religion in that the latter connotes the organized expression of faith and as such has a more restrictive application in the current context - see Satish Kumar Schumacher lecture *Spiritual Imperatives,* 30 Oct. 2004.
4. Others may use the Oath or Prayer of Maimonides, the medieval Jewish Rabbi, physician and philosopher. His healing was influential in the Islamic world.
5. Eric J. Cassell, 1978, p.48, attributed to the Spanish medical historian Pedro Lain Entralgo.
6. Caroline Myss, (medical intuitive, author of best selling *Defy Gravity: Healing Beyond the Bounds of Reason,* 2009.
7. Michael Kearney, 2000, p. 31. A very much more detailed and thoroughly researched exploration of the Hippocratic and Asklepian healing methods and their proposed integration

into modern medical care, specifically that of palliative cancer care, is included in this book, to which we shall return later.

8. Consolatory literature is examined further in a later chapter on the healing power of creativity.

9. Leslie D. Weatherhead, 1951, reprinted with further revision 1955, p. 90, and Chapter 2 in Section 1, a detailed chapter on Healing in the Early Church.

10. Ibid., 1955, p. 95.

11. 1624-1689.

12. *Chambers Biographical Dictionary* (Edinburgh: W & R Chambers, 1990).

13. Asa Briggs, 1984, p. 378.

14. Stanley W Jackson, 2001, pp. 10-18.

15. Sigmund Freud was the Austrian founder of Psychoanalysis, and he developed the process of conversational free association to replace hypnosis and the concept of the Id, Ego and Superego. He met much opposition for his theories that dreams, like neuroses, are disguised manifestations of repressed sexual desires.

16. C. G. Jung, 1995, pp.154-156.

17. Carl G Jung, Fundamental Questions of Psychotherapy, in *The Collected Works of C G Jung*, 1953-1979), vol. 16: 111-25, on p. 116, cited in Stanley W. Jackson, 2001, p. 21.

18. Henri J M Nouwen, 1994, pxvi.

19. Alfred Adler, 1930, p.11. Cited in Leslie D. Weatherhead, *Psychology Religion and Healing* (London: Hodder and Stoughton, 1955) p. 271.

20. Claire Dunne, 2000, p.149.

21. All thoughts on the attitude to religion of Jung, Freud and Adler are sourced from Leslie D. Weatherhead: *Psychology Religion and Healing* (London: Hodder and Stoughton, 1955) from where this Adler quotation also taken at p.278.

22. Eric J Cassell, 1978.

23. Eric J Cassell, 1991, Preface to first edition in second edition p.v.
24. Ibid., p. vi.
25. http://www.thehastingscenter.org/About/Default.aspx 31 March 2009 'Since 1969, Hastings Center projects have been at the forefront of explicating ethical problems raised by the rapidly changing fields of medicine and biology, and influencing policy and scholarship.'
26. Eric J Cassell, 2004, Preface to second edition, xi- xv.
27. Cassell 1991 Preface to first edition in second edition, p. ix.
28. Cassell 2004 Preface to second edition, p. xiv.
29. Cassell 1991 Preface to first edition in second edition, p. ix.
30. Leslie D Weatherhead, 1955, p. 482.
31. Weatherhead led the City Temple church from 1936-1960. See http://www.city-temple.com/History.asp There is a Healing and Counseling Centre at St Marylebone Parish Church opened 1987 combining innovative health care through an NHS doctor's surgery offering many complementary therapies http://www.stmarylebone.org.uk/HandC01.htm
32. Leslie D. Weatherhead, 2008.
33. Larry Dossey, 1993.
34. Michael Kearney, 2000, in Foreword by Balfour Mount p viii.
35. Sam H.Ahmedzai (1997) 'Five years: five threads' (editorial, *Progress in Palliative Care*, 5(6), 235-7
36. C. Farsides and E Garrard (1997) "Resourse allocation in palliative care," in *New Themes in Palliative Care*, D Clark, J Hockley, S Ahmedzai (eds). (Open University Press Philadelphia) pp 49-59.
37. Michael Lerner, 1996.
38. This is explored in much more detail in Michael Kearney, 2000. Now see *Place of Healing: Working With Nature And Soul At The End* (Spring Journal paperback, August 27, 2009)
39. Michael Kearney, 1996, cited in Michael Kearney, *A Place of Healing*, 2000, foreword by Balfour Mount p. iv.

40. Cecil Helman, 2006, p. 5.

41. Ted Kaptchuk and Michael Croucher, 1986, pp. 26, 37, cited in Michael Mayne, 1987, p. 38.

42. David J. Hufford, '*An analysis of the field of spirituality, religion and health.*' See www.metanexus.net/tarp/pdf/TARP-Hufford.pdf [PDF, 72 pages], also at http://www.templeton-advancedresearchprogram.com/pdf/TARP-Hufford.pdf accessed 9 March 2009

   Founded in 1997, Metanexus is a global interdisciplinary institute that 'promotes the transdisciplinary approach to the most profound questions of nature, culture, and the human person. Metanexus serves an ever-growing network of locally-acting, globally connected scholars, researchers, teachers, students, and ordinary citizens committed to exploring our world from a rich diversity of perspectives.'

43. For information see for example Presbyterian Health, Education and Welfare Association, http://www.pcusa.org/nationalhealth/parishnursing/ 'an idea born out of the understanding of the healing ministry of the church and the need to return to health care that focuses on the whole person to emphasize wellness, disease prevention, and health promotion.' Sourced 23 November 2009.

44. Joan Borysenko, 'Putting the Soul Back in Medicine' article sourced at http://joanborysenko.com/html/news_artcl4.html 18 November 2005 now available as chapter 4 in *Healing our Planet, Healing Ourselves: The Power of Change within to Change the World,* at *http://www.healingourplanet.com/*

45. Integrative Medical Clinic, Santa Rosa, http://www.imcsr.com/ sourced 23 November 2009.

46. http://www.medicine.mcgill.ca/newsletter/autumn-2004.pdf McGill *in Focus, Medicine Edition,* Autumn 2004 Newsletter of McGill University Faculty of Medicine Montreal, article, 'A Curriculum for the New Century: Donald Boudreau's

Legacy,' accessed 11 February 2009.

Chapter 8

1. From Larry Dossey front cover endorsement of Norman Shealy and Dawson Church, 2008.
2. Cecil Helman, 2006, p. 77.
3. World Health Organization, The Promotion and Development of Traditional Medicine (*WHO Technical Report Series 622*) (Geneva: WHO 1978), cited in Cecil Helman, 2006, p.163.
4. See chapter 4 note 6, how Barack Obama realized he diminished himself by not having empathic regard for his grandfather's needs, and how this same understanding would serve him well in the White House
5. Barack Obama , 2006.
6. Term attributed to The Honourable Sir Maxwell MacLeod by Alastair McIntosh See chapter 2.
7. David J. Hufford, *An Analysis of the Field of Spirituality, Religion and Health (S/RH)*, paper for the Metanexus Institute.
8. Andrew Rissik, a review in The Times of Ted Kaptchuk and Michael Croucher, 1986, based on the documentary television series of the same name, cited in Michael Mayne, 1987, p. 38.
9. Viktor Frankl, (1905 to 1997), 1973, p.16, latest edition, Souvenir Press Ltd (April 19, 2004). A 2008 Kindle edition is also available.
10. Story related by Larry Dossey, 2000, p. 53, followed by critical analysis of non local studies and positive responses obtained from non local prayer and healing intentions.
11. David Aldridge, 1993, cited in Michael Lerner, 1996, Chapter 9 p. 135. This is an excellent and comprehensive textbook in this field.
12. Michael Mayne, 1987, p. 22.
13. Michael Mayne, 2006, pp. 236, 238.

14. Larry Dossey, *Healing Words,*1997. My copy was the 1993 first edition.

15. See his website at http://www.dosseydossey.com/larry/default.html 10 March 2009.

16. Larry Dossey, 1989.

17. Definitions of the 3 Eras taken from Larry Dossey, article, *The Forces of Healing: Reflections on Energy, Consciousness, and the Beef Stroganoff Principle,* revised from the keynote address and welcome originally presented at Exploring the Forces of Healing, the Second Annual *Alternative Therapies* Symposium; April 1997; Orlando, Fla.

18. Larry Dossey, 2000, also a HarperCollins e-book; 1 edition July 24, 2007)

19. Professor of Psychiatry & Behavioral Sciences and Associate Professor of Medicine, Dr. Koenig is founder and former director of Duke University's Center for the Study of Religion, Spirituality and Health, and is founding Co-Director of the current Center for Spirituality, Theology and Health at Duke University's Medical Center, http://www.spiritualityandhealth.duke.edu/sth/index.html sourced 10 March 2009.

20. Harold Koenig and Malcolm McConnell, 2001.

21. Harold G. Koenig, 2004.

22. See David J. Hufford, 'An analysis of the field of spirituality, religion and health,' and Metanexus, note to Chapter 7.

23. Jon Kabat-Zinn, in foreword to M. Lerner *Choices in Healing,* 1996, p. xvii.

24. Larry Dossey, 1993, p. xv Preface.

25. Larry Dossey, 1997, p.44.

26. See for example Michael Mayne, 1995.

27. Larry Dossey, Article, *The Forces of Healing: Reflections on Energy, Consciousness, and the Beef Stroganoff Principle,* Revised from the keynote address and welcome originally

presented at Exploring the Forces of Healing, the Second Annual *Alternative Therapies* Symposium; April 1997; Orlando, Fla.

28. J. J. Means, 1997, vol. 51 No. 3.

29. Larry Dossey interview with Dennis Hughes on the Role of Prayer and Meditation in Medicine, *Share Guide: The Holistic Health Magazine and Resource Directory*, at http://www.shareguide.com/Dossey.html sourced 20 March 2009.

30. E. J. Cassell, 1982, 306:639-45.

31. Whole Person Care Working Group, 'Spirituality and Health: Developing a Shared Vocabulary,' in *OMNI: Journal of Spirituality and Religious Care*, 2003, at http://www.omc.ca/omni/archives/000040.html posted 30 September 2003, sourced 23 November 2009.

32. Chapter 4, Hope for our Destiny: a New Era of Responsibility.

33. Conti-O'Hare, Marion, 2002, pp. 141, 144.

34. Conti-O'Hare, website, http://www.drconti-online.com/ Question: How has trauma affected my life? Uncover: What can I remember about the major instances or patterns of my personal or professional trauma? Experience: What are my feelings about these events or patterns? Search for Meaning: What do these feelings and experiences mean to me? Transform and Transcend: I change my world view by resolving trauma and becoming a wounded healer.

35. Ibid.

36. J. J. Means, 2002, Vol. 56, No. 1.

37. Fetzer Institute.

38. http://www.psr.org/documents/history.pdf achievements sourced 9 March 2009

39. McGill University Faculty of Medicine Montreal, article, 'A Curriculum for the New Century: Donald Boudreau's Legacy,' in Newsletter *Focus, Medicine Edition*, Autumn 2004.

40. http://www.mcgill.ca/wholepersoncare/ 10 March 2009.

41. McGill University Faculty of Medicine Montreal, article, 'A Curriculum for the New Century: Donald Boudreau's Legacy,' in Newsletter *Focus, Medicine Edition*, Autumn 2004.

42. Gwish, http://www.gwish.org/ extract from their mission, Christina Puchalski, MD, MS, sourced 10 March 2009.

43. http://www.noetic.org/about.cfm 10 March 2009.

44. http://www.noetic.org/research/dh/faqs.html with detailed information and research results on distance healing, 10 March 2009.

45. Gwish, http://www.gwish.org/ survey conducted by Drs Puchalski and Cleary sourced 10 March 2009.

46. Larry Dossey 1997 and website.

47. Natalie Rogers, website at http://www.nrogers.com/ 10 March 2009

48. Stella Adler, American actress

Chapter 9

1. Dana Lynne Andersen, Californian spiritual artist who founded Awakening Arts Network, a global resource nexus connecting artists throughout the world who are engaged in creating art that is 'evolutionary' and 'transformative'. See http://www.awakeningarts.com/ sourced 29 November 2009.

2. Trungpa, C., 1996.

3. L'Arche International Communities. See
http://www.larche.org/home.en-gb.1.0.index.htm,
L'Arche USA at http://www.larche.org/usa-l-arche-in-your-region.en-gb.30.0.news.htm
and L'Arche UK at http://www.larche.org.uk/ sourced 23 April 2009.

4. Henri J. M. Nouwen, 1994, p. 3.

5. Ibid., p. 5.

6. Patience Wheatcroft, *The Times* on January 13th 2006 in an article entitled 'Bloodlust at the click of a Mouse.'

7. Ibid. Full story at http://www.skaiciumiestelis.lt/index.php?id=19&lang=lt. The work appeared in 2006 in the *Journal of Experimental Social Psychology.*

8. Consul B. John Zavrel, *Arun Gandhi: The Pursuit of Truthfulness,* on the Museum of European History, Clarence, New York site at http://www.meaus.com/arun_gandhi.htm sourced 25 November 2009. See also Arun Gandhi's own site at http://www.arungandhi.org/12.html 25 November 2009.

9. Review by Stephen A. Haines of the Canadian Edition of George Monbiot's *Heat,* 2007.

10. Anthony Storr, 1997, p. 1.

11. RSV 1 Samuel 16 v.14 and v. 23.

12. The therapeutic application of electricity to the body named after the Italian Luigi Galvani (now known as electrophysiology in medical terms).

13. Explored in depth in Paul Pearsall, 2003.

14. Sacks, 2005, p.222.

15. Don Campbell, 2002, p. 220.

16. Sacks (2005), p. 223.

17. Anthony Storr, 1997, p.126.

18. Don Campbell, 2008.

19. The Second Vatican Council, convened in 1959 by Pope John XXIII and concluded in 1965 under the direction of Pope Paul VI see http://www.vatican2voice.org/default.htm sourced 23 April 2009.

20. Campbell (2002) p. 104.

21. Ibid., p. 27.

22. Anthony Storr, 1997, p. 45.

23. Ibid., p. 48.

24. Allan Bloom, 1988, cited in Anthony Storr, 1997, p. 45.

25. Don Campbell, 2002, p. 222.

26. Michael Mayne, 2001, p. 15.

27. Irish dramatist, novelist, & poet (1854 - 1900) Said by the

character Basil Hallward, in *The Picture of Dorian Gray*, chapter 1 (1891).

28. Joel Metzger, *Sacred Mirrors: Discussing Transpersonal Art with Alex Grey*, from http://www.omplace.com/articles/SacredMirrors.html This interview was the first in a series with artists, created in association with the Institute of Noetic Sciences (IONS), for the Noetic Arts Program (NAP). These interviews present professional artists who are visionaries speaking about the growth of human consciousness though their art. See also www.alexgrey.com artist's website and http://www.noetic.org/main/SpecialInterest.cfm?p_style=1 sourced 23 April 2009.

29. See http://www.winston-churchill-leadership.com/winston-churchill-painting.html sourced 23 April 2009.

30. Conyers, Read, Presidential address delivered at the annual dinner of the American Historical Association on December 29, 1949: 'The Social Responsibilities of the Historian.'

31. Jonathan Sacks, 2005, p. 223.

32. Stanley W. Jackson, 2001, p. 8

33. Francesco Petrarca, *Letters of Old Age: Rerum senilium libri.* 2 volumes Translated Aldo S. Bernardo, Saul Levin and Reta A. Bernardo, 1992, 2: p. 381 (Sen. 10.4) cited in Stanley W. Jackson, 2001, p. 8.

34. Michael Mayne, 2001, p. 18.

35. Michael Mayne, 2006.

36. *The Times* Obituaries 4 November 2006

37. Danuta Kean, 2007

38. Helen Moore, *Art for Earth's Sake.*

39. George Monbiot, 'Civilisation ends with a shutdown of human concern. Are we there already?' 2007.

40. Abraham Maslow at http://www.abrahammaslow.net/more.html sourced 30 November 2009.

41. Rogers, Carl, 1962, p. 350.

42. Abreus, Jose Antonio,
    http://tipom.wordpress.com/2008/04/01/jose-antonio-abreus-
    acceptance-speech-of-the-venezuelan-branch-of-bnai-briths-
    human-rights-award/ sourced 12 March 2009, translation by
    Jose Bergher, Founder member of El Sistema - NYC

43. Helen Moore, *Art for Earth's Sake – a Manifesto.*

44. From Carl Rogers: 1961, Chapter 19. Written to encapsulate
    and develop the outcome of a conference in 1952 on
    Creativity sponsored by Ohio State University – for writer,
    dancer, musician, artist, educators in those fields and
    philosophers, psychiatrists and psychologists. Reprinted
    1990 p. 348.

45. Ibid p.349.

46. Jonathan Bate, 2001, p. 151 reviewed by John E. (Jack) Becker,
    1st September 2003, cited at
    http://www.cceia.org/resources/publications/to_be_read/
    834.html sourced 27 April 2009.

47. Graham Wallas, 1926.

48. Dean Keith Simonton, 1999. See also ch. 2 on Memes.

49. *Publishers Weekly* editorial review of Simonton *Origins of
    Genius* at http://www.amazon.com sourced 30 November
    2009.

50. Csikszentmihalyi Mihaly, *Creativity – Flow and the psychology
    of discovery and invention* (New York Harper Perennial) p. 6-7
    cited in Jenya Krein on Creativity: Theories, Beliefs, and
    Discoveries in *Speaking in Tongues Guided by Voices* at
    http://spintongues.msk.ru/CraneEng2.htm p. 11 sourced 25
    April 2009.

51. Kay Redfield Jamieson, 1993, p. 121. cited in Jackson lecture
    at p 35. Renowned clinical psychologist and author – sufferer
    of and expert on bipolar disorder.

52. Edward Adamson, *Art as Healing,* 1993, passage from his
    introduction. Adamson was Art Director at Netherne

Hospital (a psychiatric hospital) for some time.

53. Jane Piirto, Ph.D. *Metaphor and Image in Counseling the Talented*, http://talentdevelop.com/articles/Page133.html sourced 18 January 2010. Van Gogh
quotation also in Letter from Vincent van Gogh to Theo van Gogh, *Arles, 28 January 1889* cited at 'Van Gogh's Letters Unabridged and Annotated.'

54. Canon Peter Challen, South London Industrial Mission annual lecture 2005. This Mission closed in 2006, and is replaced by Mission in London's Economy, a London wide ecumenical Christian organization set up in 2005, http://www.mile.org.uk/ sourced 28 November 2009.
The Industrial Mission Association 'is an organization for lay and ordained people who want to be involved in, or to deepen their understanding of, the relationship between the Christian faith and the economic order....'

References

Abreus, Jose Antonio,
http://tipom.wordpress.com/2008/04/01/jose-antonio-abreus-acceptance-speech-of-the-venezuelan-branch-of-bnai-briths-human-rights-award/ sourced 12 March 2009, translation by Jose Bergher, Founder member of El Sistema – NYC.

Adamson, Edward, *Art as Healing*, published by Coventure, 1993, passage from his introduction.

Adherents.com for National & World Religion statistics - Church Statistics - World Religions at http://www.adherents.com/ for national and world religion statistics, 23 November 2009.

Adler, Alfred, *The Science of Living*, Allen and Unwin, 1930, p.11. Cited in Leslie D. Weatherhead, *Psychology Religion and Healing* (London: Hodder and Stoughton, 1955) p. 271.

Ahmedzai, Sam H., 'Five years: five threads' editorial, *Progress in Palliative Care*, 1997, 5(6), 235-7.

Aldridge, David, Is There Evidence for Spiritual Healing? *Advances* 9(4): 4(1993) cited in Michael Lerner, *Choices in Healing: Integrating the Best of Conventional and Complementary Approaches to Cancer*, Cambridge, Massachusetts and London, England: MIT Press, 1996, Chapter 9 p. 135.

Alliance of Religions and Conservation, (ARC), vision and strategy at http://www.arcworld.org/about.asp?pageID=4 8 December 2008 and
http://www.arcworld.org/news.asp?pageID=146#top
23 November 2009

Anthony Storr, *Music and the Mind*, London: Harper Collins, 1997, p. 1.

Aristotle Politics, Oxford World's Classics translated by Ernest Barker Revised R F Stalley, Oxford University Press: 1998, 1.9 1257a5, p.26 and 1258a35 p. 30.

Arnold, Johann Christoph, *The Lost Art of Forgiving – Stories of Healing from the Cancer of Bitterness* (Farmington, PA: The Plough Publishing House of the Bruderhof Foundation, 1998) pp. 16, 22, 27.

Ashford, Robert and Rodney Shakespeare, *Binary Economics: the New Paradigm* (Lanham MD: University Press of America, 1999).

Association for the Development of the Person Centered Approach, at http://www.adpca.org/

Awakening Arts Network, http://www.awakeningarts.com/ sourced 29 November 2009.

Bate, Jonathan, *The Song of the Earth,* Picador, 2001, p. 151 reviewed by John E. (Jack) Becker, 1st September 2003, cited at http://www.cceia.org/resources/publications/ to_be_read/834.html sourced 27 April 2009.

Benyus, Janine (attributed), at a Bioneers conference – from a Note from the Author Elisabet Sahtouris re her book *Earthdance: Living Systems in Evolution,* New York: Praeger, 2000, also at
  http://www.ratical.org/LifeWeb/Erthdnce/erthdnce.html

Black, Robert, Morris, Saul, & Jennifer Bryce. 'Where and Why are 10 Million Children Dying Every Year?' *The Lancet,* (2003), vol. 361: pp. 2226-2234. Cited at
  http://www.bread.org/learn/hunger-basics/hunger-facts-international.html sourced 17 February 2009

Blair, Tony, statement for *New Nation*, a newspaper aimed at the black community, on 27th November 2006 reported at: http://news.bbc.co.uk/1/hi/uk_politics/6185176.stm
  23 February 2009

Bloom, Allan, *The Closing of the American Mind*, Simon & Schuster; 1st Touchstone Ed edition (May 15, 1988) cited in

Anthony Storr, *Music and the Mind* (London: Harper Collins, 1997) p. 45.

Borysenko, Joan, 'Putting the Soul Back in Medicine' article sourced at http://joanborysenko.com/html/news_artcl4.html 18 November 2005 now available as chapter 4 in *Healing our Planet, Healing Ourselves: The Power of Change within to Change the World,* at *http://www.healingourplanet.com/*

Briggs, Asa, *A Social History of England,* Weidenfeld and Nicolson with Book Club Associates, 1984, p. 378.

Buchan, James, *Frozen Desire – the Meaning of Money*, New York: Welcome Rain Publishers, 2001, p. 48.

Cahn, Edgar S., *No More Throw-Away People: The Co-Production Imperative* Washington D.C.: Essential Books, 2000, p. 68.

Campbell, Alastair V, *Rediscovering Pastoral Care* (London: Darton, Longman and Todd, 1986) p. 38.

Campbell, Don, *Sound Spirit: Pathway to Faith* (Book & CD) (Paperback) Hay House 2008 more at http://www.mozart-effect.com/MoreOnTME/AboutDon/index.html

Campbell, Don, *The Mozart Effect: Tapping the Power of Music to Heal the Body, Strengthen the Mind, and Unlock the Creative Spirit* (London: Hodder and Stoughton, 2002) pp. 104, 220, 222.

Carey, Keith, *Hospitality: A Worldwide Islamic Tradition* 2005, at http://www.global-prayer-digest.org/monthdetails/2005/md-May-2005.asp by Keith Carey May 2005 sourced 2 February 2009.

Carolan, Trevor, *The Wild Mind of Gary Snyder*, http://www.shambhalasun.com/index.php?option=com_content&task=view&id=2071*Shambhala Sun,* May 1996, sourced 26 March 2009.

Carver, Charles, professor of psychology at University of Miami and a leading researcher studying the Thriving Response, attributed to, and cited in http://www.intuitive-connec-tions.net/2004/book-beethoven.htm Book Summary by

Clayton Montez, Atlantic University, of *The Beethoven Factor* by Paul Pearsall, *The Beethoven Factor: The new Positive Psychology of Hardiness, Happiness, Healing and Hope* (Hampton Roads Publishing, 2003), sourced 19 February 2009.

Cassell E. J., 'The nature of suffering and the goals of medicine,' *The New England Journal of Medicine,* 1982; 306:639-45 cited in http://www.omc.ca/omni/archives/000040.html Spirituality and Health: Developing a Shared Vocabulary, in *OMNI: Journal of Spirituality and Religious Care,* 2003, sourced 23 November 2009.

Cassell, *The Healers Art: A New Approach to the Doctor-Patient Relationship,* London: Penguin Books, 1978, p.48.

Cassell, *The Nature of Suffering and the Goal of Medicine* (New York 2004 Oxford University Press 2004) Preface to second edition, xi- xv.

Cassell, *The Nature of Suffering and the Goal of Medicine* (NY: Oxford University Press, first edition, 1991) Preface to first edition in second edition pp. v, vi, ix.

Centers for Disease Control and Prevention, statistics at http://www.cdc.gov/obesity/data/index.html

Challen, Peter and Rodney Shakespeare, *Seven Steps to Justice,* London: New European Publications, 2002, p. 1.

Challen, Peter, *A Ministry of Service in Economic Life – Servants, Pastors, Prophets and Fools - 60 years of servants seeking the economy that befits the Kin-dom of God,* South London Industrial Mission annual lecture 2005 sourced 4 December 2005, but no longer available at site, http://www.indus-trialmission.org.uk/cms/

Challen, Peter, *Exposing Corporate and Money Autocracy to Public Scrutiny as Major Threats to the Global Commons* at www.sustecweb.co.uk/past/sustec13-2/exposing _corporate.htm sourced 4 December 2005 (from Sustainable Economics vol. 13 no. 2 April 2005).

Chambers Biographical Dictionary, Edinburgh: W & R Chambers, 1990.

Christian Aid Report, The Climate of Poverty: Facts, Fears and Hope, May 2006.

Churchill, Winston, at http://www.winston-churchill-leadership .com/winston-churchill-painting.html sourced 23 April 2009.

City Temple church from 1936-1960. See http://www.city-temple.com/History.asp See also Healing and Counseling Centre at St Marylebone Parish Church opened 1987 at http://www.stmarylebone.org.uk/HandC01.htm

Clark, David, *Breaking the Mould of Christendom – Kingdom Community, Diaconal church and the Liberation of the Laity* (Peterborough: Epworth, 2005), pp. xvii, 11.

Clarkson, Petrusca, *The Transpersonal Relationship in Psychotherapy* (London: Whurr Publishers, 2002), p 236.

Clegg, Nick, in *Guardian Unlimited,* 'Queen's speech: legislation as a proxy for governing; we are facing a sixth immigration bill, an eighth terrorism bill and a 23rd justice bill. This is frenzied law-making.' at
http://commentisfree.guardian.co.uk/nick_clegg/2006/ 11/post_641.html sourced 17 February 2009.

Collins, Chuck, We're in This Together, *Sojourners Magazine,* February 2009, Vol. 38, No. 2, pp. 27, at
http://www.sojo.net/index.cfm?action=magazine.article &issue=soj0902&article=we-re-in-this-together 6 April 2009.)

Conti-O'Hare, Marion http://www.drconti-online.com/

Conti-O'Hare, Marion, *The Nurse as Wounded Healer: from Trauma to Transcendence,* Sudbury, Massachusetts: Jones and Bartlett Publishers. London: Jones and Bartlett Publishers International, 2002, p. 141, 144.

Cottrell, Barry, *The Way Beyond the Shaman: Birthing a New Earth Consciousness* Hampshire UK: O Books 2008, p107.

Council for a Parliament of the World's Religions (CPWR) a member of the International Interfaith Organisations

Network at
http://www.parliamentofreligions.org/index.cfm?n=1&sn=1
sourced 30 January 2009

Credit Union Movement, A Brief History, at
http://www.abcul.org/lib/liDownload/317/ABCUL%
20History%20Of%20Credit%20Unions.pdf, sourced 3 March
2009.

Csikszentmihalyi Mihaly, *Creativity – Flow and the psychology of
discovery and invention* (New York Harper Perennial) p. 6-7
cited in Jenya Krein on Creativity: Theories, Beliefs, and
Discoveries in *Speaking in Tongues Guided by Voices* at
http://spintongues.msk.ru/CraneEng2.htm p. 11 sourced 25
April 2009.

Dawkins, Richard and Steven Pinker, public debate on 10th
February 1999 at Westminster Central Hall, London, Is
Science Killing the Soul, reported in *Edge* 53, 8 April 1999, at
http://www.edge.org/documents/archive/edge53.html   6
April 2009.

Dawkins, Richard, *The God Delusion*, London: Bantam Press,
2006.

de Chardin, Pierre Teilhard, *The Future of Man*, New York:
Harper and Row, 1969, sourced
http://www.supremelaw.org/authors/teilhard/noospher.htm
24 March 2009.

de Chardin, Teilhard, *Activation of Energy*, Collins, 1970, p.95
cited in Mervyn Fernando, *Violence and the Rising Tide of
Globalisation – a Teilhardian perspective*, a lecture given in the
Netherlands for the Teilhard de Chardin Foundation, at
http://home.worldonline.nl/~sttdc/violence.htm

de Chardin, Teilhard, *Human Energy*, Collins 1969, p. 49.

De Mello, Anthony, *Awareness: the Perils and Opportunities of
Reality*, New York: Image Doubleday, 1992, p.182. Cited by
Alastair McIntosh in 'Cold War Psychohistory in the Scottish
Psyche,' *internet version from* www.AlastairMcIntosh.com

Sourced at http://www.alastairmcintosh.com/articles/2003-cold-war.htm 19 February 2009.

Donne, John, seventeenth century English poet died 1631. Famous words of prose taken from the final lines of his 1624 Meditation 17, from Devotions Upon Emergent Occasions.

Dossey, Larry, article, *The Forces of Healing: Reflections on Energy, Consciousness, and the Beef Stroganoff Principle,* revised from the keynote address and welcome originally presented at Exploring the Forces of Healing, the Second Annual *Alternative Therapies* Symposium; April 1997; Orlando, Fla. At http://twm.co.nz/dossey1.html#Healing 10 March 2009.

Dossey, Larry, front cover endorsement of Norman Shealy and Dawson Church, *Soul Medicine: Awakening your Inner Blueprint for Abundant Health and Energy,* California: Energy Psychology Press, 2008.

Dossey, Larry, *Healing Words - The Power of Prayer and the Practice of Medicine* New York: Harper Collins Publishers 1993, p. xv Preface and p.44.

Dossey, Larry, interview with Dennis Hughes on the Role of Prayer and Meditation in Medicine, *Share Guide: The Holistic Health Magazine and Resource Directory,* at http://www.shareguide.com/Dossey.html sourced 20 March 2009.

Dossey, Larry, *Recovering the Soul: a Scientific and Spiritual Search* (Bantam, 1989).

Dossey, Larry, *Reinventing Medicine: Beyond Mind-Body to a New Era of Healing,* Shaftesbury, Dorset, Boston, Massachusetts: Element Books, 2000, p. 12, p. 53 et. seq. Also a HarperCollins e-book; 1 edition July 24, 2007.

Dossey, Larry, *The Science of Premonitions: How Knowing the Future Can Help Us Avoid Danger, Maximize Opportunities, and Create a Better Life,* Plume, paperback due May 2010.

Dossey, Larry, website at http://www.dosseydossey.com/larry/default.html 10 March 2009.

Du Bois, W.E.B., *The Souls of Black Folk,* Barnes & Noble Classics, 2005.

Duke University, A study by sociologists at Duke University and the University of Arizona, reported at http://news.softpedia.com/news/Loneliness-Is-Getting-Rampant-in-America-27518.shtml 6 April 2009.

Duncan Collum, Danny and Polly, Taking Back Our Kids, *Sojourners Magazine,* January 2006, Vol. 35, No. 1, pp. 12-19, sourced at http://www.sojo.net/index.cfm?action=magazine.article &issue=soj0601&article=060110 6 February 2009.

Dunn, Claire, *Carl Jung: Wounded Healer of the Soul An Illustrated Biography,* London: Continuum, 2000, pp. 149, 199.

Edwards, Joel, *An Agenda for Change: a Global Call for Spiritual Transformation,* Michigan: Zondervan, 2008.

Eisler, Riane, *The Chalice and the Blade,* HarperCollins Publishers (Australia) Pty, 1998.

Eisler, Riane, *The Power of Partnership: Seven Relationships That Will Change Your Life,* New World Library; new edition 2003.

Energy Information Administration, Official Energy Statistics from the US Government, http://www.eia.doe.gov/cneaf/electricity/epa/epat1p1.html sourced 19 February 2009.

Erlich, Paul R., *Population Bomb,* Ballantine Books: Revised edition 1971.

Farm Aid, Keep America Growing, http://www.farmaid.org/site/c.qlI5IhNVJsE/b.2723715 /k.852A/Factory_Farms.htm sourced 23 November 2009.

Farsides, C. and E Garrard (1997) "Recourse allocation in palliative care," in *New Themes in Palliative Care,* D Clark, J Hockley, S Ahmedzai (eds)., Open University Press Philadelphia, pp 49-59.

Fernando, Dr. J. E. Mervyn, Violence and the Rising Tide of Globalisation – a Teilhardian Perspective; lecture on de

Chardin work by Founder-Director of the Teilhard de Chardin Centre for Science, Spirituality and the Future – Subodhi Institute, Piliyandala, Sri Lanka http://home.worldonline.nl/~sttdc/violence.htm sourced 25 March 2009.

Fetzer Institute, http://www.fetzer.org/ sourced 21 February 2009, and http://www.fetzer.org/AboutUs.aspx?PageID=About &NavID=7 10 March 2009.

Flew, Anthony, *There is a God*, New York: Harper One, 2007.

Food and Agriculture Organization 'Briefing Paper, Hunger on the Rise: Soaring Prices add 75 Million People to Global Hunger Rolls,' 17 September 2008, cited at http://www.bread.org/learn/hunger-basics/hunger-facts-international.html sourced 17 February 2009

Ford, Michael, *The Wounded Prophet: A Portrait of Henri J.M.Nouwen*, New York: Doubleday, Random House, 1999.

Forum for Stable Currencies website at http://www.monies.cc/forum/topic/connect/campaign.htm sourced 3 March 2009.

Frank, Anne, *Anne Frank; The Diary of a Young Girl*, Bantam 1993, from her entry Saturday 15th July 1944, p. 237.

Frankl, Viktor, *The Doctor and the Soul: From Psychotherapy to Logotherapy*, Harmondsworth: Pelican Books, 1973, p.16.

Frankl, Viktor, *The Doctor and the Soul: From Psychotherapy to Logotherapy* (London: Souvenir Press, 2004) p. 24.

Friends of the Earth International at http://www.foei.org/en/campaigns sourced December 2008. See also http://www.foe.org/

Gandhi, Arun, site at http://www.arungandhi.org/12.html 25 November 2009.

Garrison, William Lloyd, *From Slavery to Freedom: The African-American Pamphlet Collection, 1824-1909*, 'No compromise with slavery,' an address delivered in the Broadway

Tabernacle, New York, February 14, 1854 by William Lloyd Garrison. At http://memory.loc.gov/cgi-bin/query/r?ammem/rbaapc:@field(DOCID+@lit(rbaapc11000div2 Sourced 23 February 2009.

Global Justice Movement at www.globaljusticemovement.net/home/principles.htm 3 March 2009.

Global Justice Movement, http://www.globaljusticemovement.net/admin/news.htm 3 March 2009.

Gore, Al, The Climate for Change at http://www.planet-thoughts.org/?pg=pt/Whole&qid=2569&sc=t sourced January 2009

Graham, Martin, *Sizzling Faith: The Dream that got the Church on the Move!* Eastbourne: Kingsway Publications, 2006.

Greco, Thomas H., *Money: Understanding and Creating Alternatives to Legal Tender* Chelsea Green, 2001.

Greenpeace site at http://www.greenpeace.org/international/about sourced 3 March 2009.

Grey, Alex, at www.alexgrey.com.

Gwish, http://www.gwish.org/ extract from their mission, Christina Puchalski, MD, MS, sourced 10 March 2009.

Gwish, http://www.gwish.org/ survey conducted by Drs Puchalski and Cleary sourced 10 March 2009.

Haines, Stephen A., review of the Canadian Edition of George Monbiot's *Heat: How We Can Stop the Planet Burning*, London: Penguin, 2007, at http://www.amazon.co.uk sourced 29 November 2009.

Hastings Center, http://www.thehastingscenter.org/About/Default.aspx 31 March 2009.

Hawken, Paul and Amory and T. Hunter Lovins, *Natural Capitalism: Creating the Next Industrial Revolution Boston,*

Little Brown and Company, 1999, p. 52, cited in The Path to Living Economies – a collaborative Working Document of the Social Ventures Network at http://www.pcdf.org/SVN_Living_Economies.htm.

Helman, Cecil, *Suburban Shaman: Tales from Medicine's Frontline*, London: Hammersmith Press, 2006, pp. 5, 77, 163,

Henderson, Hazel, Mapping the Transition from GDP Growth to Rising Quality of Life, in *Nikkei Ecology*, 2001, cited in *The Path to Living Economies – a collaborative Working Document of the Social Ventures Network* at http://www.pcdf.org/SVN_Living_Economies.htm

Henri J. M. Nouwen *The Return of the Prodigal Son: A Story of Homecoming*, London: Darton, Longman and Todd, 1994, pp. 3, 5.

Hill, Penelope, graduate research paper at University of Southampton UK School of Social Sciences: *The Wounded Healer; Two People Getting the Help they Need*, 2006, http://www.southampton.ac.uk/socsci/counselling/research/index.html sourced December 2006.

His Holiness the 14th Dalai Lama in his Nobel Lecture December 11th 1989 http://nobelprize.org/nobel_prizes/peace/laureates/1989/lama-lecture.html 25 February 2009

His Holiness the 14th Dalai Lama, *Ancient Wisdom Modern World: Ethics for the New Millennium* (London: Abacus, Time Warner Books UK, 2000), p. 11.

His Holiness the 14th Dalai Lama, in his Acceptance Speech for the 1989 Nobel Peace Prize 10 December 1989. http://nobelprize.org/nobel_prizes/peace/laureates/1989/lama-acceptance.html

Holy Bible, RSV, Leviticus 25.10, Joshua chapters 13 to 21, 1 Samuel 16 vv.14 and 23, Ecclesiastes 1.9, Jeremiah 31.17, Matthew 5, vv. 6, 16, John 14.27, 1 Corinthians 12. 25,26, 13.4-8, 1 Timothy 6.10, Hebrews 13.2,

Hufford, David J., *'An analysis of the field of spirituality, religion and health.'* See www.metanexus.net/tarp/pdf/TARP-Hufford.pdf [PDF, 72 pages], also at http://www.templeton-advancedresearchprogram.com/pdf/TARP-Hufford.pdf accessed 9 March 2009

Humane Society of the United States, http://www.hsus.org/about_us/index.html sourced 25 February 2009

Huxley, Aldous, *Island,* London: Grafton Books, 1976, p.164, 247, 248.

Huxley, Aldous, *The Perennial Philosophy,* New York : Harper & Row, 1970, p. vii cited at http://www.youarethat.org/founda-tions/this-and-that2.htm 6 April 2009.

Institute of Noetic Science, http://www.noetic.org/about.cfm 10 March 2009.

Institute of Noetic Science, http://www.noetic.org/research/dh/faqs.html with detailed information and research results on distance healing, 10 March 2009.

Institute of Noetic Sciences (IONS), http://www.noetic.org/main/SpecialInterest.cfm?p_style=1 sourced 23 April 2009.

Institute of Transpersonal Psychology, http://www.itp.edu/about/aldous_huxley.php sourced 25 February 2009.

Institute of Transpersonal Psychology, http://www.itp.edu/about/carl_rogers.php sourced 25 February 2009 in site of Institute of Transpersonal Psychology

Integrative Medical Clinic, Santa Rosa, http://www.imcsr.com/ sourced 23 November 2009.

Interfaith Youth Core, www.ifyc.org sourced 6 April 2009

Intergovernmental Panel on Climate Change, http://www.ipcc.ch/press_information/press_information

_fact_sheet1.htm sourced 23 November 2009.

International Committee for the Peace Council, www.peace-council.org sourced 21 February 2009 and http://www.peace-council.org/accomplishments.html 25 March 2009.

International Interfaith Organisations Network at http://inter-faithorganisations.net/member-organisations/ 6 April 2009.

Jackson, Stanley, 'The Wounded Healer,' *Bulletin of the History of Medicine* - Volume 75, Number 1, pp. 1-36, Spring 2001, pp. 8, 10-18.

Jamieson, Kay Redfield, *Touched With Fire: Manic Depressive Illness and the Artistic Temperament* (New York Free Press: 1993) p. 121 cited in Jackson lecture at p 35.

Jubilee Centre, http://www.jubilee-centre.org

Jung, Carl G., Fundamental Questions of Psychotherapy, in *The Collected Works of C G Jung* trans. R F C Hull, ed. Herbert Read, Michael Fordham, Gerhard Adler and William McGuire (Princeton University Press, 1953-1979), vol. 16: 111-25, on p. 116, cited in Stanley W. Jackson, 2001, p. 21.

Jung, Carl G., *Memories, Dreams Reflections* (London: Fontana Press, 1995) pp.154-156.

Jung, Carl, *C J Jung Letters volume 2* selected and edited by Gerhard Adler in collaboration with Aniela Jaffe (Bollingen Series; Princeton: Princeton University Press, 1953) p. 316 Letter to Elined Kotschnig cited in *Clare Dunn: Carl Jung: Wounded Healer of the Soul: An Illustrated Biography,* London: Continuum 2000, p.199.

Jung, Carl, from *The Collected Works of C G Jung,* volume 10 The Undiscovered Self; Princeton University Press, 1970 pp304-305 as quoted in Claire Dunn: *Carl Jung: Wounded Healer of the Soul An Illustrated Biography* (London: Continuum, 2000) p.199.

Kabat-Zinn, Jon, in foreword to M. Lerner *Choices in Healing: Integrating the Best of Conventional and Complementary Approaches to Cancer,* Massachusetts, London: MIT Press,

1996, p. xvii.

Kaptchuk, Ted and Michael Croucher, *The Healing Arts,* BBC Publications, 1986, pp. 26, 37, cited in Michael Mayne, *A Year Lost and Found,* London: Darton, Longman and Todd, 1987, p. 38.

Kean, Danuta, *The Pornography of Misery Memoirs,* Mail Online 10 October 2007, http://www.dailymail.co.uk/femail/article-486478/The-pornography-misery-memoirs.html sourced 24 April 2009.

Kearney, Michael, *A Place of Healing: Working with Suffering in Living and Dying,* Oxford University Press, USA (November 30, 2000), p. 31. Now see *Place of Healing: Working With Nature And Soul At The End* (Spring Journal paperback, August 27, 2009)

Kennedy, Robert F., transcription of audio version of Address made 18 March 1968 at the University of Kansas, Lawrence, Kansas, sourced at
http://www.jfklibrary.org/Historical+Resources/
Archives/Reference+Desk/Speeches/RFK/RFKSpeech68
Mar18UKansas.htm 28 March 2009.

King, Martin Luther Jnr., Nobel Peace Prize Lecture December 11 1964
http://nobelprize.org/nobel_prizes/peace/
laureates/1964/king-lecture.html sourced 5 April 2009.

King, Martin Luther, Jnr., Nobel Peace Prize Acceptance Speech 10th December 1964, at
http://nobelprize.org/nobel_prizes/peace/
laureates/1964/king-acceptance.html sourced 19 February 2009.

Koenig, Harold and Malcolm McConnell, *The Healing Power of Faith: How Belief and Prayer can help you Triumph over Disease,* Paperback Simon & Schuster - April 17, 2001.

Koenig, Harold G., *The Healing Connection: The Story of a Physician's Search for the Link between Faith and Health*

(Templeton Foundation Press, 2004).

Korten, David, *Living Economies for a Living Planet* at http://www.pcdf.org/living_economies/ cited in *The Path to Living Economies – a collaborative Working Document of the Social Ventures Network* http://www.pcdf.org/SVN_Living_Economies.htm 3 March 2009, p. 10 of 40, and ref. 15.

Kumar, Satish, in 'Spiritual Imperative: Elegant Simplicity is the way to Discover Spirituality,' *Resurgence* (March/April 2005) issue 229 at http://www.resurgence.org/2005/kumar-spirit229.htm sourced 19 February 2009, and also at http://www.resurgence.org/magazine/article653-SPIRITUAL-IMPERATIVE.html sourced 3 March 2009.

Kumar, Satish, Schumacher lecture *Spiritual Imperatives*, 30 Oct. 2004 Bristol UK available at http://www.schumacher.org.uk/transcrips/ BSL04_SatishKumar_Spiritual_Imperative.pdf 2 April 2009.

Kumar, Satish, *Spiritual Compass: The Three Qualities of Life,* Green Books, 2007.

L'Arche International Communities. See http://www.larche.org/home.en-gb.1.0.index.htm, L'Arche USA at http://www.larche.org/usa-l-arche-in-your-region.en-gb.30.0.news.htm and L'Arche UK at http://www.larche.org.uk/ sourced 23 April 2009.

Lane, Belden C., *The Solace of Fierce Landscapes: Exploring Desert and Mountain Spirituality,* Oxford and New York: Oxford University Press, 1998, p. 216.

Langford, Malcolm, *Waking the Wounded: Facing our own Poverty.* Langford draws much of his inspiration from Henri Nouwen. World Vision site at http://www.worldvision.com.au/getinvolved/ faithinaction/files/grid2000_wakingthewounded.pdf sourced 17 February 2009.

Lennox, John C., *God's Undertaker: Has Science Buried God?*

Oxford: Lion Hudson, 2007.

Lerner, Michael, *Choices in Healing; Integrating the Best of Conventional and Complementary Approaches to Cancer*, Cambridge, Massachusetts: MIT Press paperback edition 1998, p.123.

Let Justice Roll, 'Faith and Community Voices against Poverty,' Living Wage Campaign, http://letjusticeroll.org/news/00936-churches-push-10-minimum-wage-2010 sourced 23 November 2009, responding to the challenge of the prophet Amos 5.24, RSV, 'But let justice roll down like waters, and righteousness like an overflowing stream.'

LETS, http://www.lets-linkup.com/080 -All%20About%20LETS.htm and http://www.lets-linkup.com/71-USA.htm 3 March 2009.

Lexington USA website, http://www.lexva.com/ sourced 26 February 2009.

Lietaer, Bernard, See www.futurenet.org/2Money/Lietaer.html for further discussion and explanation of the flaws in our money system and ideas for change to support community and sustainability, in an interview with Bernard Lietaer, Summer 1997: *Money: Print Your Own! Beyond Greed and Scarcity*, 3 March 2009.

Lietaer, Bernard, *The Future of Money – Creating New Wealth, Work and a Wiser World* (2001) cited at http://www.transaction.net/money/book sourced 3 March 2009.

Lovelock, James, *The Revenge of Gaia*, London: Penguin Books Ltd, 2006, pp. 5, 8, 25, 26, 138, 146, 162.

Lovelock, James, *The Vanishing Face of Gaia: a Final Warning*, London: Penguin Books Ltd 2009.

Lovelock, James, website, http://www.ecolo.org/lovelock/lovedeten.htm sourced December 2008.

Martin, Gary, from

(http://www.phrases.org.uk/meanings/274400.html), sourced 26 March 2009.

Maslow Abraham, at http://www.abrahammaslow.net/more.html sourced 30 November 2009.

Mayne, Michael, *A Year Lost and Found,* London: Darton Longman and Todd, 1987, pp. 22, 38,

Mayne, Michael, *Learning to Dance,* (London: Darton Longman and Todd, 2001, pp. 15, 18.

Mayne, Michael, *The Enduring Melody,* London: Darton Longman and Todd, 2006, pp. 13, 151, 154, 236, 238.

Mayne, Michael, *This Sunrise of Wonder: Letters for the Journey,* London: Fount Paperbacks, 1995.

McEwan, Ian, *The Guardian* 15 September 2001, 'Only love and then oblivion. Love was all they had to set against their murderers.'http://www.guardian.co.uk/world/2001/sep/15/september11.politicsphilosophyandsociety2 sourced 19 February 2009.

McGilchrist, Iain, *The Master and his Emissary,* Newhaven and London: Yale University Press, 2009, Chapter 7, 'Imitation and the Evolution of Culture.'

McGill Medicine at http://www.mcgill.ca/wholepersoncare/ 10 March 2009.

McGill University, http://www.medicine.mcgill.ca/newsletter/autumn-2004.pdf in *Focus, Medicine Edition*, Autumn 2004 Newsletter of McGill University Faculty of Medicine Montreal, article, 'A Curriculum for the New Century: Donald Boudreau's Legacy,' accessed 11 February 2009.

McGrath, Alister, *Dawkins' God, Genes, Memes and the Meaning of Life,* Oxford: Blackwell 2005.

McGrath, Alister and Joanna Collicutt McGrath, *The Dawkins Delusion: Atheist Fundamentalism and the Denial of the Divine,* London: SPCK 2007.

McIntosh, Alastair, *Rekindling Community: Connecting People,*

Environment and Spirituality, Schumacher Briefing, Green Books 2008.

McIntosh, Alastair, *Soil and Soul: People versus Corporate Power*, London: Aurum Press, 2004, pp. 4, 19, 128, 131, 146, 151, 176, 183, 214, 280, 284 and Chapter 14 et. seq.

Means, J. J. 'Wounded Healer/Mighty Prophet,' *The Journal of Pastoral Care and Counseling*, Spring 2002, Vol. 56, No. 1.

Means, J. J., 'Pastoral Counseling: An Alternative Path in Mental Health,' *The Journal of Pastoral Care* Fall 1997 vol. 51 No. 3.

Metanexus Institute, at http://www.templetonadvancedresearch-program.com/pdf/TARP-Hufford.pdf 29 March 2009.

Metzger, Joel, *Sacred Mirrors: Discussing Transpersonal Art with Alex Grey*, from

http://www.omplace.com/articles/SacredMirrors.html

Micah Challenge, http://www.micahchallenge.org

Michael Kearney, *A Place of Healing: Working with Suffering in Living and Dying*, in Foreword by Balfour Mount p viii., Oxford: Oxford University Press, 2000.

Michael Kearney, *Mortally Wounded: Stories of Soul Pain, Death and Healing*, Dublin: Marino Books, 1996, cited in Michael Kearney, *A Place of Healing*, foreword by Balfour Mount p. iv. (USA: Oxford University Press, 2000) Now reprinted Spring Journal, Inc. (December 1, 2007).

Mission in London's Economy, http://www.mile.org.uk/ sourced 28 November 2009.

Monbiot, George, Civilisation ends with a shutdown of human concern. Are we there already? *The Guardian*, 30 October 2007, at

http://www.guardian.co.uk/commentisfree/2007/oct/30/comment.books sourced 25 April 2009.

Monbiot, George, *Heat: How We Can Stop the Planet Burning*, London: Penguin, 2007.

Moore, Helen, *Art for Earth's Sake – a Manifesto* at

http://www.natures-words.co.uk/Art%20for%20

Earth%27s%20Sake%20-%20a%20Manifesto.pdf sourced 23 April 2009.

Myss, Caroline, *Defy Gravity: Healing Beyond the Bounds of Reason*, Kindle Edition, Hay House, 2009.

Nietzsche, Friedrich, from *Die Frohliche Wissenschaft, The Gay Science* (1882, 1887) paragraph 125 Walter Kaufmann ed. (New York: Vintage, 1974), pp.181-82, sourced http://www.fordham.edu/halsall/mod/nietzsche-madman.html 25 March 2009. Also *The Gay Science* (Philosophical Classics) Friedrich Nietzsche with Thomas Common (Translator)(New York: Dover Publications, 2006)

Nobel Laureates Statement on the occasion of the one-hundredth anniversary of the Nobel Prize, Stockholm, December 11, 2001.
http://www.wagingpeace.org/articles/2001/12/11_nobel-statement.htm sourced 23 November 2009.

Nouwen, Henri J. M. *The Wounded Healer,* London: Darton, Longman and Todd, 1994, pp. xvi, 81, 83, 84, 88, 89, 92,

O'Hare, Conti, *The Nurse as Wounded Healer; From Trauma to Transcendence,* Massachusetts: Jones and Bartlett Publishers, 2002, pp. 39-42.

Obama, Barack, *The Audacity of Hope*: *Thoughts on Reclaiming the American Dream*, Edinburgh: Canongate Books, 2008 p67, 68. Also published in USA, New York: Crown Publishers, 2006.

Obama, Senator Barack, *'Call to Renewal'* Keynote Address to a Sojourners conference in 2006,
http://www.sojo.net/index.cfm?action=news.display_article&mode=C&NewsID=5454 sourced 19 February 2009.

O'Dell, Larry, 25 February 2007, 'Virginia Apologizes for Role in Slavery,' *The Washington Post.*
http://www.washingtonpost.com/wp-dyn/content/article/2007/02/25/AR2007022500470.html
sourced 23 February 2009.

On the Move International, The Free Barbeque Ministry,

http://www.onthemoveinternational.org/ and
http://www.onthemove.org.uk/ 26 March 2009.

Palmer, Martin with Victoria Finlay, *Faith in Conservation: New Approaches to Religions and the Environment*, The World Bank Washington DC 2003, pp. 3, 72, 77, 78, 83-85, 91, 93, 132, 134, 141. Full credit is given to the individual contributors in the endnotes to Chapter 1. See Note 26 to Chapter 1.

Palmer, P., *A Place called Community*, Pennsylvania: Pendle Hill, 1987, p.15 cited in David Clark, *Breaking the Mould of Christendom – Kingdom Community, Diaconal Church and the Liberation of the Laity* (Peterborough: Epworth, 2005), p. 11.

Patel, Eboo, *Acts of Faith: the Story of an American Muslim, the Struggle for the Soul of a Generation*, Boston: Beacon Press, 2007a

Patel, Eboo, Building the Beloved Community; Values of Religious Pluralism in *Frank, the magazine of the Clinton School of Public Service* (Winter 2007b), p. 58, available online at http://www.frankmagazine.org/Patel.asp cited in http://www.parliamentofreligions.org/_includes/files/syllab i/Meyer,%20Patel-%20Interfaith%20Action%20.pdf sourced 25 March 2009.

Pearsall, Paul, *The Beethoven Factor: The new Positive Psychology of Hardiness, Happiness, Healing and Hope*, Hampton Roads Publishing, 2003.

Peck, M. Scott, *The Different Drum The Creation of True Community – the First Step to World Peace*, London: Arrow Books 1990a, p.17, 19, 20, 325, and Chapter XI.

Peck, *People of the Lie: The Hope for Healing Human Evil*, London: Arrow, 1990b, p. 249.

Petrarca, Francesco, *Letters of Old Age: Rerum senilium libri*. 2 volumes Translated Aldo S. Bernardo, Saul Levin and Reta A. Bernardo, Baltimore: John Hopkins University Press, 1992, 2: p. 381 (Sen. 10.4) cited in Stanley W. Jackson, 2001, p. 8.

Physicians for Social Responsibility,
    http://www.psr.org/documents/history.pdf   achievements
    sourced 9 March 2009 published January 31, 2008 at
    http://www.ic.nhs.uk/pubs/opadjan08 sourced 3 March 2009.
Planet Thoughts, www.planetthoughts.org
Pope, Alexander, from *Part II* of *An Essay on Criticism*.
Presbyterian Health, Education and Welfare Association,
    http://www.pcusa.org/nationalhealth/parishnursing/
    Sourced 23 November 2009.
Publishers Weekly editorial review of Simonton *Origins of Genius* at
    http://www.amazon.com sourced 30 November 2009.
Putnam, Robert, Lewis Feldstein and Donald Cohen, *Better
    Together, Restoring the American Community*, New York: Simon
    & Schuster, 2005.
Qur'an 007.031.
Read, Conyers, Presidential address delivered at the annual
    dinner of the American Historical Association on December
    29, 1949: 'The Social Responsibilities of the Historian.'
    From the *American Historical Review*, Vol. 55, No. 2.
    (Jan.1950), pp. 275-285, at
    http://www.historians.org/info/AHA_History/cread.htm
    sourced 25 November 2009.
Remen, May, Young, and Berland, 'The Wounded Healer'
    Saybrook Review, (1985), 5 (1) pp. 84-93.
Rissik, Andrew, a review in The Times of the book Ted Kaptchuk
    and Michael Croucher, *The Healing Arts*, BBC Publications
    1986, based on the documentary television series of the same
    name, cited in Michael Mayne, *A Year Lost and Found*,
    London: Darton, Longman and Todd, 1987, p. 38.
Roddick, Anita,*Take it Personally: How Globalization Effects (sic)
    You*, London: Thornson, 2001, From Introduction, quoted in
    http://www.pcdf.org/SVN_Living_Economies.htm#N_2_
Rogers, Carl, *A Therapist's View of Psychotherapy: On Becoming a
    Person*, London: Constable, 1961, pp. 27, 348, 349, 350,

Chapter 19.

Rogers, Carl, *A Way of Being*, Boston: Houghton Mifflin, 1980, p. 356.

Rogers, Natalie, http://www.nrogers.com/ 10 March 2009

Sacks, Jonathan, *The Times*, 5 January 2008, Count your Blessings and Begin to Change your Life.

Sacks, Jonathan, *To Heal a Fractured World*, London: Continuum, 2005, pp. 3, 222, 223, 273, 108, 109 and Chapter 20: On Dreams and Responsibilities.

Sahtouris, Elisabet, *Earth Dance: Living Systems in Evolution*, Chapter 1 p. 5 1999 at http://www.ratical.org/LifeWeb/Erthdnce/chapter1.html sourced January 2009.

Sahtouris, Elisabet, *Earthdance: Living Systems in Evolution*, New York: Praeger, 2000, also at http://www.ratical.org/LifeWeb/Erthdnce/erthdnce.html

Sanhedrin tractate of the Talmud cited in Henri J. M. Nouwen, 1994, p. 81.

Sawyer, D, *Aldous Huxley: A Biography*, New York: The Crossroad Publishing Company, 2002, p. 95, cited at http://www.itp.edu/about/aldous_huxley.php sourced 25 February 2009.

Schluter, Michael and John Ashcroft, Editors, *Jubilee Manifesto: a Framework, Agenda and Strategy for Christian Social Reform*, Leicester: Inter-Varsity Press, 2005, pp. 207, 217.

Schoon, Darryl, *The United States Fiat Money & The Federal Reserve System*, June 23, 2008 at http://www.financialsense.com/fsu/editorials/schoon/2008/0623.html sourced 2 December 2009.

Scientific and Medical Network, at http://www.scimednet.org/aims.htm, and their journal, *Network Review*, Summer 2009, p. 3, Oliver Robinson, John Clark and David Lorimer, 'Crisis as Opportunity: Seizing the Moment for a New Renaissance, a Manifesto for Change.'

Second Vatican Council, convened in 1959 by Pope John XXIII and concluded in 1965 under the direction of Pope Paul VI see http://www.vatican2voice.org/default.htm sourced 23 April 2009.

Selby, Peter, *Liberating God, Private Care and Public Struggle,* London: SPCK, 1983, publisher's note, back cover.

Sentamu, John, inauguration sermon 2005.

Shakespeare, Rodney and Peter Challen, *Seven Steps to Justice,* London: New European Publications Limited, 2002.

Shealy, Norman and Dawson Church, *Soul Medicine: Awakening your Inner Blueprint for Abundant Health and Energy,* Santa Rosa, CA: Energy Psychology Press, 2008.

Shri Venkateswara(Balaji) Temple of UK
http://www.venkateswara.org.uk/ReadNews.aspx?
NewsID=1 sourced 23 November 2009.

Simonton, Dean Keith, *Origins of Genius: Darwinian Perspectives on Creativity,* USA: Oxford University Press, 1999.

Simpson, George, *A Thesis, Conflict and Community: A study in social theory,* New York: Liberal Press, 1937, cited in David Clark, 2005, p.11.

Sinclair, Upton Beall, *I, Candidate for Governor: And How I Got Licked* (1935), reprint University of California Press, 1994, p. 109.

Singleton, John, *At the Roots of Methodism: Covenant services mark New Year* Jan. 28, 2004, at
http://archives.umc.org/interior.asp?ptid=2&mid=3004 sourced 25 February 2009.

Skoloff, Brian, The Associated Press, Friday 26 October 2007, at http://www.truthout.org/article/much-us-could-see-a-water-shortage sourced 23 November 2009.

Skoloff, Brian, The Associated Press, Friday 26 October 2007, http://www.truthout.org/article/much-us-could-see-a-water-shortage sourced 23 November 2009.

Slovic, Professor Paul, University of Oregon: Report to

Conference of American Association for the Advancement of Science. Reported in The Times 17 February 2007.

Smith, David, *Being a Wounded Healer: How to Heal Ourselves while we are Healing Others*, Madison, WI: Psycho-Spiritual Publications, 1999, cited in O'Hare 2002 p. 41.

Snyder, Gary, at http://www.tomradulovich.com/?p=55 26 March 2009.

Social Ventures Network - Living Economies – The Path to Living Economies www.pcdf.org/SVN_Living_Economies.htm 28 March 2009, p. 6 of 40.

Sojourners, www.sojo.net

Spencer, Nick and Robert White *Christianity, Climate Change and Sustainable Living,* London: SPCK, 2007.

Spiritual Alliance to Stop Intimate Violence, (http://www.saiv.net/about.htm).

Spirituality, Theology and Health at Duke University's Medical Center, http://www.spiritualityandhealth.duke.edu/sth/index.html sourced 10 March 2009.

Statistics on obesity, physical activity and diet: England, January 2008, at http://www.ic.nhs.uk/pubs/opadjan08 sourced 3 March 2009.

Stern, Sir Nicholas, UK Government Chief Economist: Stern Review on the Economics of Climate Change. October 30th 2006 H M Treasury. Now available from Cambridge University Press 2007 *The Economics of Climate Change: The Stern Review.*

Stop Climate Chaos Coalition, http://www.stopclimatechaos.org/

Storr, Anthony, *Music and the Mind,* London: Harper Collins, 1997, pp. 45, 48, 126.

The Campaign for Interest-Free Money at http://www.interest-freemoney.org/index.htm 3 March 2009.

The Industrial Mission Association at

http://www.industrialmission.org.uk/cms/

The Rt. Reverend James Jones, Bishop of Liverpool, in the Foreword to *Jubilee Manifesto, a framework, agenda & strategy for Christian Social Reform*. Ed. Michael Schluter and John Ashcroft, Inter-Varsity Press, 2005, p. 11.

The Times Obituaries 4 November 2006

Thomas Merton: *New Seeds of Contemplation*, New York: New Directions Publishing Corporation 1972, pp. 112, 122 and Chapter 16 'The Root of War is Fear.'

Thompson, Judith and James O'Dea, *Shift* Issue 7, May 2005, 'Social Healing for a Fractured World; a Summary Report to the Fetzer Institute.' Sourced at

http://www.shiftinaction.com/node/1677 19 February 2009.

Tony Blair Faith Foundation, http://tonyblairfaithfoundation.org/

Trungpa, C., 1996, *Dharma Art*, Shambala Publications, Boston, Mass. Sourced 23 April 2009 at

Tudge, Colin, *So Shall We Reap (How everyone who is liable to be born in the next ten thousand years could eat very well indeed; and why, in practice, our immediate descendants are likely to be in serious trouble)*, 2004 Penguin Books.

Tutu, Desmond, talk, *Forgive and Begin to Heal*, University of Florida, Tampa, January 2006, reported by Waveney Ann Moore in the St. Petersburg Times, sourced 6 April 2009 at http://www.sptimes.com/2006/01/20/news_pf/Tampabay/Tut u__Forgive_and_beg.shtml

United Methodist Church website at

http://www.umc.org/site/apps/nlnet/content3.aspx?
c=lwL4KnN1LtH&b=1752979&ct=6635959   sourced   22
February 2009

van Gogh, Vincent, to Theo van Gogh, *Arles, 28 January 1889* cited at 'Van Gogh's Letters Unabridged and Annotated,' sourced 29 November 2009 at

http://www.webexhibits.org/vangogh/letter/19/574.htm

Wallas, Graham, *The Art of Thought*, 1926.

Wallis, Jim, *Seven Ways to Change the World: Reviving Faith and Politics,* Oxford: Lion Hudson, 2008, Chapter 12, p. 232.

Wallis, Jim, *The Great Awakening; Seven Ways to Change the World,* HarperOne, Reprint edition 2009.

Wallis, Jim, *Rediscovering Values: On Wall Street, Main Street, and Your Street,* Howard Books, 2010.

Weatherhead, Leslie D, *Psychology Religion and Healing,* London, Hodder and Stoughton, 1951, reprinted with further revision 1955, pp. 90, 95, 278, 482 and Chapter 2 in Section 1.

Weatherhead, Leslie D., *Psychology Religion and Healing,* new edition Stewart Press: 2008.

Wheatcroft, Patience, *The Times* on January 13th 2006 in an article entitled 'Bloodlust at the click of a Mouse,' full story at http://www.skaiciumiestelis.lt/index.php?id=19&lang=lt. The work appeared in 2006 in the *Journal of Experimental Social Psychology.*

Whole Person Care Working Group, 'Spirituality and Health: Developing a Shared Vocabulary,' in *OMNI: Journal of Spirituality and Religious Care,* 2003, at http://www.omc.ca/omni/archives/000040.html posted 30 September 2003, sourced 23 November 2009.

Williams, Peter S, *A Sceptic's Guide to Atheism,* Milton Keynes: Paternoster, 2009.

World Bank poverty statistics available for 2005 as at March 2009 at http://web.worldbank.org/WBSITE/EXTERNAL/NEWS/ 0,,contentMDK:20040961~menuPK:34480~pagePK:36694 ~piPK:116742~theSitePK:4607,00.html 28 March 2009.

World Health Organization, The Promotion and Development of Traditional Medicine (*WHO Technical Report Series 622*) (Geneva: WHO 1978), cited in Cecil Helman, *Suburban Shaman,* 2006, p.163.

York Minster http://www.dioceseofyork.org.uk/files/adminandinfo393-

1.doc sourced 6 April 2009.

Zavrel, Consul B. John, *Arun Gandhi: The Pursuit of Truthfulness*, on the Museum of European History, Clarence, New York site at http://www.meaus.com/arun_gandhi.htm sourced 25 November 2009.

B O O K S

MySpiritRadio